SUBTERRANEAN CITY
Beneath the streets of London

First published 2000
by Historical Publications Ltd
32 Ellington Street, London N7 8PL
(Tel: 020 7607 1628)

ISBN 0 948667 69 9
British Library Cataloguing-in-Publication Data
A catalogue record for this book is available from the British Library

Typeset in Palatino by Historical Publications Ltd
Design of jacket by Brian Christiansen of C & C Graphics
Reproduction by G & J Graphics, London EC2
Printed by Edelvives in Zaragoza, Spain

SUBTERRANEAN CITY
Beneath the Streets of London

Antony Clayton

HISTORICAL PUBLICATIONS

FOR BOB AND DOREEN CLAYTON

The Illustrations

The following kindly permitted reproduction of illustrations:

British Telecom: *77, 123*
Building Design: *129*
Country Life: *131*
London Borough of Camden: *15*
Antony Clayton: *59*
Roderick Coyne and Alsop & Störmer: *128*
Docklands Light Railway: *127*
Dennis Gilbert / View and Foster & Partners: *130*
Guildhall Library, City of London: *9*
Hulton Getty Picture Library: *118, 120*
Imperial War Museum: *124*
Royal Borough of Kensington & Chelsea: *6, 97, 109*
Library of Congress, Washington: *107*
London Canal Museum: *18*
London Transport Museum: *96, 104, 105, 119*
Nigel Pennick: *122, 125*
Post Office: *116*
Tim Smith: *67*
Thames Water Utilities: *39, 42, 43* and back jacket

All other illustrations were supplied by the publishers.

CONTENTS

Preface

Though London is a city with nearly 2000 years of habitation it often seems as if there were an inverted city beneath our feet as extensive and fascinating as the one above. Ever since the Romans established a settlement by the Thames *c*AD43 wells were dug, mosaic pavements were laid, burials were made, the ground was disturbed. Living above this rich palimpsest we carry out our urban tasks, aware of its subterranean counterpart when we travel on the tube, leave the car in an underground car park, visit a basement night club or restaurant or use one of the increasingly rare unprivatised underground public toilets. The intention of this book is to provide a view of this buried world in all its manifestations. Roman remains, medieval wine cellars, Victorian utility subways and modern nuclear bunkers can all be found in the subterranean city.

Looking back I am aware of three pieces of fictional inspiration which concentrated my imagination on underground London. In the dim past I recall a particularly creepy episode of the *Dr Who* television series taking place in the sinister tunnels of the London Underground, in which the Doctor had to defeat his hirsute adversaries the Yeti.[1] Much more vivid was the first occasion I viewed the Hammer horror film *Quatermass and the Pit* (alternate title in the USA *Five Million Miles to Earth*), in which the history of human evolution is upset by an extraterrestrial entity in Hobb's Lane Underground station. In 1988 a conspiracy thriller by Stephen Poliakoff, *Hidden City* starring Charles Dance, enjoyed a brief cinematic release and reignited my interest in unknown aspects of the city, with its use of unusual underground locations.

In recent years I have been struck by the number of artists who have been setting their works in subterranean locations. Some of the more effective examples have been: the recreation of prehistoric cave paintings by John Berger and Artangel at the abandoned Underground station at Aldwych, Robert Wilson's theatrical use of the vast caverns beneath the railway viaducts on Bankside for his installation *HG* in 1995 and in 1999 Mimmo Paladino's sculptures placed within the beautifully symmetrical brick vaults beneath the Roundhouse in Chalk Farm, accompanied by Brian Eno's ambient atmospheres. Turner Prize-nominated artists Jane and Louise Wilson have produced evocative videos from a variety of underground sites such as the Greenham Common missile silos and control rooms and the service passages beneath the Houses of Parliament.[2]

During the time spent writing this book I often listened to music to inspire or soothe me, in particular that of the latter-period Miles Davis.[3] It was only later that I discovered that *Agharta*, the intense double album he recorded in 1975 prior to his premature 'retirement', derived its title from a mythical underground realm.[4] Suddenly it was all beginning to make sense ...

Whilst seeking to update information on subterranean London I have to acknowledge the (under)groundbreaking research of the late Richard Trench and Ellis Hillman whose *London Under London* revealed this hidden world to many for the first time. Readers of that work hoping to undertake further research were frustrated, however, by the omission of footnotes or any bibliographic references; a second edition introduced a cursory bibliography but failed to correct the textual errors in the first edition. I have aimed to provide a more detailed set of references in this present work and a more comprehensive bibliography. Another intrepid explorer was Peter Laurie, whose various revisions of *Beneath the City Streets* have provided so much fuel for speculation and debate regarding the more secretive structures and tunnels that form a warren under central London.[5] Journalist Duncan Campbell has also written a number of stimulating articles and books on the role clandestine underground structures play in the 'security' of the nation. Less well-known but equally useful sources of subterranean information are the two booklets written by Nigel Pennick in the 1980s: *Tunnels Under London* and *Bunkers under London*.[6] Despite these earlier researches it seemed timely to examine once more the massive amount of burrowing beneath the city as more information has become available and as huge contemporary underground projects such as the Jubilee Line Extension have recently been completed.

In the course of writing this book I have tried, unsuccessfully in many places, to resist the urge to don an anorak. Those eager troglodytes seeking further detailed information are directed to the footnotes and bibliography. The plethora of books that cover aspects of the London Underground system and the capital's numerous railway lines are packed with sufficient facts and number crunching to keep the most ardent trainspotter or researcher satisfied. When writing about railway and engineering matters an author may be diagnosed as suffering from acronym fatigue, so I have attempted to keep these somewhat irritating time-savers to a minimum in the text. Given the amount of articles in the popular press on aspects of underground London that appeared in 1999 and 2000 during the course of the preparation and writing of this book it would appear that interest in this subject is increasing. I hope that the follow-

ing will help to assuage some of that interest.[7] It is intended that a book on this protean subject will be revised every few years and the author welcomes any corrections, clarifications or fresh information on aspects of this fascinating subterranean world.

Acknowledgements

Jill Barber, Llinos Thomas, Susannah Rayner and the rest of the staff at the City of Westminster Archives Centre, Peter Collins, Adrian Cornish, Jon Sims and rest of the staff of the ever-dwindling Westminster Reference Library, Kieron Tyler of the Museum of London Archaeology Service for assistance and advice, Jerome Farrell, Michael Delicata-Bennett of the Brunel Engine House, Roger Cline, Kevin Flude, Steven Patterson (the man with the Macintosh), the staff of the Guildhall Library, the staff of the library of the Institution of Civil Engineers, the staff of the British Library, Psyche Ameen, Johnny Green, Richenda Power, Goldberry Broad, Jane and John King, John Richardson, Audrey Adams and lastly to Acorn Broad, who has patiently pored over the Powerbook correcting my English.

Footnotes to the Preface

[1] The episodes were entitled *The Web of Fear* aired between 3 February and 9 March 1968. As it was too expensive to film in the Underground, the Greenwich Foot Tunnel was used, whilst most of the subterranean scenes were shot on realistically designed sets. See David J Howe, Mark Stammers & Stephen James Walker *Doctor Who, the Sixties* (Doctor Who / Virgin Books, 1992), 98-99.

[2] *Jane and Louise Wilson* exhibition catalogue with an essay by Peter Schejeldahl (Serpentine Gallery, 1999).

[3] Music inspired by the world below is also a fertile subject. Titles that come to mind in a far from definitive list would include The Jam's *Down in the Tube Station at Midnight* and *Going Underground*, The Stranglers' *Down in the Sewer*, Coil's *Lost Rivers of London* and Petula Clark's *Don't Sleep in the Subway*. Stanley Holloway described life beneath the streets in *Down Below*, David Bowie plumbed the depths with the *Subterraneans* whilst The Moles asserted that *We are the Moles* . Punning titles using Underground stations would enlarge the list considerably. One goth group – Balaam and the Angel – almost succeeded in combining a pair of Northern Line

stations in their name.

[4] The most scholarly analysis of these hyperborean, subterranean country / world myths is Joscelyn Godwin's *Arktos, the Polar Myth in Science, Symbolism and Nazi Survival* (Thames & Hudson, 1993). Anyone else interested in lost civilisations and chthonic entities should probably stick with H P Lovecraft or Jules Verne's *Journey to the centre of the Earth*.

[5] Following in his father's footsteps, Laurie's son Adam, owner of AL Digital, bought a decommissioned nuclear bunker, formerly part of RAF Ash, not far from Sandwich in Kent. Within this concrete fortress featuring bomb-proof doors and walls five metres thick, "a wide range of hosting and data warehousing options are available, with varying levels of access and security to suit both corporate and individual applications," internet servers being the principal clients. Information from http://www.thebunker.net. See also Stephen McLaren 'E-commerce joins the underground economy' *The Independent* 23 January 1999, 13.

[6] Since these early forays into print this author has written numerous New Age books and evolved into, "an authority on northern European geomancy, runemaster, practising geomant and traditional symbolic craftsman." Author biography in John Matthews & Chesca Potter eds. *The Aquarian Guide to Legendary London* (Aquarian Press, 1990), 314.

[7] For example, a number of articles on underground London appeared in the *Evening Standard* and the 'Space' supplement of *The Guardian*. A magazine for graffiti artists even encouraged its readers to visit this hidden world in order to wreak spray-can havoc, see *Graphotism*, No 17 1999. One hallucinatory article claimed that, "The subterranean tram system – comprising many hundreds of miles of clay pipes embedded in concrete a few feet beneath London's pavements – could soon be put to new use, carrying cable television." (*Evening Standard* 11 January 1999.) Incidentally, while the author cannot endorse the dubious and potentially dangerous pursuit of so-called 'urban exploration' there are numerous sites on the internet devoted to this subject for those who are interested.

Many of the buildings mentioned in this book, such as the Cabinet War Rooms, London Canal Museum or the crypt of St Paul's Cathedral can be easily visited all year round. London's extensive Underground lines can similarly be explored and tours are sometimes arranged to the 'ghost' stations at Aldwych and Down Street. One of the best opportunities to visit the subterranean city and observe aspects of the water supply and sewerage systems is during the admirable London Open House weekend that occurs each September.

CHAPTER ONE
An Introduction to the Subterranean City

At the most remote end of the crypt there appeared another less spacious. Its walls had been lined with human remains, piled to the vault overhead, in the fashion of the great catacombs of Paris. Three sides of this interior crypt were still ornamented in this manner. From the fourth the bones had been thrown down, and lay promiscuously upon the earth, forming at one point a mound of some size.

Edgar Allan Poe in *The Cask of Amontillado*

GEOLOGY OF THE LONDON AREA

'*Sous les Pavés, la Plage*' ('beneath the paving stones the beach') was a particularly evocative graffito from the Paris student riots of 1968, when cobblestones were torn up from the streets to be hurled at the police. Although sand can be found in certain outcrops in the London area the city is mostly underlain by rocks and sedimentary strata formed over hundreds of millions of years. London lies within the Thames Basin, a large syncline, which consists of a sandwich of geological layers, with the chalk outcrops of the Chilterns forming part of the northern rim and those of the North Downs the southern.[1] Much deeper down the oldest rocks from the Silurian Age, roughly 425 million years ago, are folded into an arched anticline that may once have been a ridge until covered by the seas in which the chalk formed. If a hole were drilled from Tottenham Court Road through 1200 feet of rock the deepest layer encountered would consist of the Devonian Palaeozoic rocks laid down several hundred million years ago and underlying the entire London region.[2]

Heading upwards, rocks of the Jurassic period form another layer 65 feet thick, followed by 160 feet of Gault Clay and 28 feet of Upper Greensand. On this rests a massive 655 feet thick layer of chalk, whose formation can be traced back to the deposition over at least ten million years of the bodies of billions of creatures. The sedimentation occurred at a time when the London region lay beneath a vast sea that stretched to the Pennines in the north and the Welsh Marches to the west. This chalk forms the depression of the London Basin and reaches into the centre in small outcrops as far as Greenwich Park. Over this chalk a layer of Thanet Sands extends for 21 feet, above which is a stratum of 52 feet of sediments known as the Woolwich and Reading Beds. These consist of mixed coloured sands, clays and pebble-beds of flint or quartz and concretions of various materials originally laid down in shallow, partly brackish water. Known by miners centuries ago as Shepherd's Plaid, this stratum varies between 25 feet and 80 feet in thickness throughout most of the London area. It outcrops only at intervals between Dulwich, Plumstead and Eltham and is mainly water bearing, where sand and gravel occur.

Immediately above this stratum to the south of the Thames, the Blackheath Tertiary Beds are responsible for the barren soil of the plateau in south London after which they are named and for the open spaces further south at Plumstead, Chislehurst and Hayes Common. At Tottenham Court Road, however, the Woolwich and Reading Beds are overlain by the famous London Clay that, beneath this part of central London, extends for a mere 64 feet. Much of the London Underground has been carved through this clay and an engineer with much experience of tunnelling through it describes it thus:

> "London blue clay is a sedimentary deposit. Starting as a very fluid mud about 70 million years ago, its water content was gradually reduced by pressure from the weight of superincumbent materials until it reached its present stiff, over-consolidated and relatively impermeable state. It is composed of very fine particles and has a complex mineral composition. The presence of ferrous oxide of iron gives it its characteristic greenish-blue colour, but weathering changes the state of oxidation of the iron, and near the top of the stratum its colour changes to brown ...At Wimbledon its thickness is over 400 feet and at Highgate about 350 feet, but due to denudation arising from changes in land levels its thickness is less than 100 feet towards the middle of the basin."[3]

The London clay is overlain by a series of sandy deposits once laid down by the waters of a shallow sea, known as the Claygate beds. In certain parts of London, especially Hampstead and Highgate, the Bagshot Beds form another sedimentary layer. They accounted for Hampstead's fame as a spa in the eighteenth century, as there are numerous springs at the junction of the sand and the impervious clay. Great quantities of sand on the Heath were dug up to fill sandbags in the Second World War. Continuing with the borehole in central London, the last twenty feet or so consists of gravel, alluvium and made ground before the pavement is reached, although human intervention has disturbed the shallower layers. There are no *natural* caves in the London region as both clay and chalk are unsuitable for cave formation.

'JACK CADE'S CAVERN'
Some mysterious underground caverns were, however, re-discovered in south London more than two hundred years ago. The area, known geologically as the Blackheath Tertiary Beds, was once extensively quarried for deposits of chalk, limestone, sand and gravel. Beneath the pebbly soil are layers of clay and sand and under those a thick layer of chalk. This chalk layer is nearest the surface at the escarpment known locally as 'The Point', on the western edge of Blackheath. In 1780 a local builder discovered an entrance to a series of three caverns excavated from the chalk and connected by passages, which reached to a depth of 160 feet below the surface. The three excavations became known as the main chamber, the inner chamber and the well chamber. The whole complex was dubbed 'Jack Cade's Cavern' after the rebel leader who had assembled an army on Blackheath in 1450. A flight of steps was constructed down to the caverns, which became a local curiosity and later, in the nineteenth century, an unusual venue for entertainments. During the 1850s the public were permitted to visit the caves for 4d or 6d for a tour by torch-light. Following the installation of a bar, a chandelier and a ventilation system powered by bellows, the caverns were used for drinking parties and balls. During one masked ball in 1853 the lights were extinguished and panic ensued. This incident, coupled with the growing unsavoury reputation of the caves, led to the entrance in Blackheath Hill being sealed in 1854. However, local legends accrued around the caverns and their existence was not forgotten.

There was an unsuccessful attempt to rediscover them by the local council in 1906,

1. Visitors to 'Jack Cade's Cavern' in the 1850s.

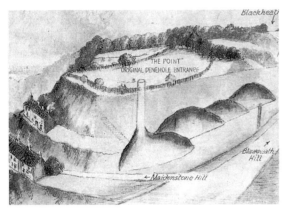

2. A Sphere magazine conjecture of a Denehole on Blackheath of which 'Jack Cade's Cavern' was part.

but in 1938 a determined effort to explore the caverns was made with the aim of utilising them as air-raid shelters. The original entrance could not be located, so a shaft was sunk at the rear of 77 Maidenstone Hill, which intercepted a short stretch of passage whose walls had been carved with names and dates of previous visitors. The end of the passage was blocked and a second passage had to be excavated around it, which eventually joined up with a clear area leading to the caverns. The explorers found the wreckage of the bar and noted that the brass pulley for the chandelier remained in the roof. Further explorations revealed the former well chamber, which had been sealed off, containing a dry well 21 feet deep. This chamber and the passage leading to it were also heavily inscribed with initials and graffiti, the oldest dating to 1780, as well as a prominent carving of the devil. Rubbish was cleared away, the cavern roofs were supported by wooden props and a new ventilation shaft was inserted, but the plan to convert it to an air-raid shelter was eventually abandoned as there was felt to be insufficient cover.[4]

A popular explanation for these features is that they are examples of Deneholes, which frequently occur in south London and north Kent. Deneholes consist of shafts sometimes as deep as eighty feet with a pattern of caves at their base, which do not extend for any great distance and which do not link up with similar excavations. Their name derives from the legend that they were used to hide from the invading Saxons and Danes in the long period following the withdrawal of the Roman legions in the fifth century. It is more likely that they are survivals of very early chalk mines and their discovery can account for many cases of 'secret tunnels'.[5] 'Jack Cade's Cavern' was probably a mine dug to supply chalk during the construction of St Paul's cathedral in the late sixteenth or early seventeenth centuries. There have been many instances of subsidence in the area around the caverns, a notable incident involved the loss of a

horse in a 15-ft hole in Kidbrooke in 1798; similar subsidence was recorded in 1878 and 1880. A little further to the north a series of underground brick conduits supplied water to the palace at Greenwich and these have in the past been mistaken for secret passages.[6]

THE EARLY ARCHAEOLOGY OF CENTRAL LONDON

Walk down a charming narrow alleyway behind the Old Bell Tavern in Fleet Street past the groaning bowed walls of St Bride's churchyard and enter the church. Follow the sign to the crypt, pointing down a short flight of steps to the right and you will encounter the fascinating archaeological history of underground London at first hand. The evidence of nearly 2000 years of human occupation, religious belief and construction are visible and labelled in this relatively unknown display. One of the few benefits resulting from the destruction of large swathes of the City of London during the bombing raids of the Second World War was the opportunity afforded to archaeolo-

3. A Map of Roman London featuring the recently discovered amphitheatre on the site of the Guildhall Yard.

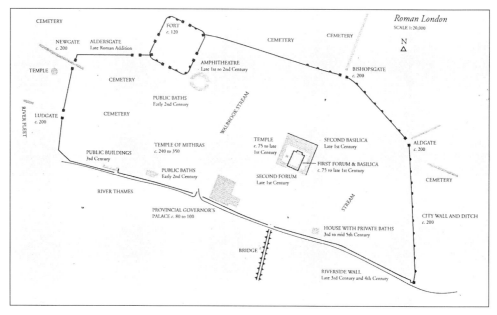

gists to reveal the buildings and artifacts of previous ages and civilisations stretching back to the Romans. A small area of tessellated pavement can be glimpsed, reflected in a mirror in the corner of St Bride's crypt, a survival of what has been claimed to be one of the earliest buildings in the City.

One of the earliest human interventions in the soil of the City was a pre-Roman burial on the future site of the Tower of London. Following the successful Roman invasion in AD43 a settlement was established near the River Walbrook on Cornhill by AD50. The Roman presence is acknowledged as declining around AD410, when the legions were recalled to defend Rome from hostile incursions. During this period of roughly 350 years an important Roman city was constructed, whose major buildings have since been discovered through archaeological investigations, principally since the Second World War.[7] The important structures so far found include a reconstructed forum and basilica of the early second century, the largest such complex in Britain, discovered beneath Gracechurch Street. The forum measuring 545 x 548ft included on its northern side the basilica 172 x 548ft, the centre of law and administration, with an apse at the east end.

A visit to the bath house was an integral part of a Roman Londoner's day. The largest suite was located at Huggin Hill, terraced into the hillside and heated by a subterranean hypocaust system. Significant bath houses have also been found in Milk Street and near the former Billingsgate Market, the latter providing some of the latest evidence of Roman occupation in the City. The discovery of the temple of Mithras beside the covered-over river Walbrook in 1954 was one of the most important and

4. The Mithraeum of Roman London. A reconstruction by Alan Sorrell.

publicised finds of recent years. The fort in the north-western corner of Roman London, whose western gate can be viewed beneath the Museum of London and the so-called Governor's Palace, now thought to be a collection of grand buildings, were further significant finds that increased our knowledge of the importance of Roman London. The most recent major discovery was the uncovering of a small part of the amphitheatre on the site of the Guildhall Art Gallery.[8] Evidence of the dress and appearance of Roman Londoners is rare, but the unearthing of a stone coffin containing a decorated lead sarcophagus at Spitalfields in March 1999 caused considerable excitement. The skeleton inside was that of a young woman and the contents included a long glass phial and a jet box dating to the fourth century AD.

The previously confused situation regarding the Anglo-Saxon settlement, mentioned in a handful of documents, but lacking archaeological evidence within the City walls, was clarified spectacularly by remarkable discoveries during the excavation at Jubilee Hall in Covent Garden in 1985. Although a small ecclesiastical community probably existed on the western side of the City, close to the first St Paul's founded in 604, the secular trading port referred to as "a mart of many nations" by Bede in 703 was located to the north of the Strand (the shoreline at that date) in the present-day Covent Garden area. Known as Lundenwic, it flourished between the seventh and ninth centuries, before Viking raids in the ninth century forced King Alfred to reoccupy and fortify the old Roman walled city of Londinium, the new settlement being named Lundenburgh.[9] Evidence for the western Saxon settlement was found, including sunken buildings of timber and wattle and daub, alleyways, pottery, rubbish pits and human burials.

Given the depth of modern foundations and the huge amount of redevelopment in central London in the last fifty years it is unlikely that any further major archaeological finds on the scale of the forum or amphitheatre will be made. However, during the course of the excavation of the Jubilee Line Extension more evidence of London's early history emerged.[10] Thorney Island, on which the Houses of Parliament sit, was formed between two branches of the River Tyburn as they entered the Thames. Proof that the island had been occupied by pre-historic peoples was provided by a neolithic leaf-shaped arrowhead and fragment of polished axe. During the excavation of the new Westminster station late Bronze Age or Iron Age pottery was found. The Romans also appear to have built on Thorney Island, although the remains of walls and foundations have yet to be discovered.

The site of London Bridge Jubilee Line Underground station was probably the most interesting for archaeologists, as it was from near here that the first bridge across the Thames was established, close to the site of the present London Bridge. The promise of the site was amply fulfilled and a great deal of information was gained about the growth of this area so close to the City, especially during the Roman period. A road deck was installed along Borough High Street in Easter 1995 with services such as water and electricity pipes and cables suspended beneath it so that work could continue below. Timber and clay houses that once lined the main road leading up to the Roman bridge were discovered, together with a layer of fire debris, that indicated that the settlement south of the river may have been destroyed, like its counterpart to the north, by Boudicca and her marauding followers in AD 61. The houses, shops and warehouses were rebuilt after this conflagration and by the end of the second century Roman Southwark may have had a population of over three thousand. Samian ware pottery, brooches, oil lamps, glass and coins provided evidence of the everyday items used by these early settlers.

BURIAL GROUNDS, CEMETERIES AND CATACOMBS

Much of underground London may lack the thrill elicited by penetrating the complex labyrinth of catacombs beneath Paris or Rome but a number of its Victorian cemeteries have smaller catacombs amongst the monuments and mausolea.[11] As the population of London grew and the number of burials increased, the central area and its parish churchyards, in use since the middle ages, became grotesquely overcrowded and by the nineteenth century posed a significant health hazard. The sight of body parts protruding through the soil was also a factor in the closure of these congested graveyards. John Evelyn in his diary describes the overflowing churchyards packed with bodies, "one above the other, to the very top of the walls, and some above the walls." Charnel houses were increasingly used as repositories for the stacked bones of the dead, disinterred to accommodate new

burials; a rare example survives at Hythe Church in Kent.

One of the oldest burial grounds in London can still be visited along the City Road, opposite John Wesley's House and Chapel. Bunhill Fields was once a large field in the manor of Finsbury, the name derived from a hill of bones and was leased by the Corporation of London from 1315. The hill was formed from the remains of the charnel house at St Paul's churchyard which were deposited on this site in 1549. The Corporation intended to use it in 1665 as a burial ground for the victims of the Great Plague and at that time it was walled and enclosed, although plague burials do not seem to have been made there. Unconsecrated, Bunhill Fields was later used for the burial of Nonconformists and such dissenting luminaries as John Bunyan, Daniel Defoe, Dr Isaac Watts, Susannah Wesley and William Blake. Closed after the Burials Act of 1852 it saw its final burial in 1854; it is estimated

5. Bunhill Fields burial ground in 1876.

6. *A perspective view of Brompton Cemetery made in 1849.*

that 120,000 bodies lie there. It is still preserved by the Corporation as the only cemetery remaining in the City.

Sir Christopher Wren envisaged new extramural cemeteries following the destruction resulting from the Great Fire of London, with impressive architect-designed memorials and mausolea. John Evelyn made plans for a universal cemetery for all London parishes extending straight for a mile across North London. The church objected, as these schemes would interfere with the money they made from burial fees. In the nineteenth century the rapid increase in population and rise in the death toll from visitations of cholera after 1832 placed even more strain on the already overcrowded parish churchyards of the city. The London Cemetery Company was formed in January 1832 and the first of its private cemeteries at Kensal Green was opened in July that year. Between 1837 and 1841 Parliament authorised the establishment of six additional commercial cemeteries in a ring around what was then the periphery of London: Abney Park, Brompton, Highgate, Nunhead, Tower Hamlets and West Norwood.

Kensal Green includes brick-vaulted catacombs with space for 10,000 bodies and the Anglican chapel once had a lift to lower coffins from the interior to the catacombs below. Brompton, established in 1840, features a series of catacombs beneath its impressive colonnades entered through iron gates decorated with various symbols of death. When Nunhead was built two areas of catacombs were situated to the east of the gates, the larger consisting of a brick barrel-vaulted chamber with 144 cells, entered by a staircase together with a brick catacomb shaft 17 feet deep. The neglected and vandalised cemetery was bought by Southwark Council in 1975 and the dilapidated catacombs sealed. Highgate, the most famous of the seven, was consecrated in May

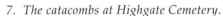

7. The catacombs at Highgate Cemetery.

1839 with an extension on the east side of Swain's Lane opening in 1857.[12] From the chapels on the western side a tunnel was excavated under the road to the new cemetery and coffins were raised and lowered into it on each side by means of a hydraulic system. In the older cemetery the tomb-flanked Egyptian Avenue leads to the magnificent Circle of Lebanon, catacombs placed on either side of a circular passageway. Highgate cemetery contains 166,600 bodies in 51,000 graves and covers 37 acres.

The commercialisation of cemeteries disturbed certain reformers such as Edwin Chadwick, who complained about their high costs for interment. A burial in a brick vault could cost as much as £50. The Metropolitan Interments Act passed in 1850 was an attempt to improve the situation by appointing a Board of Health with powers to lay out new cemeteries. Old churchyards were closed and further burials forbidden; in addition the Act empowered the Board

to compulsorily purchase private cemeteries if required. The Board encountered many difficulties, however, and following the repeal of the 1850 Act a Burial Act was passed in 1852, which instead provided powers for local vestries to elect their own burial boards to determine where burial grounds would be located and to oversee them. A number of Burial Acts followed over the years that were finally rationalised in the Local Government Act of 1972. Anthony Trollope and Charles Voysey were enthusiastic supporters of the Cremation Society founded in 1874, but it was not until 1902 that London's first crematorium opened at Golders Green. The total area covered by London's cemeteries is about 3000 acres.

CRYPTS, VAULTS AND CELLARS

A number of atmospheric ancient crypts survive beneath historic churches, mainly in the City of London. Medieval cellars and vaults can still be found beneath the pave-

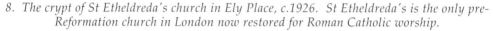

8. The crypt of St Etheldreda's church in Ely Place, c.1926. St Etheldreda's is the only pre-Reformation church in London now restored for Roman Catholic worship.

ments throughout London. The largest and most visited crypt is that beneath St Paul's Cathedral in which Lord Nelson and the Duke of Wellington lie amongst many other notables, including the building's architect, Sir Christopher Wren. Sequestered St Etheldreda in Ely Place, a church that was originally built as the chapel to the town house of the Bishop of Ely, contains a crypt dating from the middle of the thirteenth century. St Bartholomew the Great at Smithfield, the oldest church in the City, has a Norman crypt that served, following the Dissolution of the Monasteries, as a wine cellar. A secular crypt occasionally open to inspection is that beneath the City's Guildhall, which is the largest in London to survive from the medieval period. The western part is thought to date from the thirteenth century and was probably the undercroft of an earlier Guildhall, whilst the eastern dates back to the fifteenth century. Amidst the sturdy pillars of Purbeck marble and the ragstone and Reigate stone walls the records of the City were stored during the Great Fire of 1666 and were saved from destruction.

The Carmelites or White Friars had a cemetery and a series of monastic buildings to the south of Fleet Street that were mostly built in the thirteenth century. Despite the dispersal of London's monastic communities and subsequent depredations a small fragment of their friary remains. Along Whitefriars Street in Britton's Court, beneath the site of a former newspaper building, a room twelve feet square constructed mainly of chalk blocks with a ribbed stone ceiling, once formed part of the prior's house. Originally constructed around 1420, it was later used as a coal cellar until it was purchased and restored by the *News of the World*. In 1986 the building was vacated when the newspaper relocated to Wapping. After redevelopment in 1988-89 the structure was once more preserved under the Freshfields building that now dominates the site.

9. The west crypt of the medieval Guildhall, as restored in 1973.

Beneath the tower of the church of All Hallows Staining in Mark Lane lies the crypt from another church. St James in the Wall was an ancient hermitage in Monkwell Street near Cripplegate, which passed into the ownership of the Clothworkers' Company in the sixteenth century. William Lambe, a member of that guild, bought the church in 1543 and left it to his company. The crypt, dating from the twelfth century, was moved and rebuilt beneath All Hallows Staining, close to the Clothworkers' Hall, where it can be visited today by arrangement. All Hallows-by-the-Tower exhibits Roman and Saxon remains in its undercroft. St Mary-le-Bow has a Norman crypt, a meeting place for the ecclesiastical Court of Arches, the curving Romanesque style of these arches giving their name to the church. The extensive crypt under St Martin-in-the-Fields in Westminster has been successfully converted into a popular café.

Two of London's most interesting wine cellars are situated close to one another in the centre of Westminster. Berry Brothers & Rudd, the traditional wine merchants at 3 St James's Street, have access to extensive cellars, some on two levels, that stretch for a considerable distance beneath the surrounding streets, capable of storing up to 18,000 cases of wine. Off Whitehall, Cardinal Wolsey once owned a wine cellar 64 feet long, 32 feet wide and twenty feet high, one of the few survivals from his residence York Place, which became the Whitehall Palace that burnt to the ground in 1698. The cellar is preserved beneath the Ministry of Defence and the construction of a new block for the MOD in 1947 would have necessitated its destruction, had it not been physically moved underground to a more convenient location. This complex engineering feat involved the 1000 ton structure being placed on a concrete platform, resting on

10. Cardinal Wolsey's old wine cellars, originally in the episcopal town house, York Place, in Whitehall.

two hundred steel rollers, which moved it 43 feet 6 inches to the west. After its former location was excavated a further twenty feet, the cellar was rolled back and lowered to a position roughly beneath its original site, the whole process having taken two and a half years.[13]

Countless wine and coal cellars still exist beneath London's streets, many of them converted to new uses. Similarly, pub cellars can harbour historic secrets; the beer barrels of the Viaduct Tavern opposite the Old Bailey sit among the remains of the gloomy cells of Giltspur Street Compter, a debtors' prison demolished in 1865. The Olde Cheshire Cheese, approached down the narrow alleyway of Wine Office Court off Fleet Street, conceals layers of atmospheric cellars going back to the medieval period. Areas of underground London have been used for entertainment purposes for many years as bars, clubs or restaurants such as Quaglino's. The Criterion Theatre at Piccadilly Circus is completely under-

ground, as is the Pit at the Barbican. In 1999 Fabric, another of London's burgeoning 'superclubs', opened beneath Smithfield Market at 77a Charterhouse Street, occupying fourteen arches formerly lined with cork and used for meat cold storage. A massive series of spaces capable of holding 2500 people, the club contains beautiful brick walls and vaults interspersed with steel walkways and staircases: it achieved publicity for its minimalist unisex toilets.

Hidden away below Strand Lane behind the closed Aldwych station, lies a 'Roman' bath, a plunge pool about 16ft x 7ft with an apsidal end, which probably only dates as far back as the eighteenth century. Close by, the importance of the tram in the history of public transport is illustrated by the Kingsway Tram Tunnel, constructed under the road named after King Edward VII and opened in 1906. The tunnel was extended to the Victoria Embankment in 1908, where it served as a link between the north and south London tram systems. It included

11. The Olde Cheshire Cheese in Wine Office Court, off Fleet Street.

12. Entrance to the underground Criterion Theatre in Piccadilly Circus.

13. The so-called 'Roman Bath' in Strand Lane, probably an 18th-century plunge pool.

two subterranean stations at Holborn and Aldwych and was enlarged in 1931 to accommodate double-decker trams. Becoming finally redundant as trams were phased out in London, it closed in 1952. The southern section was converted in 1964 into a traffic underpass, the northern section becoming a GLC flood-control centre.

Also nearby and, prior to the construction of the Victoria Embankment much closer to the Thames, stood the Adelphi (built 1768-72), an ambitious residential development, whose Piranesian arched underground vaults are the only survival of the Adam brothers' original ambitious and beautiful scheme.[14] Known as the Adelphi Arches, they were constructed in order to level the sharply sloping site and provide solid foundations. The groined vaults were built over a system of underground streets, designed to facilitate access to the wharves at the foot of the Adelphi Terrace, below which were further vaults. The lower vaults were prone to flooding at high tides and the Government therefore refused to lease the cellars for storing gunpowder in the late eighteenth century. Guns were stored there in 1848, however, in the expectation of violence at the Chartist demonstrations in central London. Also in the nineteenth century the arches were used as stables and cows were even kept there under artificial light in a subterranean farm. In 1850 Thomas Miller could write that, "Thousands who pass along the Strand never dream of the shadowy region which lies between them and the river – the black-browed arches that span right and left, before and behind, covering ... ground on which the rain never beats, nor the sunbeams sleep, and at the entrance of which the wind only seems to howl and whine, as if afraid of venturing

14. *A single-deck tram emerges by the Embankment from the Kingsway Tram Tunnel c.1926, to connect with south London lines. A man with a flag warned oncoming traffic of its imminence.*

15. *By 1931, the tunnel had been deepened to allow for double-decker trams such as this one photographed in 1952, the year the tunnel was closed.*

*16. The Adelphi scheme fronting the Thames and its foreshore, designed by the Adam Brothers.
Goods could be off-loaded and taken through arches beneath the buildings, to the Strand.*

further into the darkness."[15]

The building of the Victoria Embankment from 1864-70 blocked the direct access from the Thames and from this time the Arches were used as coal and wine cellars. They also became criminal dens where "the most abandoned characters have often passed the night, nestling upon foul straw". It was observed that "many a street thief escaped from his pursuers in these dismal haunts before the introduction of gaslight and a vigilant police".[16] In 1936-38 the Adam houses above the vaults were demolished to be replaced by the present monolithic block that adopted the name Adelphi. One writer on underground London was shortly afterwards shown the remains of the cellars strung with stalactites and confessed, "I had no idea that I should be introduced to long subterranean passages, with high-arched doorways, dark tunnels running off at right angles for fifty yards or so, bewildering turnings, and at last, at the foot of a few steps, a dark little chamber that looked rather threatening to me".[17] Lower Robert

Street, once a gloomy winding tunnel, still survives as an entrance to an underground car park and certain vaults can be seen beneath the Royal Society of Arts, another building by the Adam brothers.

In Camden Town a number of underground passages and vaults dating back to the nineteenth century survive close to the Roundhouse. A subway was provided for horses to enable them to reach the goods station formerly to the south. The impressive brick vaults beneath the Roundhouse were used effectively in the summer of 1999 for an installation art work by Mimmo Paladino with atmospheric 'ambient' sounds supplied by Brian Eno. The Chancery Lane Silver Vaults, originally the Chancery Lane Safe Deposit Co., were established in 1882 and used by Hatton Garden silver dealers and jewellers to store goods, but gradually merchandise began to be sold from the vaults themselves. Following the destruction of their former premises in the Blitz the London Silver Vaults were reopened in their underground site in 1953. The guards are

17. The Victoria Embankment blocked the through use of the arches beneath the Adelphi scheme. Many of the arches became vaults for wine or coal, such as this one photographed c.1926.

no longer allowed to carry guns. Today over thirty silver dealers are based in these secure subterranean vaults. Harrod's, besides having its own artesian well, includes an extensive underground domain with a tunnel that links it with its warehouse in Trevor Place and side tunnels and cellars for storing frozen food and wine together with a cell in which shoplifters can be temporarily incarcerated. In the heart of fashionable Clerkenwell lies an atmospheric warren of underground cells and passageways that were once part of the Clerkenwell House of Detention. The three storeys above ground were demolished in 1890 but ventilation tunnels, a laundry, kitchen and transportation cells remain. (Formerly open to the public the building was closed in the summer of 2000.)

Beneath the massive brick edifice of the new British Library on Euston Road four levels of huge basements descend nearly 75 feet, as deep as the warren of London Underground tunnels that run close to the building. The basements are equipped with advanced air-conditioning and filtration systems that provide optimum conditions for the preservation of the twelve million books stored there. The volumes occupy some of the 190 miles of purpose-built shelving with advanced systems for protection from fire and water damage. The spoil from the excavation of the basements was added to the existing slag hill near Beckton Power Station which now features a dry ski-slope. Underground car parks have also staked a large claim on the subterranean city with some of the largest examples in Bloomsbury and Finsbury Squares.

ICEHOUSES AND CANALS

Amongst the secluded streets behind King's Cross, beside Battlebridge Basin, is another unusual subterranean survival housed in the London Canal Museum. In the days before ice could be produced in every home it had to be found locally or imported, usually from Norway and stored prior to its despatch to fishmongers, butchers and others in the catering trade. The storage areas consisted of deep ice wells, where the large bulk of the ice helped to preserve it, after having already lost one third of its weight in transit from Norway to London. For the last stretch of the journey the large blocks were transported along the Regent's Canal by barge. At King's Cross the ice was stored in wells in a warehouse owned by

18. *Conjectured plan of the inner workings of Gatti's ice house in New Wharf Road, near King's Cross. Drawing by Brian Alldridge for the London Canal Museum, 1996.*

19. *The eastern entramce to the Regent's Canal tunnel at Islington. Barge operators had to propel their craft through this by lying flat on the boat and pushing their legs against the tunnel walls. Illustration by T.H. Shepherd, published in 1829.*

Carlo Gatti (1817-1878), a famous restaurateur and producer and populariser of ice cream. Two ice wells 34 feet across and 42 feet deep were excavated between 1858 and 1863 before the building was constructed. Subsequent accumulations of rubbish have been gradually removed recently to reveal more of these impressive spaces, some of which could reach one hundred feet in depth. In the Victorian era the ground floor was used by horse-drawn ice carts for collection and delivery. Gatti's wells are a reminder of the former scarcity of everyday commodities we now take for granted.[18]

The Regent's Canal, opened on 1st August 1820 from the Grand Junction Canal at Paddington to the Thames at Limehouse, includes along its route two tunnels in the heart of London. Already an expensive excavation, the cost of the Maida Hill tunnel was increased when work had to be undertaken following the discovery of a spring en route, but the 272-yard long bore was eventually successfully completed. The Islington tunnel is 960 yards long. Progress along both tunnels, before mechanised barges, involved 'legging', whereby two men would lie on their backs on the barge and 'walk' along the walls carrying the vessel with them.

Footnotes for Chapter One

[1] A detailed study is *British Regional Geology: London and the Thames Valley* 4th ed. compiled by M G Sumbler (HMSO, 1996).

[2] See R S R Fitter *London's Natural History* (Collins, 1945), 8-14.

[3] H G Follenfant *Reconstructing London's Underground* (London Transport, 1974), 10-11.

[4] See Neil Rhind *Blackheath Centenary 1871-1971, a short history of Blackheath from earliest times* (GLC, 1971) pp2-3 and Jeremy Errand *Secret Passages and Hiding Places* (David & Charles, 1974), 146-149.

[5] The Chelsea Speleological Society has published detailed records of caves and mines in south-east England that can be ordered on the internet at http://www.demon.co.uk/stoneweb/css. The study that covers Greenwich and Blackheath is *CSS Records Vol. 15 Caves and Tunnels in South-East England Part 7*.

[6] John Stone "Greenwich: its underground passages, caverns etc." in *Transactions of the Greenwich Antiquarian Society* Vol 1 1914, 262-277.

[7] The best recent surveys are Dominic Perring *Roman London* (Seaby, 1991) and Gustav Milne *English Heritage Book of Roman London, Urban archaeology in the nation's capital* (B T Batsford/English Heritage, 1995).

[8] Nick Bateman 'The discovery of Londinium's amphitheatre: excavations at the Old Art Gallery site 1987-88 and 1990' in *London Archaeologist* Vol 6 No 9 Winter 1990, 232-241, published quarterly by the London Archaeologist Association and a useful source for recent discoveries. MOLAS the Museum of London Archaeology Service publishes an annual report which also updates London's archaeology.

[9] A good account of this period that includes the discoveries of the 1980s is Alan Vince *Saxon London: an Archaeological Investigation* (Seaby, 1990).

[10] Museum of London Archaeology Service *The Big Dig, Archaeology and the Jubilee Line Extension* (MOLAS, 1998).

[11] The best guide to London's cemeteries is Hugh Meller *London Cemeteries, An Illustrated Guide and Gazetteer* (3rd ed. Scholar Press, 1994) See also James Stevens Curl *A Celebration of Death* (Constable, 1980), ch vii.

[12] See Felix Barker and John Gay *Highgate Cemetery, Victorian Valhalla* (John Murray, 1984) .

[13] Michael Harrison *London Beneath the Pavement* (Peter Davies, 1971), 223-224.

[14] *Adelphos* is the Greek for brother.

[15] Quoted in F L Stevens *Under London, a chronicle of London's underground lifelines and relics* (J M Dent, 1939), 97.

[16] Quoted in Ben Weinreb & Christopher Hibbert eds. *The London Encyclopedia* (Papermac, 1983, rev. ed. 1995), 7.

[17] F L Stevens *op. cit.*, 96.

[18] The London Canal Museum 12-13 New Wharf Road London N1 9RT. For more on ice storage see Sylvia Beamon and Susan Roaf *The Icehouses of Britain* (Routledge, 1990) and Tim Buxbaum *Icehouses* (Shire Publications 1992).

CHAPTER TWO

Buried Waters

'London's rivers,' said Mr Snell. 'You can bury them deep under, sir; you can bind them in tunnels, you can divert them and stop them up and forget about them, you can lose the map, and wipe the name out of mind, but in the end where a river has been, a river will always be.'

'There's hundreds and hundreds of miles of it [sewers] under London. We have teams of flushers working, but it takes them a while to get round. Unless we gets a problem it might be more than a year before we come past somewhere.'

Dorothy L. Sayers and Jill Paton Walsh in *Thrones, Dominations* (Hodder & Stoughton, 1998)

THE 'LOST RIVERS' OF LONDON

London's fields were once intersected by many rivers feeding into the Thames: only a few of them are visible above ground today. They provided valuable sources of fresh water and fish, but as a result of the huge growth of the capital's population in the nineteenth century became fetid hazards to public health and were therefore culverted and subsequently covered over to become part of the expanding sewerage system.[1] In central London to the north of the Thames once flowed the Westbourne, Tyburn, Fleet and Walbrook and to the south the Effra, Falcon, Peck and Neckinger amongst others. The Wandle, Beverley Brook, the Ravensbourne and of course the River Lea have survived despite being canalised, partially built over or diverted over the centuries. At Dulwich and Sydenham in south London these rivers originated in the hills from springs where the porous, water-bearing chalk meets the non-porous London Clay in its thinnest layers. In the Hampstead-Highgate massif there are a number of springs where the sand and gravel rest on the impervious clay. These so-called 'lost rivers' of London are recalled in literature and numerous paintings and illustrations and are powerfully evocative of the meta-

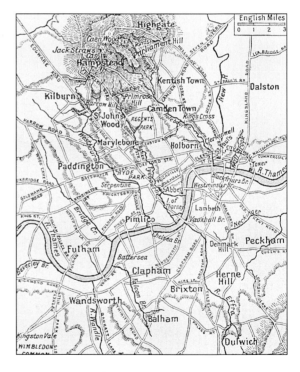

20. *A map of the central London rivers, now mostly covered over.*

morphosis of the London landscape over the last two thousand years. The courses and features of some of the more important of them are described below.[2]

28

THE FLEET

The existence of the river Fleet, which gave its name in the medieval period to the important thoroughfare Fleet Street, was one reason for the Roman establishment of the first settlement close to the Thames around AD50, as it provided a secure western barrier and an inlet for boats to dock. The Fleet derives its name from an Anglo-Saxon word meaning a tidal-inlet.[3] In its higher reaches it was known as Hole Bourne, the River of Wells and Turnmill Brook, owing to the number of mills powered by its fast-flowing water. Rising to the west on Hampstead Heath where the Hampstead Ponds store its waters, one stream runs south near Hampstead Heath station and follows the course of Fleet Road to Camden Town. To the east another stream emanates from the grounds of Kenwood

21. The river Fleet near Hampstead, sketched in 1854.

House; it runs through the man-made Highgate Ponds and meets the Hampstead waters in the old railway lands opposite Kentish Town Station. In 1826, when in flood near Camden Town, this watercourse was reported to be 65 feet wide. From this point the river flowed to St Pancras Way, past the ancient church of (Old) St Pancras to the area once called Battle Bridge, now more familiar as King's Cross. Following a heavy downpour, the author, who once lived nearby, remembers hearing the storm waters rushing beneath St Pancras Way along the course of the vanished river.

From King's Cross the Fleet continues down King's Cross Road, where it once flowed through the grounds of Bagnigge Wells, a popular eighteenth-century spa. Past Mount Pleasant and on towards the Metropolitan Line along Farringdon Road, which runs in its former valley, the Fleet caused havoc when it burst in on the construction works of that railway. Streets to the south bear witness to the former passage of the Fleet, such as Turnmill Street where a number of water mills were once located. In the nineteenth century the area had acquired an unsavoury reputation as it was close to the notorious criminal rookery at Saffron Hill, used by Dickens as the location for Fagin's den. Further south the river was joined by the Faggeswell Brook running its incarnadine way from the slaughterhouses of Smithfield. In the thirteenth century tanners and cutlers had established themselves along its banks and from 1343 the butchers of Newgate Street were allowed to cleanse entrails from a wharf to the south near the Fleet Prison. The shape of the river valley is clear from the steepness of Snow Hill and the presence of the 1400-feet long Holborn Viaduct, constructed between 1863 and 1869 to bridge these slopes once so treacherous for horse-drawn transport. One of the statues in niches on the buildings beside the viaduct is of Sir Hugh Myddelton, pioneer of the New River water supply.

22. *One of the Highgate Ponds, constructed as reservoirs to harness the supply of the Kenwood arm of the Fleet river.*

Newcastle Close and Old Seacoal Lane recall the days when ships carrying coal from the North East would be berthed here and Turnagain Lane the earlier impossibility of continuing further. A bridge spanned the river at Fleet Lane, where the Knights Templar and later the Knights Hospitaller had a wharf and where patients for St Bartholomew's hospital could be landed. John Stow (1525-1605) in his *Survey of London* mentioned four other bridges over the lower section of the Fleet at Cow Bridge, Holborn Bridge, Fleet Bridge and Bridewell Bridge. Sir Christopher Wren's (1632-1723) plans for rebuilding the City after the Great Fire included grand wharves and quays along the side of the Fleet in its southern stretch and the northern bank of the Thames. He did get the chance to build a new bridge over the river at Holborn in 1674, as the Fleet was deepened and canalised in this final section. Even by the fifteenth century the Fleet was referred to as a ditch and was becoming increasingly polluted. Jonathan Swift (1667-1745) gives a colourful account of the polluted state of the Fleet by the beginning of the eighteenth century in *A Description of a City Shower* published in 1710:

> Now from all parts the swelling Kennels flow,
>   And bear their Trophies with them as they go:
>   Filth of all Hues and Odours seem to tell
>   What Street they sail'd from, by their Sight and Smell.[4]

In 1732 the Fleet was arched over from Holborn Bridge to the Punch tavern in Fleet Street. The Fleet Market, removed from its former incarnation as the Stocks Market on the site of the Mansion House, successfully traded on the site above the river from 1737 until 1830 when it closed. In 1765 the section from Fleet Street to the river was similarly covered over and the Fleet began the long process of its transformation into a sewer. The upper reaches from Camden Town to King's Cross were covered in by the early nineteenth century, following extensive development in the area. The section from

23. *Today's King's Cross Road, looking south, just south of the Bagnigge Wells pleasure gardens. The river Fleet, which went through the grounds of Bagnigge Wells, is to the right. Tile kilns are on the other side of the road.*

Hampstead to Camden Town was diverted into a high-level intercepting sewer in 1872. At the end of its route the river once disgorged its contents into the Thames between the site of the Blackfriars monastery and the Bridewell Palace, built for Henry VIII from 1515-20 and used as a prison from the late sixteenth century up to 1855. Today, the Fleet sewer discharges into the Thames from an arched tunnel entrance, four and a half miles from Hampstead, beneath Blackfriars Bridge.[5]

A recent archaeological investigation of the lower Fleet River valley discovered previously unknown northern and southern eyots (islands) on the eastern side that survived until the late twelfth century.[6] A Roman milling complex existed on the

24. *Interior of the Fleet ditch at the back of Field Lane, a road displaced by the construction of the southern end of Farringdon Road.*

25. The mouth of the river Fleet at Blackfriars, a sketch of 1749. To the west were the remains of Bridewell Palace.

northern eyot and wharfage on the southern, that were abandoned in the third or fourth centuries. By the late eleventh century the northern eyot was the location for London's earliest prison, named after the river that surrounded it, saving the trouble of digging a moat. The Fleet prison was a grim edifice beside the increasingly rank waters of its river, although the moat had been filled in by Stow's time. Rebuilt after the Great Fire of 1666, it numbered amongst its hundreds of unfortunate debtor inmates Hogarth's father and William Penn; it was destroyed again in the Gordon Riots of 1780. Rising from the ashes once more, the prison was later used by Charles Dickens as the place of incarceration for Samuel Pickwick.

From the more amenable circumstances of retirement in Dulwich, Pickwick wrote his *Speculations on the source of Hampstead Ponds with some Observations on the Theory of Tittlebats.* The prison was closed in 1842 and demolished in 1846. The ancient watercourse has not been completely forgotten however, as a letter was printed in *The Guardian* on 20 March 1996 from a group that "want to convert Farringdon Road back into the course of the old Fleet River". This wildly optimistic, almost certainly unrealisable, but imaginative and exciting project would banish one of the City's traffic-clogged streets and enable the Fleet to flow once more through the heart of the metropolis.

THE TYBURN

The River Tyburn is another lost river, whose course can still be traced through the streets and topography of central London.[7] From its main source, the Shepherd's Well near Fitzjohns Avenue in Hampstead, it flows through Swiss Cottage and thence beneath Regent's Park and Marylebone Lane. The latter's winding course reflects that of the buried river, its name deriving from St Mary by the bourne, or stream. The sloping streets to the east of Berkeley Square such as Hay Hill indicate the valley of the Tyburn, which then flows beneath Green Park and Buckingham Palace, and along the line of Tachbrook Street before finally discharging into the Thames to the west of Vauxhall Bridge, where the outfall is clearly visible.[8] In 1860 the underground enthusiast John Hollingshead (1827-1904) descended into the sewer from a point near St John's Wood Chapel and followed its course through narrow tunnels and eventually "through an iron tube, about three foot high and two feet broad, which conveys the sewage over Regent's Canal, through the crown of the bridge."[9]

After passing beneath Baker Street, Hollingshead was able to stand upright, and some distance later was halted by his guides, who informed him that they were standing directly beneath Buckingham Palace. On hearing this news, "my loyalty was at once excited, and, taking off my fan-tailed cap, I led the way with the National Anthem, insisting that my guides should join in." The veteran traveller Eric Newby (b.1919) also walked along the Tyburn in 1963 at a time when the final stage of the river was still open near the Sewer Depot in Grosvenor Road.[10] Finding "a fine unmounted pair of antlers" and "a folio Bible in Welsh" in the river he proceeded underground, walking towards Piccadilly. Newby asked his experienced sewerman guide if there were anything special about the sew-

26. Marylebone, from the site of the present Wigmore Street, showing the Tyburn in the foreground. From a print of 1750.

age from Buckingham Palace. "Well, you can take it from me, that what comes down hasn't got 'By Appointment' on it", was the reply.[11] Overpowered by the atmosphere he emerged from a manhole cover at the corner of Moreton and Tachbrook Streets.

THE WESTBOURNE

The River Westbourne is also of interest, again originating on the heights of Hampstead and once flowing in the open through Kilburn, Maida Vale and Paddington to Hyde Park. In 1730, following Queen Caroline's orders, its course here was dammed to form Long Water and the Serpentine. At Albert Gate, where the river leaves Hyde Park, it was crossed by a bridge, Knightsbridge, and continues beneath Kinnerton Street and Cadogan Lane to Sloane Square, where a large pipe conveys it above the Underground railway tracks

inside the station. From beneath Holbein Place it splits, one branch discharging into the Thames near Chelsea Royal Hospital and another at the Grosvenor Canal dock, beside the railway bridge leading to Victoria station. By 1834 its lower reaches had been covered over and by 1856 a similar fate had befallen the remainder of the river.

Following the expansion of Bayswater and the perceived need for drainage and sewerage a proposal was put forward in 1808 that the houses in the new streets would discharge their effluent into the submerged Westbourne, just before it entered the Serpentine. Faced with the noisome prospect of a polluted lake in a popular central London park it was decided instead to divert the river away to the east into what became known as the Hyde Park Tunnel Sewer. This was completed in 1813, flowing east under the park on its north side, from Albion Street

27. *The river Westbourne contained in an iron pipe over the platforms and track of Sloane Square station.*

28. *The Westbourne crossing the main road at 'Knight's Bridge' on its way to Chelsea.*

before it runs south to rejoin the course of the river on the south side of Knightsbridge. From there the Westbourne ran as an open watercourse known as the Ranelagh Sewer. The vicissitudes of the Westbourne were to continue with the development of Belgravia by the 2nd Earl of Grosvenor in the 1820s and further discharges into its waters augmented by those from building developments further to the north. By 1834 the lower reaches were covered over to prevent the "miasmic influence" of the open sewer's fumes.

The Grand Junction Waterworks Company built a pumping station in 1820 by the Thames near the Royal Hospital, Chelsea, with Boulton and Watt engines, to obtain drinking water from the river rather than from the Grand Junction Canal, which had been its former source. As a contemporary illustration makes clear the intake equipment (or dolphin) for the potential drinking water was situated a few feet into the Thames, directly where the fetid waters from the Westbourne/Ranelagh Sewer drained into the river. It is little wonder that the wealthy inhabitants of Belgravia were to complain about the poor quality of their drinking water.

29. *Extract from a map of London c.1558, showing the Moorfields area. The City wall with Moor Gate is to the south and the Moor Field itself, used mainly for recreation and drying clothes is to its north. To the east of the Field is the river Walbrook (see opposite page) which has been diverted into the moat around the City wall.*

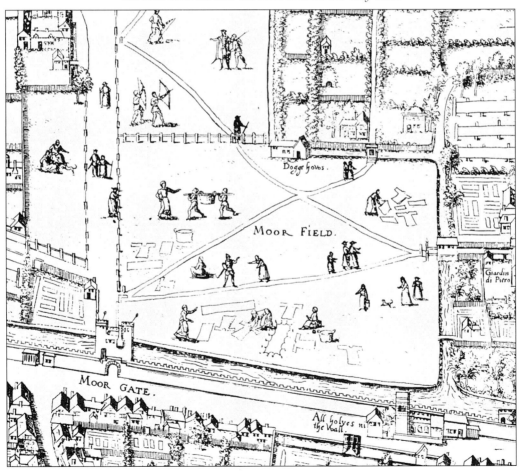

30. St Margaret's Lothbury, as rebuilt after the Great Fire, on vaults over the Walbrook.

THE WALBROOK

The Walbrook, that once bisected the City, has its origins in Moorfields, the once swampy land to the north of the City walls, "the great marsh or sheet of water washing the walls of the city on the north side." The stream passed through the city wall to the west of the church of All Hallows-by-the-Wall and ran south west to be crossed by a bridge, which it was the responsibility of the prior of Holy Trinity within Aldgate to repair. It then flowed through Tokenhouse Yard to St Margaret's Lothbury, built on vaults above the waters and then curved to the south-west to pass beneath the site of the Bank of England. The Walbrook was observed there during building works in the eighteenth and nineteenth centuries. Flowing to the east of what is today James Stirling's No.1 Poultry, it formed a small valley where the Romans erected their temple to Mithras on its banks. Many years later it flowed against the wall of the chancel of St Stephen Walbrook church, which at first stood on the west side of the watercourse. The actual route of the river is about 150 feet to the west of the street named after it and its presence can be detected by a still discernible dip along Cannon Street between Budge Row and Walbrook.

From here it proceeded under the Horseshoe Bridge to reach Cloak Lane, where a monument marks the site of the church of St John the Baptist upon Walbrook, destroyed for the construction of the Metropolitan District Railway. This thoroughfare is probably named after the sewer (Latin *cloaca*) that ran down the street into the Walbrook. College Street nearby was once known as Elbow Lane, commemorating the sharp turn the Walbrook took here as it flowed towards the Thames. At this point it formed the boundaries of the City wards of Dowgate and Vintry and was only between twelve to fourteen feet wide, but could nevertheless be treacherous. The indefatigable Elizabethan chronicler, John Stow, records that on 4 September 1574 after a heavy rainstorm, "a lad of eighteen years old, minding to have leapt over the channel ... was taken into the stream, and carried from thence towards the Thames with such a violence, that no man with staves or otherwise could stay him till he came against a cartwheel ... before which he was drowned, and stark dead".[12] Following complaints about its polluted and noisome state this lower section was culverted and covered over from the middle of the fifteenth century, although the final Dowgate section was open for many years. Even before Stow's time the Walbrook, "which was of old time bridged over in divers places, for passage of horses and men ... the channel being greatly straitened ... the same by common consent was arched over with brick, and paved with stone, equal with the ground wherethrough it passed, and is now in most places built upon, that no man by the eye discern it, and therefore the trace thereof is hardly known to the common people".[13] Today it is known as the London Bridge Sewer, running 30-35 feet below the City's streets and disgorging its contents into the Thames from an outlet about 120 feet to the west of Cannon Street station.[14]

LOST RIVERS SOUTH OF THE THAMES

The area covered by the northern reaches of Wandsworth, Lambeth and Southwark consisted of desolate marshland until the nineteenth century. Whilst south London still enjoys rivers such as the Wandle meandering towards the Thames, others have gone the way of their counterparts to the north. One of the now-hidden rivers is the Effra, a name derived from the Celtic *'yfrid'*, meaning a torrent. The source of the river is still debated. The Upper Norwood hills seem to be the generally accepted area, whence it flowed through Norwood Cemetery and beside Croxted Road, where it was joined by a tributary near the Half Moon

pub by Herne Hill station. Following the north-eastern side of Brockwell Park and across Rush Common it reached Brixton. From there it ran along the eastern side of Brixton Road as far as St Mark's church Kennington, where it turns west. Even today it is still possible to visualise the Effra running down Brixton Road, if the river of traffic can be temporarily blotted out. Some of the houses here are set back from the road behind a grass verge that resembles a river bank. The river at this point was twelve feet wide and six feet deep as it ran to Kennington church, then along the south side of the Oval passing under South Lambeth Road at Cox's Bridge to discharge into the Thames just upstream from Vauxhall Bridge.[15] The lower reaches of the Effra were being used as a sewer by the seventeenth century, but it was still running in the open through

31. Martin's farm in Loughborough Road off Brixton Road, next to the river Effra.
A sketch of 1784.

Dulwich in the middle of the nineteenth century. Some writers claim to have identified a still extant stretch of the Effra in Dulwich village at Belair, where it forms a long pond and a pleasant ornamental feature.

The Falcon Brook, once known as the Hidaburna, rises near Tooting Common and Balham, the two streams joining near Clapham Common, before tracing a course across Wandsworth Common towards Clapham Junction. The eighteenth-century Falcon pub on the corner of Falcon Road recalls the course of the river, named in the sixteenth century after the 'falcon rising' crest of the St John family, once lords of Battersea Manor. Battersea was known in the Saxon period as Badric's Island, created by the Falcon as it divided near Falcon Grove. One branch went west through York Gardens to enter the Thames at Battersea Creek upstream from the heliport. The other follows the Clapham Junction to Victoria railway line, passes the famous Dogs' Home and enters the Thames just to the east of Battersea Power Station.

The stream called Neckinger ran from Bermondsey Abbey to the Thames, but it probably rose to the west in St George's Fields near the Imperial War Museum, passing near the Elephant and Castle before running east towards the Lock Hospital and crossing Great Dover Street. From there it flowed through the grounds of Bermondsey Abbey, entering the Thames at St Saviour's Dock where a luxury flat-flanked inlet still exists. The river's unpoetic name is derived from the 'Devil's neckinger' or neckerchief, a popular term for the hangman's noose used in the execution of pirates at a spot close to the river's outlet to the Thames. The Neckinger also flowed around Jacob's Island, notorious for its squalor in the nineteenth century and called the 'capital of cholera'.

LONDON'S WATER SUPPLY

When the Romans first established their settlement on the site of the present City one of the major factors for choosing that location was the presence of the Walbrook, running between the two small hills with water-bearing gravel terraces, known today as Ludgate and Cornhill and the wider Fleet running to the west. These were convenient sources of fresh water and fish. Clay pipes were laid to convey the waters of the Walbrook through the City to public conduits and baths. Abundant supplies of fresh water were therefore always available from the Thames and its tributaries, supplemented by wells. During the medieval period water was also taken from various springs, streams and wells, which became centres of social activity. Mystery plays were performed at the *Fons Clericrum* or Clerks' Well, that gave its name to present day Clerkenwell. There were important wells at Holywell in Shoreditch and St Clement's Well near Clement's Inn on the north side of the Strand; Wellclose Square off Cable Street also reminds us of a local water source.[16] In 1183 William Fitzstephen in his famous brief description of London could happily describe the "excellent suburban springs, with sweet, wholesome, and clear water that flows rippling over the bright stones".[17]

Already by the thirteenth century chroniclers were complaining about the poor state of these local sources of supply. It was realised that water would have to be brought in from further afield and a system of conduits was developed to meet the growing need. The Tyburn Conduit was constructed in 1236 to convey water by gravity from present-day Stratford Place (in Oxford Street) on a route close to Conduit Street as far as St James's Church Piccadilly, and then eastwards following the edge of the hill. Through Soho the Conduit continued eastwards to the north of the Strand and Fleet Street, crossing the Fleet river at Fleet Bridge to discharge its contents in Cheapside, a total distance of over 3000 yards. Here it was freely available to be carried away in jugs from the Great Conduit at the east end and the Little Conduit at the west. Water could also be purchased from the carts of water-carriers, who formed a guild in 1496 calling themselves the Brotherhood of Saint Christopher of the Waterbearers. Its use by London's tradesmen was often subject to assessment and charging. The conduit at Cheapside was made to run with wine to celebrate special royal occasions such as Edward I's return from the Holy Land in 1274 or following the coronation of Henry VI in 1432. In the fifteenth century the Charterhouse received a supply of water by aqueduct from Canonbury and St Bartholomew's priory and hospital were reported to have an independent supply in pipes that had "run of old".

Also in the fifteenth century Westminster Abbey leased to the City some springs adjoining the Westbourne near Paddington that were soon connected by lead pipe to the Tyburn Conduit. The Standard Conduit at Cornhill, first erected in 1401, was used for measuring distances to the capital. By the middle of the sixteenth century there were many conduits in London, the cost of whose construction and maintenance was met by various prominent citizens and civic dignitaries.[18] For example, in 1577 William Lambe rebuilt the conduit at Holborn – his name is remembered today in Lamb's Conduit Street. The London Bridge Waterworks provided the earliest pumped water supply in 1581 from beneath the first northern arch of London Bridge, where a waterwheel pumped the supply to Cornhill. Pieter Morice, who paid a yearly sum of ten shillings for this privilege, had proved the efficacy of this technology when he directed a jet of water over the steeple of St Magnus the Martyr. A second wheel was built by Bevis Bulmar in 1594 which could raise water at the rate of 216 gallons per minute. Both

32. *A familiar figure in London's streets was the water carrier, who collected water at wells and sold to individual houses.*

waterwheels were rebuilt after the Great Fire but were removed by 1822.

In 1606 and 1607 the City obtained Acts to bring water from Chadwell and Amwell in Hertfordshire to London. In 1608, Edward Colthurst offered to carry out the project, but soon after he began the City resumed responsibility, only then to entrust the scheme to goldsmith Hugh Myddelton (c.1560-1631) in 1609, in which year construction began again.[19] The New River, actually a canal, took only four years to excavate and when completed was 38 miles in length and ten feet wide. After his own resources were exhausted Myddelton sought help from James I, who eventually paid for

33. *The wheels and pumps of London Bridge Waterworks, built by Pieter Morice and opened in 1581. Underneath the arches nearest to the northern shore near Pudding Lane, they were engulfed by flames in the Great Fire and rendered useless as a fire fighting tool.*

half the total cost in return for a half-share in the profits. By keeping to the hundred-foot contour the design allowed a gradual flow downhill to its reservoir at New River Head, the Round Pond near Sadler's Wells. However, as it was a commercial enterprise, water from the New River was only supplied to paying customers: privatisation of water supplies had begun. The Society of Hampstead Aqueducts was established in 1693 to supply the Holborn district with water from four reservoirs on Hampstead Heath fed by the Fleet river. By the early eighteenth century private water companies were becoming increasingly dominant. Given the massive growth of London at the turn of the nineteenth century the New River in its lower reaches was channelled through underground pipes. In 1946 the river was terminated at Stoke Newington, where a lavish baronial pumping station had been erected. It continued to be the major source of water for the City and north London

34. *Sir Hugh Myddelton.*

35. *The New River Head, Clerkenwell, near Sadler's Wells. Drawing by Wenceslaus Hollar, 1665, perhaps made in comparative safety away from the Great Plague in the City.*

36. *Building a new reservoir for the New River Company on the site of today's Claremont Square.*

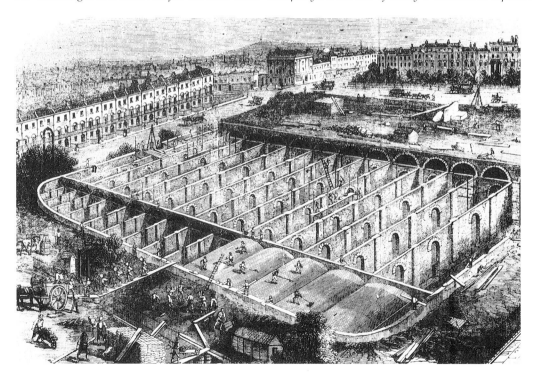

37. *Elm water pipes in Soho, outside St Anne's church. They were part of the system which conveyed water from near Stratford Place, off Oxford Street, to the City of London.*

until the late 1980s, when it was supplemented by the Thames Water Ring Main. Today the former route can still be easily traced through the streets of north London.[20]

Following the development of steam pumping machinery several private companies were set up in the eighteenth and nineteenth centuries to supply water to London from the tidal Thames. The Chelsea Waterworks Company was established in 1723 to be followed by the Southwark (1760), Lambeth (1785), Vauxhall (1805), West Middlesex (1806), East London (1807), Kent (1809) and the Grand Junction (1811) water companies, leading to fierce competition and a quest for profits. Connections were made to the homes of paying customers by small pipes or 'quills' and as supplies could be erratic wealthier customers subscribed to a number of companies. Though the Chelsea Company had laid the first iron main in 1746, it was not until the Metropolitan Paving Act of 1817 compelled water companies to lay their pipes in iron that this material, previously avoided owing to the increased cost of manufacture, was used widely. During the early nineteenth cen-

38. *Chelsea Waterworks looking towards Westminster Abbey. A print of 1752 by J. Boydell.*

39. *A satirical print, entitled 'Monster Soup', published in 1828, dedicated to the London water companies. It depicts the horrendous quality of their water supply.*

40. *Death rowing in the Thames, the source of much of London's drinking water. A drawing in Punch, 1858.*

41. *Death dispensing water at the sort of street standpipe found by Dr John Snow to be the source of cholera.*

tury the quality of water supplied by these concerns was rapidly declining, as it was drawn from the increasingly foul Thames. The link between polluted drinking water supplies and cholera was publicised in 1849 in Dr John Snow's (1813-1858) pamphlet *On the Mode of Communication of Cholera*. Even so, it was only after considerable campaigning by public spirited reformers such as Edwin Chadwick (1800-1890), that Parliament at long last acted.

The Metropolis Water Act of 1852 constituted an important step forward in improving London's appalling water supply by appointing a London Water Examiner. The companies had to cover all reservoirs within five miles of St Paul's, filter all domestic supplies through sand beds and could only take water from the Thames above Teddington Lock. Together with the requirement to provide a constant supply of water these measures resulted in a significant drop in mortality in central London, although they were not readily adopted by all the water companies. After years of criticism and many abortive Water Bills a Royal Commission in 1900 recommended that the companies be taken over and that a government body should be created. The Metropolis Water Act was passed in 1902, creating a Metropolitan Water Board that took over the eight private water suppliers at a cost of £40 million. Large scale reservoir and waterworks building proceeded, including the King George VI reservoir at Staines in 1947. On 1 April 1974 the Metropolitan Water Board was replaced by the Metropolitan Division of the Thames Water Authority and in 1989 Thames Water was established as a private company with a principal operating subsidiary, Thames Water Utilities, intended to supply water and provide sewerage services.

Most of London's water was carried from the Thames and River Lea through cast-iron pipes laid by the Metropolitan Board of Works but age, increasing pressure and the weight of London's traffic have taken their toll and contributed to increasingly serious leakages and bursts. Thames Water today has 20,000 miles of mains, between two and sixty inches in diameter, spread over 5000 square miles, together with 50,000 miles of sewers, 98 water treatment and 355 sewage treatment works. In the past the River Lea, on the eastern side of London, was also a source of water with its reservoirs at Coppermills. Eventually, however a 19-mile tunnel had to be dug in 1955 from Hampton to Coppermills near Lea Bridge to compensate for the relative paucity of water further east. Roughly three-quarters of London's water supply is drawn from the Thames to be stored in the large reservoirs at Hampton, Ashford, Kempton Park, Walton-on-Thames, Stanwell and Wraysbury and then cleaned and pumped to customers in central London. The expense of this pumping system, which was prone to breakdown and the need to distribute water more efficiently around London, led to the construction of the Thames Water Ring Main.

THE THAMES WATER RING MAIN

At the time of writing anyone walking past the former Islington headquarters of Thames Water along Amwell Street is greeted by the surreal sight of a huge decorated pipe on a trailer sitting forlornly in the car park. This was part of a display advertising the construction of the Thames Water Ring Main, the longest tunnel constructed in Britain and claimed to be the world's most advanced urban water control system. Excavated mechanically at an average depth of 130 feet, the 50 mile-long Thames Water Ring Main has a diameter of 7½ feet. 'Dorothy', one of the three 55-ton cutting machines, churning deep beneath the London streets, broke the world record for tunnelling when it removed 550 yards in five days. The Thames Water Ring Main was excavated from 21 access shafts with little disturbance to those living nearby or above, taking eight

years to complete from 1986 to 1994 at a cost of £250 million. Lasers were employed in the navigation of the tunnelling machines and the exact position of each shaft was plotted with the aid of the satellite-based Global Positioning System. Many of the experienced tunnellers joined the project after finishing work on the Channel Tunnel and then went on to the Jubilee Line Extension. The majority of the excavation was through London clay and did not present too many problems, although a one mile stretch of tunnel was flooded when a section of Thanet sand was encountered beneath Tooting Bec Common. The treacherous ground had to be chemically frozen before tunnelling could recommence. At such a great depth the tunnellers avoided pipes, drains and cables and could use the pressure of the clay to bond the concrete segments of the tunnel in place.

42. (Above) Standing in the newly made Thames Water Ring Main tunnel.

43. (Right) The water meter tower at Shepherds Bush roundabout.

The huge project was built in phases in order to link the five large water treatment works on the Thames in the west with centres of demand in London and with reservoirs to the east along the River Lea. The final phase was completed near Ashford Common treatment works. Massive structures incorporating nineteen-ton valves have been built underground at the twelve points where the tunnels link with shafts that connect the main to the shallower water distribution network.[21] Beneath the Park Lane roundabout in Mayfair a vast pumping station was constructed 130 feet down. Similar installations exist at Shepherd's Bush roundabout and Barrow Hill next to Regent's Park.

Though the general flow of supply is from west to east the main is built so that water can flow in either direction. As the tunnel forms a massive loop enclosing London maintenance can be made easier by closing a section and diverting water away from the affected area. For gravity to keep the water moving the tunnel must be full and local usage is monitored by flow meters situated in the network. Information is relayed by a specially developed optical fibre cable that will not degrade in water, which runs along the side of the tunnel and sends messages to the twelve pumping stations. Sensors are placed on the tunnel walls and the interior of the main can be observed on closed-circuit television. The data is displayed at the new £3.2 million control centre in Hampton which monitors pressures, flows, water levels and the quality of most of the capital's water supply. The system is also designed to minimise inconvenience from burst mains by re-routing the supply when problems occur. The Thames Water Ring Main is part of a sophisticated London-wide water control system that can supply up to 1300 megalitres of water every day, half of London's drinking water. It should guarantee that Londoners enjoy good quality drinking water for many years to come.

WELLS

Some Londoners do not have to rely on piped water as they have their own supply drawn from a well. About fifty properties in central London enjoy this privilege as they include boreholes or artesian wells sunk through the London clay to extract some of the millions of gallons of water held in the chalk aquifers. Sadler's Wells was initially famous in the seventeenth century for its healthy spring waters and the rebuilt theatre now sells patrons designer bottles of its own water drawn from a 200-foot borehole. Harrod's has three boreholes that penetrate 500 ft below the store and deliver over one thousand cubic metres of water each day, saving an estimated £200,000 a year in water bills. The Army and Navy store in Victoria Street and the former Simpson's of Piccadilly (now appropriately a branch of Waterstone's) similarly tap these limitless resources. The Bank of England used its underground liquid assets for all purposes until the water was discovered to be too rich in minerals – its drinking water is now taken from the mains supply. The Abbey National headquarters in Baker Street bottled and sold its natural water for charity in the 1980s. The Dolphin Square apartment complex along Grosvenor Road, which includes a swimming pool, is supplied by four boreholes. The new office block for members of Parliament, Portcullis House, recently built above the reconstructed Westminster tube station, is served by an underground water supply used during the construction works for the Jubilee Line Extension.[22]

Despite these extractions from beneath the city's streets Thames Water plans to sink fifty new boreholes around London to counteract the rise in London's water table, which has been creeping upwards, owing to a decline in industrial usage since the 1970s. Ironically, it was also thought that some of this increase is due to excessive leakage from water supply pipes. In 1997 it was revealed that Thames Water was losing 38% of its water in this way, a situation which is currently being addressed. 68 million litres of groundwater will be pumped out each day at an initial cost of £10 million, with costs of £2 million each year thereafter. Some of it could be used for drinking water, or for industrial use or street cleaning, or otherwise discharged into London's extensive sewerage system.

SEWERS

Waste disposal was a matter of concern for the authorities in the City from the medieval period onwards. Rubbish and excrement lay in the streets, to be occasionally washed away by heavy rain into ditches and streams, that then carried it to the Thames. As early as 1290 the White Friars living near the Fleet, complained that the stench from the polluted river was affecting their health and preventing them from carrying out their religious duties. In the reign of Edward III (1327-1377) the City was ordered to provide twelve carts to remove sewage and rubbish. Householders along the Walbrook were ordered to keep rakes for removing obstructions to the stream. By the middle of the fourteenth century rakers were having to remove waste from the streets once a week. Richard II (reigned 1377-1399) in a statute announced that, "none shall cast any garbage or dung or filth into ditches, waters or other places within or near any city or town on pain of punishment by the Lord Chancellor at his discretion." Human wastes were mostly disposed of in outdoor privies discharging into cesspools. These were periodically cleared by nightmen, rakers or gong-fermors, who transported it to the fields and market gardens then in close proximity to the London streets. It could be a precarious job: in 1326 Richard the Raker fell into a cesspit and drowned, "monstrously in his own excrement". Cesspools also leaked, sometimes into local watercourses and wells, a potential source

44. Nightmen, who removed the contents of dung heaps and cesspits at night.

of ill health. Many years later Samuel Pepys could still record that, "Going down into my cellar ... I put my foot into a great heap of turds, by which I find that Mr Turner's house of office is full and comes into my cellar, which doth trouble me".[23]

In 1531 an Act created the Commissioners of Sewers and established eight commissions to regulate London's primitive system of sewers, and to survey streams, ditches, bridges and weirs. They had the powers to fine offenders and to appoint officers to enforce their orders. This was followed by a number of local Acts empowering commissioners to construct new sewers, although these were intended for surface water rather than human waste. The connection of cesspools or house drainage to street sewers was forbidden at that time. Those

45. *The Fleet sewer in c.1830, before the rebuilding of the sewer system by Bazalgette.*

46. *Deepening the sewer in Fleet Street in 1845.*

sewers that were constructed were still inadequate. Even after the destruction wrought by the Great Fire had provided an opportunity to improve water supply and sewerage, plans such as those put forward by Sir Christopher Wren (1632-1723) were ignored. The Rebuilding Act of 1667 contained powers to enlarge and clean the City sewers, but these lapsed when the rebuilding was complete. Through complacency and inefficiency the City, by the mid-nineteenth century, possessed only fifteen miles of sewers.

The introduction of the water closet was eventually to seriously affect the quality of the water in the Thames. The prototype has been attributed to Sir John Harington (1561-1612) in the late sixteenth century, but was improved upon by Joseph Bramah (1748-1814). Between 1778 and 1797 Bramah supplied more than 6000 water closets, which were to become widely used in London by the middle of the nineteenth century.[24] Following the passage of the Metropolitan Buildings Act of 1844 it became mandatory to connect cesspools and drains to sewers. By this time there were three million people in London, dwelling in an estimated 300,000 buildings. Most of these were situated above a cesspool, which sometimes overflowed into the lower rooms. The creation of the Metropolitan Commission of Sewers in 1847 resulted in the amalgamation of the eight bodies surviving from the sixteenth century. By 1850 legislation required that new properties were to include water closets and that cesspools were to be abolished. The effect of these 'improvements' was that the entire contents of the proliferating water closets were released into the sewers, originally only designed to carry surface water. The effluent was thus carried to the Thames, which rapidly assumed a cloacal character. Even more worrying, the first serious outbreak of cholera occurred in 1831-32 to be followed by more virulent outbreaks in 1848-49 when

47. Joseph Bazalgette.

14,000 died, 1853-54 and 1865-66. Doctor John Snow (1813-1858), flew in the face of the prevalent belief that disease was spread by inhaling a noxious 'miasma'. He proved, through careful monitoring and recording of the incidence of cholera amongst the poor drawing water from a pump in Broad Street, Soho during the outbreak of 1854, that cholera was spread through contaminated drinking water. A pub bearing his name is situated close to the site of the pump from which the unfortunate residents obtained their tainted water.

In the sultry summer of 1858 pollution of the river had become so serious that London experienced the 'Great Stink' as members of Parliament were forced to abandon the House of Commons close to the putrid Thames. Fortunately, the great Victorian engineer, Joseph Bazalgette (1819-1891), had been appointed Chief Engineer to the new Metropolitan Board of Works in 1856. From 1859, under Bazalgette's direction, a massive construction programme commenced that would transform the riverside and

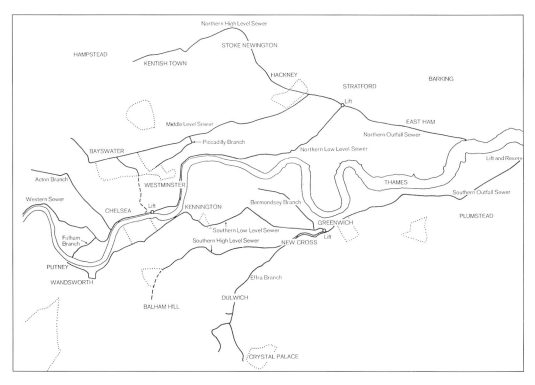

48. Map of the main sewers proposed by Bazalgette. Work began in 1859.

provide London with a cleaner, more efficient sewerage and drainage system.[25] The essence of his plan was to build three levels of intercepting sewers north and south of the river, those north of the river running eastwards to Abbey Mills and then on to the huge treatment works at Beckton beside Barking Creek. The high-level sewer ran for nine miles, at depths of between twenty and 26 feet, from Hampstead Heath to Old Ford on the River Lea, intercepting sewage and surface water from the older drains and sewers. The middle-level sewer at a depth of up to 36 feet ran twelve miles from Kensal Green, with branches from Piccadilly and Gray's Inn Road, to Old Ford where its flow was combined with that of the high-level into the northern outfall. The tunnels were designed to be egg-shaped, in order to ease the flow and encourage a scouring action along the walls. The lowest level sewer to the north was built into sections of the

Victoria Embankment which was opened in 1870. The tunnels of the District Line were incorporated into this impressive and complex structure. Additionally, the Albert and Chelsea Embankments were constructed as part of this grand scheme.

South of the river Bazalgette proposed a low-level sewer from Putney, a low-level branch sewer from Bermondsey, a high-level sewer from Roehampton and a high-level branch sewer from Norwood. They would all meet at Deptford pumping station, where the low-level sewage would be lifted and the whole flow carried to the southern outfall at Crossness, whose complex of buildings and machinery were opened by the Prince of Wales (later King Edward VII) in 1865. At Beckton and Crossness the sewage was not treated but discharged into the Thames on the ebb tide. Nevertheless the rapid improvement in Thames water quality in central London

49. *The shoreline of the Thames near Somerset House before the construction of the Victoria Embankment.*

50. *Sectional drawing of the main drainage pipes being laid near Old Ford, Bow in 1859.*

51. Commencement of the high-level sewer near Victoria Park, Hackney.

was significant. At Crossness the effluent was lifted 21 feet to a reservoir, to await discharge. This was accomplished by the use of four 47-ton beam engines, the largest ever built, provided by James Watt & Co., that continued in service until 1953.[26] The northern outfall works were finished in 1864, but the whole of Bazalgette's ambitious and life-saving programme, consisting of 1300 miles of mostly brick-built sewers, was not completed until 1875. Today Bazalgette's bust occupies a niche along the Embankment near Hungerford Bridge, a small monument to one of the least appreciated designers of London's fabric.

Bazalgette's works still remain at the core of London's sewerage system, which has been considerably expanded since then. The sewers did not have sufficient capacity for storm water so, in 1878, pumping stations were installed at the outlets of the Effra and Falcon rivers. In 1879, following severe flooding, twelve miles of storm relief sewers were built. In 1887 it was decided to precipitate the sewage chemically at Beckton and Crossness, allowing only the effluent to run into the Thames, the sludge being removed in ships to be dumped at sea. Many improvements were carried out under the London County Council, successor to the Metropolitan Board of Works, between 1900 and 1914 and between 1919 and 1935, but water quality had reached a new nadir by 1950. In 1964 a plant was built at Crossness for treating sewage with bacteria and the Beckton works was enlarged to become, by 1974, the largest in Europe. The very poor quality of the Thames water was dramatically improved and the first live salmon since 1833 was caught at West Thurrock.[27] Sewerage is now the responsibility of Thames Water Utilities who, in 1998, opened a £165 million sludge incineration plant at Beckton and a sludge-powered generator at Crossness as an alternative to dumping at sea, curtailed by European directives. The generator at Crossness produces enough electricity to power the entire sewage works, whilst at Beckton sufficient is generated to be sold to the National Grid. As a result Thames Water's sludge-boat, the *SS Bazalgette*, finally became redundant. Bark-

52. *An aqueduct built at Abbey Mills, Stratford, in connection with Bazalgette's main drainage works.*

53. *Building the Embankment at Chelsea.*

54. A Penstock Chamber, a sluice for controlling water flow with a gate which opened by lifting upwards.

55. *Intercepting sewers at Hammersmith in the 1920s.*

ing Power Station has been rebuilt as a combined cycle gas turbine (CCGT) station by Thames Water, where energy is generated by igniting the methane gas naturally present in sewage and is then exported to the National Grid.

Today there are around 50,000 miles of sewers beneath the streets of London, only 5% of which are more than three feet in diameter. The main intercepting sewers, which traverse London from west to east, can reach fifteen feet in height and occasionally open out into large subterranean chambers where sewers join. A small team of about eighty employees of Thames Water have to enter the sewers in groups of between five and eight to perform a variety of vital tasks, including re-pointing ancient brickwork, poisoning rats and scraping off the fat that lines the walls. Their numbers have been cut in recent years, as it was considered too expensive and dangerous to send people into the ageing capillary network. Much of their inspection work is now done remotely by small tractors, equipped with powerful lights and video cameras, relaying their pictures from the depths back to operators on the surface. These peripatetic machines survey between 375 and 500 miles of sewer each year in the Thames region. Common problems revealed are blockages, pipes deformed and cracked by tree roots, or unexpected pipes installed illegally that break through the tunnel walls.

56. *Crossness at the southern outfall of the new sewage system. It was opened in 1865.*

The narrower sewers can be relined by inserting new plastic pipes or by placing over the tunnel mouth a long membrane coated with resin, which is forced into the sewer by pumping water into it and bonded to the wall with hot water. Side pipes are reconnected by a CCTV tractor equipped with a rotary cutting tool.

One additional recent problem has been the build up of fatty deposits on the sides of tunnels, a result of the detritus produced by the host of fast food outlets in the West End, with Leicester Square and Piccadilly being identified as the worst fatspots. A representative of Thames Water has complained that, "It's like concrete ... there are instances where we've had between 30 and 40 inches solid where we could barely push a stick into it".[28] The only way to remove this troublesome coating is by digging it out, although experiments, as yet unsuccessful, have been undertaken with fat-eating bacteria. Whilst the modern sewers of central London are not inhabited by the alligators of New York urban legend there is a declining population of brown rats (*Rattus norvegicus*) and thriving colonies of cockroaches. According to scientific research cockroaches can survive on a diet of human faeces and used medical swabs and within central Westminster, with its numerous restaurants and hotels, a colourful variety of species has been discovered. The oriental cockroach (*Blatta orientalis*) can be found beneath the streets of Chinatown and the American cockroach (*Periplaneta americana*) thrives close to the outlets of the larger hotels. With their extensive laundries and kitchens, they keep the temperature in the sewers directly underneath at 30 degrees Centigrade.[29]

VICTORIAN PUMPING STATIONS

Bazalgette's new sewerage system required three major pumping stations to lift the effluent as it travelled by gravity for most of its course along the natural gradient of the London Basin. These were the Western in Pimlico, Abbey Mills in north-east London and Deptford in the south. With its distinctive minaret tower, the Western Pumping Station at Grosvenor Road has intrigued many travellers in and out of Victoria Station. Built between 1872 and 1876 by the Metropolitan Board of Works it originally contained eight plunger pumps worked by four steam-driven beam engines, each of 90 hp. In 1937 the station was replanned and the electric and diesel pumps installed at that time are still running today. Sewage from an area about 4200 acres west of the station enters the works through Low Level One, a 6' 9"-diameter sewer. If the weather is dry the pumps raise the sewage about 18 feet into the east Low Level, where

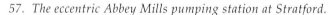

57. The eccentric Abbey Mills pumping station at Stratford.

58. The Moorish interior of the Abbey Mills pumping station.

it gravitates without the need for further pumping, down to Abbey Mills further east. With heavy rainfall the flow in the sewer is increased and, in order to prevent flooding, storm water is diverted to the river.

Abbey Mills Pumping Station, because of its elaborate Venetian Gothic appearance, has been nicknamed the 'cathedral of sewage'. Built between 1865 and 1868 to the designs of Bazalgette, it originally had a pair of ornate chimneys on either side that had to be demolished during the Second World War in case they were used as landmarks for German bombers. Although the attractive buildings remain, all the original plant has been removed. Abbey Mills is situated next to the Northern Outfall Sewer embankment containing four nine-foot diameter iron pipes that carry over 100 million gallons of sewage each day. Deptford Pumping Station opened in 1864 and contained four beam engines that lifted the sewage twenty feet to the Southern Outfall Sewer that ran from there to Crossness.

POST MODERN PUMPING STATIONS

The extensive redevelopment of Docklands in recent years required widespread improvements in the area's infrastructure, especially in the fields of sewerage and drainage. Between 1985 and 1997 the London Docklands Development Corporation (LDDC) built over 12½ miles of public trunk sewers and four major pumping stations to deal with waste water. Over £120 million was invested in sewerage and drainage, with substantial contributions from Thames Water Utilities. The new pumping stations, designed by major British architects, are distinctive buildings that also perform a vital drainage function for the occupants of Docklands. One of the first to be constructed and perhaps the most memorable was the Isle of Dogs Pumping Station which is intended to resemble a vividly coloured 'temple to summer storms'.

As a result of the Victorian development of main drainage, sewage from the Isle of Dogs gravitates north into the Low Level

59. The new Isle of Dogs Pumping Station 'a temple to summer storms'.

Intercepting Sewer One at Bromley-by-Bow, then passes to Abbey Mills, from where it is pumped finally to Beckton Sewage Works. As a low-lying peninsula the Isle of Dogs had been frequently subject to flooding, which was particularly bad in the 1870s, following persistent heavy rain. A storm water pumping station was provided by the Metropolitan Board of Works in 1885, to relieve the main sewer in Manchester Road and to pump excess flows into the Thames. One hundred years later the redevelopment of the 'Enterprise Zone' at the heart of the Isle of Dogs required the installation of 4½ miles of main sewers and the construction of the Millwall Cutting Subway, an underwater box culvert constructed across a dock passage to carry water, gas mains and sewerage. The overall drainage scheme for the Isle of Dogs was designed by Sir William Halcrow and Partners.

It was also decided to replace the pumping station situated in Stewart Street, a site that today faces directly across the river to the Millennium Dome. The new pumping station superstructure is an often-quoted paradigm of British postmodern architecture, a striking structure by John Outram (b.1934) completed in May 1988. The colourful symbolism of the external brickwork and the imposing 10-feet diameter fan, which removes any build up of methane, conceal a concrete substructure and a control and supply maintenance room for the ten submersible pumps. Subterranean incoming flows pass through a pair of mechanically-raked screens into an inlet chamber, then through slots into the main sump. From there the pumps raise the water an average 27 feet to a surge tank, from where it can run by gravity through twin outfall mains into the Thames.

Redevelopment further east into the former Royal Docks again necessitated extensive drainage works. It was decided by the LDDC and Thames Water that the new sewerage infrastructure would have a separate system for surface water drainage.

The existing sewerage system in that area had combined sewage with surface water, draining east to Beckton via the North Woolwich Pumping Station. A new system of sewers was therefore created that drained west to a new storm water pumping station situated by the tidal basin of Victoria Dock that pumped the surplus water directly into the Thames. The Tidal Basin Pumping Station is another eye-catching landmark building, that opened in April 1989, designed in this case by Richard Rogers (b.1933) and Partners with engineering by Sir William Halcrow and Partners. Its sculptural forms of circular tanks painted bright blue and associated colourfully painted structures are placed above a reinforced concrete caisson 92 feet deep. The station contains sixteen submersible pumps which discharge into a high level chamber from where flows gravitate to the river. At the time of its commissioning it was the world's largest surface water pumping station using submersible pumps. Like the Stewart Street building it is unstaffed and supervised remotely by telemetry lines to Abbey Mills.

The architectural practice of Nicholas Grimshaw (b.1941) and Partners (responsible for the spectacular Waterloo International Terminal) also designed the pumping station at North Woolwich, the largest individual project within the Docklands sewerage strategy and the final element in the drainage of the Royal Docks. Opening in late 1997 it replaced the former pumping station built around 1900. The characteristic high-tech style is demonstrated by its dramatically curved aluminium roof and smaller ancillary building housing two standby generators and switchgear. The pumping station caters for the new trunk foul sewers and the existing local combined sewers and discharges sewage into the Northern Outfall Sewer and excess storm water into the Thames.

In close proximity to the Victorian splendour of Abbey Mills Pumping Station lies its sleek, modern successor, designed by Allies and Morrison and completed in 1997. Resembling a gleaming church without its spire, this pumping station incorporates new low-level culverts, which pump sewage to be discharged at a higher level. The air intakes and extractors on either side of the pitched roof are a distinctive feature.

Footnotes for Chapter Two

[1] The best account of these largely forgotten watercourses remains Nicholas Barton's *The Lost Rivers of London*. First published in 1962 a revised edition was issued in 1992 by Historical Publications.

[2] A few hours can be profitably spent tracing the routes of these rivers through the streets of central London, noting the still visible evidence of their courses and valleys. A good guide is Andrew Duncan *Secret London* (New Holland, 1995) which includes walks along the lower courses of the Westbourne, Tyburn and Fleet.

[3] J Ashton *The Fleet* (1890) is one of the older histories.

[4] Jonathan Swift *The Poems of Jonathan Swift* Vol I ed. Harold Williams. (Clarendon Press Oxford, 1958), 139

[5] On a more sinister note, for those who subscribe to conspiracy theories, the discovery of the hanging body of the Vatican banker Roberto Calvi, a member of the Italian P2 Masonic lodge, at this very point underneath the bridge led to theories of Masonic involvement in his 'suicide'. See David Yallop *In God's Name*. (Corgi, 1987).

[6] W McCann ed. *Fleet Valley Project Interim Report* (Museum of London Archaeology Service, unpublished report, 1993).

[7] A short history is J G Waller 'The Tybourne and the Westbourne', extract from the *Transactions of the London and Middlesex Archaeology Society* 1st Series Vol 6 1890.

[8] According to Nicholas Barton *op. cit.* 34-42, the

southern course of the Tyburn has been the subject of conflicting theories.

9   John Hollingshead *Underground London* (Groombridge & Sons, 1862) ch v.

10   This section was covered over in the 1970s.

11   Eric Newby *A Traveller's Life* (Collins, 1982), 198-9.

12   John Stow *A Survey of London written in the year 1598* ed. Henry Morley with an introduction by Antonia Fraser (Sutton Publishing, 1999), 232.

13   *ibid.*, 143.

14   Despite Trench and Hillman's (*op. cit*) claims that the Walbrook valley was the site of the Roman port the Walbrook was too shallow to be navigable, the wharves and warehouses being situated largely between present-day Southwark and Tower bridges. Its name may derive from the Old English *Wealas* or 'stream of the strangers' probably referring to the ancient Britons who became known as the Welsh from the same word, or may simply mean the brook by the wall.

15   Barton *op.cit.*, 51-54.

16   See C J Foord *Springs, Streams and Spas of London* (Fisher Unwin, 1910) and S Sunderland *Old London Spas, Baths and Wells* (J Bale, Sons & Danielson, 1915).

17   Included as a preface to John Stow *A Survey of London written in the year 1598* ed. Henry Morley with an introduction by Antonia Fraser (Sutton Publishing, 1999), 24.

18   Metropolitan Water Board *London's Water Supply* (1953) and H W Dickinson *Water Supply of Greater London* (Newcomen Society, 1954) cover this early period. A good summary is provided in Ben Weinreb and Christopher Hibbert *The London Encyclopedia* (Papermac 1983 rev. ed. 1995), 953-959.

19   For his life see J W Gough *Sir Hugh Myddelton, Entrepreneur and Engineer* (Oxford University Press, 1964).

20   A statue of Sir Hugh Myddelton stands on Islington Green. A pleasant few hours can be spent following the course of the New River through Islington and Hackney. See Mary Cosh *The New River* 2nd ed revised (Islington Archaeological & History Society, 1988) for an informed guide.

21   Martin Whitfield 'Water company sheds light on invisible tunnel' *The Independent* 15 August 1994, 4.

22   Graham Ball 'The answer to drought: a well in the cellar' *The Independent on Sunday* 5 May 1996, 6.

23   Samuel Pepys *The Shorter Pepys* selected and edited by Robert Latham (Penguin, 1987), 87, entry for 20 October 1660.

24   For a more comprehensive history of this important invention see Lucinda Lambton *Temples of Convenience* (St Martin's Press, 1995) and L Wright *Clean and Decent* (Routledge, 1980).

25   Details of the works and contracts and the history of sanitation in London are covered in a recent publication by Stephen Halliday *The Great Stink of London, Sir Joseph Bazalgette and the Cleansing of the Victorian Capital* (Sutton Publishing, 1999).

26   These impressive engines are being restored at Crossness, which can be visited. See http://www.tanton.ndirect.co.uk/crossness/.

27   For an account of the long battle to clean up the Thames see Leslie B Wood *The Restoration of the Tidal Thames* (Adam Hilger Ltd, 1982).

28   *New Scientist* 'The World Below' supplement with the edition for 1 April 1995, 18-19. Not an April Fool prank.

29   *ibid.*, 8.

CHAPTER THREE

Pipes and Tunnels

'The lift chamber is sheer old fashioned luxury, roomy and well-benched. The teak and polish of pre-war steamers. There are uniformed operatives, pitched by the mechanical repetition of duty into secret mindscapes. Passengers are no longer a reality. The cage has become a time-travelling module, connected to the outside world by a surveillance window: it's a Nautilus on wires, lowered into depths far stranger than Brother Thames can provide.'
Iain Sinclair in *Lights out for the Territory* (1997), describing the interior of the passenger lift for the Greenwich-Isle of Dogs Foot Tunnel.

'It would have been a sight worth seeing, the laying of the first gas pipe - and a picture worth drawing. The landing of Julius Caesar, the signing of Magna Carta and the death of Harold furnish more romantic groupings for historical painters; but no one can say that they were of more historical importance.'
Charles Dickens in 'The Genii of the Lamps' in *All the Year Round*, 1861.

GAS SUPPLY

The introduction of gas lighting in England dates from the beginning of the nineteenth century. Experiments with coal gas to provide lighting had been made earlier, most notably by Philippe Lebon in France, but the first plant to produce gas on a commercial scale was developed by William Murdock (1754-1839), an employee of Boulton & Watt. From lighting his house in Redruth in Cornwall with gas he proceeded to install, in Boulton & Watt's Soho Foundry, a gas-making plant which illuminated the building. Gas lighting appealed to the owners of mills and factories as it was less of a fire risk than candles or oil lamps and, more importantly, enabled their businesses to run efficiently through the night; not such good news for their workers however. The first large-scale project was for a cotton mill in Salford in 1806, where Boulton & Watt installed six retorts and nine hundred gas lights. The engineering firm failed to capitalise on this new source of energy and it was left to one of their

60. An early gasworks in Horseferry Road, Westminster, depicted in the Illustrated London News in 1842.

apprentices, Samuel Clegg, to forge ahead and install gas factory plants on his own from 1805.

Clegg was soon to team up with a recent immigrant from Germany, Friedrich Albert Winzer (1763-1830), who anglicised his name to Frederick Winsor. Winsor had conceived the idea of a public gas supply from a central manufacturing works and set up an office at 97 Pall Mall, close to the residence of the Prince of Wales. He demonstrated his flair for publicity by placing gas illuminations, with the Prince's permission, along the top of the wall of Carlton House on 4 June 1805 on the occasion of King George III's birthday. It was recorded that, "the Mall continued crowded with spectators until near twelve o'clock, and they seemed much amused and delighted by this novel exhibition".[1] Following this spectacle he was allowed to illuminate Pall Mall with thirteen lamp posts, each with three gas-jet globes supplied by pipe from carbonising iron furnaces in his house, for an experimental period from January to April 1807.

In 1812 Winsor, with Clegg's engineering assistance, established the Gas Light & Coke Company with a charter to light the City of London, Westminster and Southwark. Their first works were set up in Great Peter Street Westminster. Within two years the parish of St Margaret's Westminster was lit by gas

and there were gas lamps along Westminster Bridge. By 1823 London had 122 miles of gas mains, increasing to 600 miles by 1834 and when Victoria became queen in 1837 gas was firmly established as a source of illumination. The diameter of the gas mains grew from 16 inches in 1820 to 36 in 1850 and to the standard 48 by 1870. The success of Winsor and Clegg's venture inspired the formation of rival gas companies, such as the City of London (1817), the Imperial (1821), the Independent in north London and the South London, South Metropolitan and Phoenix to the south.[2] Competition became fierce and led to absurd situations. In one example, from the 1840s consumers in Oxford Street and Tottenham Court Road were supplied by four separate companies from five different gas works. In 1851 a gas cooker was on display in the Great Exhibition, although it was not until the end of the century, when electricity had become more of a threat, that the heating properties of gas were to be exploited more widely.

61. Gasholders at the Imperial Gas Company's works at Bethnal Green in 1858.

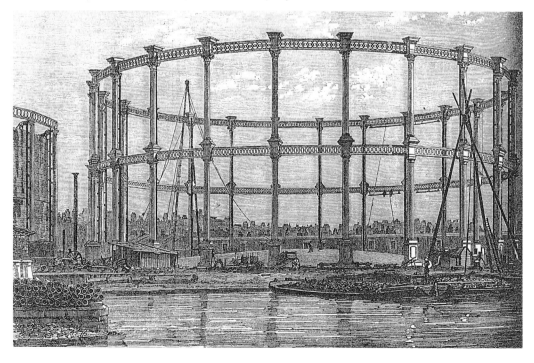

62. *Gustav Doré's dark study of men and women working at Lambeth Gas Works in an atmosphere reminiscent of Hades.*

63. *Purifiers, otherwise known as scrubbers, at the Nine Elms gasworks.*

64. *Laying gas mains c. 1880.*

By the 1840s Buckingham Palace, the newly rebuilt Houses of Parliament and many West End theatres were lit by gas. Within ten years there was a period of consolidation amongst the gas producers, with those south of the Thames agreeing to supply only specific districts. By 1854 the companies north of the river had come to a similar arrangement. Charles Pearson (1794-1862) established the Great Central Gas Consumers Company in order to challenge the companies' pricing policies, offering gas from his own company at lower rates. The war between the rivals culminated in the 'Battle of Bow Bridge' in which workmen from the Great Central were prevented from bringing their gas main through one of the few bridges over the River Lea. The Great Central company was eventually taken over by the Gas Light & Coke Company. A major problem with gas production was the possibility of explosions in urban centres. The most serious accident in London occurred in October 1865, when the gasometer of the London Gaslight Company at Nine Elms exploded, causing nine deaths.

Seeking to expand production, the Gas Light & Coke Company bought a cheap site of 540 acres in East Ham in 1867, where a large new works was built using coal landed directly from the Thames. This massive enterprise opened in 1870 eventually to become the world's largest coal gas works, at its peak serving four and a half million customers. The township that grew up around it was named Beckton after the Governor of the company Simon Adams Beck. Coal gas manufacture ceased there in 1969 and the area was substantially redeveloped in the 1980s, with housing built on the site of the redundant industrial works. In nineteenth-century London rival companies attempted to follow suit, but the Imperial Company gas works at Bromley-by-Bow was not as technically advanced. A period of amalgamation ensued, culminating in the absorption by the Gas Light & Coke Company of its competitors in north London by the 1870s. The South Metropolitan built a huge gas works at Greenwich and assumed, south of the river, the dominant position enjoyed by the Gas Light & Coke Company to the north.

Whilst electrical power supply was developed in the 1880s, the installation of gas lighting in working class homes prior to the First World War, following the invention of the incandescent mantle and use of the prepayment meter, still made gas a more economically attractive proposition. Although gas continued to be a popular source of

65. Women stokers working at the South Metropolitan gasworks during the First World War.

66. Men working in the blacksmith's shop at Beckton gasworks, c.1926.

energy many gasworks and storage facilities were eventually closed down or converted. In 1937 the Horseferry Road gasholders, some of the first in London, were dismantled and a government 'citadel' built within the deep circular enclosures. On nationalisation in 1948 the Gas Light & Coke Company became North Thames Gas and the South Metropolitan evolved into South Eastern Gas. The number of gasworks was greatly reduced and gas production was developed based on the use of oil, rather than coal. Later came conversion from coal gas to North Sea gas, which was carried out in London from 1968 to 1976. British Gas was privatised in 1986 and demerged in 1997 into two separate companies: Transco which owns and maintains the national and regional pipelines, and Centrica (trading under the name British Gas) which supplies the gas. Since 23 May 1998 Londoners have been able to choose from fifteen different gas supply companies in the deregulated market.

Installation and maintenance of gas pipes has been improved by the introduction of a number of remotely controlled mechanical devices. The Rotamole is a compact tubular machine, driven by a compressed air piston that batters its way forward as its head rotates and can be monitored and steered from above ground. The vast network of ageing cast-iron gas pipes under London has required relining with polyethylene, which expands to fit securely against the walls. In order to restore the branch connections from the pipe an articulated electronic device resembling a metallic snake is employed. Travelling along until sensors alert it that a branch has been encountered, the device uses a drill to reopen the connection through the plastic lining. New plastic pipes can also be joined and sealed to the network underground by these 'pigs', a generic name for the variety of such objects that inspect, clean or repair pipes.

LONDON HYDRAULIC POWER COMPANY

Another source of energy was that derived from high pressure water pumped at 700 lb per square inch through a network of pipes buried beneath the streets and owned by the

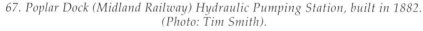

67. Poplar Dock (Midland Railway) Hydraulic Pumping Station, built in 1882.
(Photo: Tim Smith).

London Hydraulic Power Company (LHPC). Power was provided for office and hotel lifts, car hoists in garages, safety curtains at Drury Lane and Her Majesty's theatres and primitive vacuum cleaners in the homes of a handful of London's wealthier inhabitants. In addition hydraulic power was used for the revolving stages at the London Palladium and Coliseum theatres, the picture lift at the Royal Academy and the organ console lift in the Odeon Marble Arch. Some of the company's pipes may be seen on a tour of what is now St Pancras Chambers, formerly the Midland Grand Hotel fronting St Pancras Station, where they powered hydraulic lifts.

The LHPC commenced generating hydraulic power at central stations in 1884, the first pumping station being situated 200 yards east of Blackfriars bridge at Falcon Wharf. Power was extracted from the water by utilising the potential energy stored in it by raising it to a high pressure. Water was taken from the Thames, filtered, warmed to guard against freezing and pumped by steam engines into an accumulator, a large tower at the pumping station containing a weighted vertical ram to produce the required pressure.[3] A few of these accumulator towers still exist and some good examples remain in Docklands, where hydraulic power was once utilised to run cranes, warehouse hoists, dockgates and capstans.[4]

At the company's peak in the 1930s the cast-iron hydraulic pipes were pumping 33 million gallons of water each week and extended for 187 miles under London, passing over the Thames through Vauxhall, Waterloo and Southwark bridges. When the Tower Subway was made redundant by the opening of Tower Bridge in 1894 another north-south conduit was available, which the LHPC bought for £3000 in order to install its mains. The Rotherhithe Tunnel was utilised to provide a supply from Wapping to Rotherhithe and Bermondsey. Premises once served by the LHPC can be identified by the company's distinctive stop-cock covers with a raised chequerboard margin and the initials LHP set into the pavement outside. Hydraulic power was eventually to be superseded by the inevitable spread of electricity as an energy source. The LHPC ceased operating in the late 1970s, leaving its 300 10-inch cast-iron mains sunk under London at an average depth of about three feet. In 1977 Mercury Communications acquired the LHPC, inheriting their invaluable network serving the City and West End – their engineers needed only to thread Mercury's optical fibre cables through the already existing pipework. Apart from the digging entailed by the removal of valves and difficult bends, months of expensive engineering works and road excavations were avoided. The underground work was also made considerably easier by the meticulously detailed records and plans kept by the Victorian engineers.

ELECTRICITY

Electric current was first produced by electro-chemical means by the Voltaic pile devised by Allesandro Volta (1745-1827) in 1800 and the later cells of John F. Daniell (1790-1845) in 1836 and Georges Leclanché (1839-1882) in 1866. Batteries capable of storing electricity were invented in France in the 1870s. The principle of electric arc light was demonstrated by Humphry Davy (1778-1829) at the Royal Institution in 1808, using a battery of 2000 cells. Some years later in 1821, Michael Faraday (1791-1867) discovered electro-magnetic rotation, the principle behind the electric motor. Through a series of ground-breaking experiments at the Royal Institution, Faraday had by 1831 discovered electro-magnetic induction, the principle behind the electric transformer and generator. The design of dynamos advanced until in 1870 Zenobe Theophile Gramme (1826-1901) produced the ancestor of the modern dynamo. With improvements by the Swiss engineer Emil Burgin

68. *The newly opened Savoy Theatre, in the Strand, in 1881. It was the first public building to be lit by electricity.*

and Colonel R.E.B. Crompton (1845-1940) in England it was manufactured as the Crompton dynamo, a device that supplied current to many of the earliest electrical installations in Great Britain. William and Ernst Werner Siemens (1823-1883 and 1816-1892 respectively) had also produced a similar dynamo that was to be a rival for many years.

Through the medium of carbon arc lamps electricity was initially used for illumination in lighthouses, with the arc being struck between the opposed tips of horizontally arranged electrodes. Paul Jablochkoff (1847-1894), a Russian engineer, designed a lamp in which the carbon electrodes were opposed vertically and parallel with each other, resulting in improved performance. By combining the Jablochkoff candle with Crompton's version of the Gramme dynamo the first public electric lighting installations were now capable of transforming the London landscape. By the late 1870s the West India Docks, Billingsgate Market, part of the Thames Embankment and Holborn Viaduct were electrically lit.

In 1879 Crompton produced the first portable generating set with the aid of an agricultural portable engine which he parked in the mews behind his house in Porchester Gardens in order to light the interior, the first private rooms to be illuminated in this manner.[5] Joseph Swan (1828-1914), a Newcastle chemist, devised a vastly improved filament utilising carbonised paper, whilst almost simultaneously Thomas Alva Edison (1847-1931) had been developing a lamp with a filament of carbonised thread. Owing to the resulting patent problems in this country they formed a joint company, the Edison and Swan United Light Company in 1883, adopting a carbonised extruded cellulose filament that facilitated the widespread use of electric light. The light provided by the incandescent lamp was not as overbearing as the dazzling illumination from an arc lamp. Despite the

69. Building works for the new Westminster Bridge, lit by electricity. From the Illustrated London News 1855.

efforts of the Gas, Light & Coke Company to denigrate this power source the popularity of electricity grew and inevitably new companies emerged to exploit it. Speculation became rife and millions of pounds of investors' money vanished through fraud or incompetence. On the opening night of the Savoy Theatre in 1881, Richard D'Oyly Carte (1844-1901) demonstrated the hundreds of Swan lamps in the auditorium that bathed the interior in electric light. The appreciative audience witnessed the first public building in the country to be completely lit by electricity. In an attempt to regulate the supply of electricity the Electric Lighting Act of 1882 gave vestries and local authorities the right to purchase any private electricity company in their district after 21 years, later amended to 42 years when it was found that this threat affected the companies' ability to raise capital.

70. *The grandiose electricity sub station in Duke Street, built 1903-5.*

'THE MICHELANGELO OF DEPTFORD'

Sebastian Ziani de Ferranti (1864-1930), born in Liverpool, had been fascinated with electrical engineering from an early age and as a teenager had visited one of Crompton's early lighting installations at Alexandra Palace and sought out the pioneering engineer for a discussion on the subject. While studying during the evenings at University College he was given a job by the Siemens brothers in the Experimental Department of their works at Charlton. During his time there he invented an improved ac generator, or alternator, an arc lamp and a meter for measuring electricity consumption. Shortly afterwards, in 1886, he was approached by Sir Coutts Lindsay (1824-1913), proprietor of the fashionable and controversial Grosvenor Gallery in New Bond Street. In 1883 Lindsay had installed an electricity generating system in the gallery's basement using simple transformers connected in series to supply power to a small local area. Following complaints about variable supply Ferranti was consulted and

so impressed Lindsay that he appointed him Chief Engineer at the age of 21. Together they established the London Electricity Supply Corporation in August 1887, after Ferranti had completely redesigned and re-equipped the station, doubling the voltage to 2400 by connecting transformers of his own design in parallel and installing two of his own 750 hp alternators capable of generating enough electricity to light 26,000 lamps. Thanks to Ferranti's ingenuity the company expanded rapidly to supply an area from the Thames to Regent's Park and from Kensington to the edge of the City.[6]

Ferranti, however, had grander ambitions for electric power and envisaged widespread distribution from a single massive power station that he proposed to build at Deptford. The site was chosen for its proximity to the Thames with its convenient supplies of water and coal brought in by barge. The power-house he designed had an ultimate capacity of 120,000 hp, which by overhead mains would supply current at 10,000 volts to a series of sub-stations, where it would be

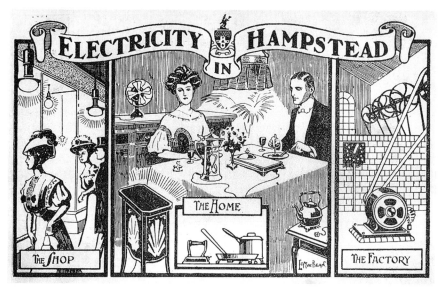

71. *Once it became feasible to light streets by electricity, a number of London local authorities supplied their own power. Among these was Hampstead Vestry who by the beginning of the 20th century was supplying electricity for home gadgets. This postcard advertises the supply facility and the various uses for it.*

reduced to the street mains pressure of 2400 volts. When it reached the house the electricity would be converted to 100 volts for domestic lighting. At Ferranti's planned capacity Deptford would then have had sufficient energy to have lit the whole of London.

He devised improved high voltage cables and obtained permission to run them alongside railway lines, both above and below ground and across bridges. Unfortunately for Ferranti's visions a 'battle of the systems' broke out between the alternating current of the London Electric Supply Corporation and those advocating the supply of direct current supplied from a series of small local generating stations. A Board of Trade inquiry in 1889 decided that local supply companies should be awarded contracts by the respective parish vestries and Ferranti's plans for a single source of power were defeated. Many years after these events Ferranti was recognised as the originator of the idea for a National Grid, whose construction was eventually accomplished between 1926 and 1934.[7] Electricity was also

instrumental in the rapid growth of the underground railway network – the City & South London Railway, with locomotives powered by Crompton traction motors, being in 1890, the first underground electric railway in the world.

By the end of the nineteenth century there were thirty power stations in London controlled by sixteen companies. The multiplicity of undertakings that sold electricity divided roughly into private concerns in the City and West End and municipal ownership in the East End. Attempts by the London County Council to unify London's supply met with little success, but the industry was finally nationalised in 1947, with most of London becoming part of the London Electricity Board. The Electricity Supply Act of 1926 had earlier established the National Grid controlled by the Central Electricity Board, whereby electricity could be transmitted around the country to where it was most needed. Power could be bought from the Grid by private companies and local municipalities at a fixed rate. To ease supply in central London and provide extra income for London Underground many miles of electricity cables run through the tube tunnels. Since privatisation the National Grid Company still owns and operates the transmission network and the wholesale electricity market, but supply to consumers is carried out in England and Wales by twelve regional electricity companies. London Electricity (parent company Energy Corporation based in the US) is the principal supplier for the capital.

RECENT ELECTRICITY SUPPLY PROJECTS

Across London there are 12,000 substations taking power at 11,000 or 6,600 volts from larger converter stations and transforming this energy down to 405 or 240 volts for distribution to individual customers. In the heart of the West End, forty feet beneath Leicester Square, lies a relatively new electricity substation on three levels. Equipped with three large transformers it is entered by a disguised trap door to the left of the Half Price Ticket Booth, a structure that also doubles as a ventilation shaft. Opened in May 1991, after two years work, this substation supplies the West End with its power. It links to a new 1¼ mile tunnel that connects it with another substation at Duke Street near Grosvenor Square. Tunnels such as these, intended for high-voltage electricity cables, run about 80 to 100 feet below the surface. Another of these tunnels crossing the City, about one mile in length and 6½ feet in diameter, had to negotiate the deep piling beneath the Barbican Centre and passed within twenty inches of the foundation piles on each side.

In April 1996 the Energy Minister, Tim Eggar, inspected a recently completed electricity tunnel intended to safeguard the capital's power supplies into the 21st century. In late 1989 plans were announced for the digging of the 6¼ mile tunnel 130 feet under central London intended to carry a 400,000 volt electricity cable. The route of the ten-feet wide electricity tunnel would be from Pimlico under the Thames to Battersea then to Clapham and Wimbledon. Ventilation shafts and access points were required in locations such as Clapham Common and Battersea, but could be disguised as parts of buildings.[8] According to the National Grid the tunnel is the deepest in London, fifty feet below the average depth of tube line and constitutes the capital's longest cable link (though the Thames Ring Water Main is equally as deeply embedded). The latest tunnel to carry 132kW cables is being excavated beneath the City Road during 2000. A boring machine, formerly owned by Thames Water, is digging the 8½ ft diameter tunnel 82 ft below the streets. Work has been managed by 24seven, the company formed as a result of the merger between the distribution businesses of London and Eastern Electricity.[9]

In 1998 the substation at West Ham was reinforced and a new cable tunnel was burrowed under the Thames conveying twelve 11kV circuits to the Greenwich Peninsula in order to supply the considerable requirements of the Millennium Dome. As power stations have been relocated further from the centre of the capital the brick monoliths that dominated Battersea and Deptford have closed, to be joined by Chelsea's Lots Road in 2000. The former Bankside generating station opposite St Paul's Cathedral has been spectacularly reborn as the Tate Modern art gallery and reopened to the public on 12 May 2000. The electrical hum in the turbine hall that greets visitors betrays the presence of transformers in the section of the vast building that has yet to be fully converted from its former function.

VICTORIAN UTILITY SUBWAYS

Several miles of purpose-built subways large enough to walk through, carry the pipework of the public utilities across central London. The inconvenience of continually digging up the streets to lay pipes for utility companies was prevented by the prescience of the Victorian engineers who constructed these subways beneath their new major roads. Buried at a depth of about ten feet the tunnels carried early gas, water and hydraulic power pipes and later electricity supplies. According to the London County Council (Subways) Act 1893 the intention was to "secure the more effectual use of such subways so as to limit the breaking up or interference with the streets," a function they admirably fulfil today. They form yet another underground labyrinth consisting of nine miles of tiled subway tunnel connecting Islington to Soho and the Embankment to the City of London.

The oldest was built under Garrick Street and the new Cranbourn Street, opened in 1861. John 'Subway' Williams and William Austin had previously lobbied the Commissioners for Metropolitan Improvements for this form of subterranean servicing. One of the most extensive networks radiated out from Piccadilly Circus and Trafalgar Square, incorporating manholes and gratings for ventilation. An interesting account written shortly after the reconstruction work at Piccadilly Circus station, when a service tunnel was constructed beneath the booking hall, describes a journey along these utility subways. From below looking up through the gratings in the busy streets over his head the author could see, "the roofs and upper windows of Piccadilly's shops and hotels. I enjoyed this splendid isolation-to be within a few feet of crowded streets and yet to be alone, gazing from this queer angle at the roofs of Piccadilly."[10] From there he walked under Charing Cross Road and beneath the booking office at Leicester Square station. A circular tunnel to contain diverted utilities was also constructed during the extensive modernisation of Oxford Circus station as part of the Victoria line works in 1968, a project which took nine months.[11]

The Victoria Embankment (1864-70) also carries a utility subway, with access through a door in the base of Boudicca's statue near Westminster Bridge, that runs all the way to Blackfriars and then to the Bank of England. A subway also runs beneath Shaftesbury Avenue preventing the delays caused by roadworks in this busy thoroughfare. Similar networks exist beneath parts of the City, some installed in preliminary works for Holborn Viaduct in 1863 and others beneath Queen Victoria Street in 1867-71 and to the north of London Bridge. One access shaft to the central London subways is situated at the junction of Kingsway and Theobalds Road. This section was part of the extensive early twentieth-century metropolitan improvement scheme including Aldwych that transformed this once decaying slum area.

A service subway was also incorporated into the tunnels running from City Thameslink station to Farringdon built in 1992 when the bridge over Ludgate Hill was dismantled. In Docklands there exist similar conduits to accommodate the vast mass of telecommunications technology necessary for the transmission of global capitalism.

The subways provide ideal working conditions for maintenance, safely concealed from London's weather and traffic. They are owned by the local councils who charge rental fees to each utility. Engineers from the earthquake-damaged Japanese city of Kobe visited Camden to view the subways as inspiration for the rebuilding of the infrastructure of the metropolis that will rise to replace it.[12] The original gas and water pipes lining the tunnels have been more recently supplemented by the conduits of modern technology: electricity wires and telecommunications cables.

THE EARLY TELEGRAPH SYSTEM

One of the earliest important applications of electricity was in powering electric telegraphs to send signals over considerable distances. Francis Ronalds (1788-1873) laid an early telecommunications cable beneath his garden in Upper Mall, Hammersmith in 1816. A 525-foot long wire was threaded through glass tubes and placed in a four foot tar-lined trench for insulation. Ronalds successfully transmitted electricity along this wire, but soon abandoned his experiments. William Fothergill Cooke (1806-1879), who had worked with Ronalds, pursued his interest in electricity, studying it in Prussia and returning to England in 1836 during the railway boom. In partnership with Professor Charles Wheatstone (1802-1875), who had already transmitted electricity through long-distance cables, he patented a telegraph system in 1837. They obtained permission from the London & Birmingham Railway to install a telegraphic

signalling apparatus between Euston station and the engine house at Camden Town, to aid in the early operation of hauling trains up the steep incline by rope cable from the former to the latter. This cable-haul was made unnecessary by the development of more powerful locomotives. Although Cooke and Wheatstone's system worked well the railway company refused to adopt it, preferring instead the method of signalling by pneumatic warning whistle.

Isambard Kingdom Brunel (1806-1859) heard about it, however, and as chief engineer of the Great Western Railway, ordered that the system be installed along the thirteen miles of track between Paddington and West Drayton. This had been accomplished by April 1839 and marked the first commercial use of electricity. It also proved extremely effective and was extended to Slough in 1843. Not only did it convey the news to London on 6 August 1844 of the birth of Queen Victoria's second son, but the

72. In the boiler room at the Central Telegraph Office in 1874.

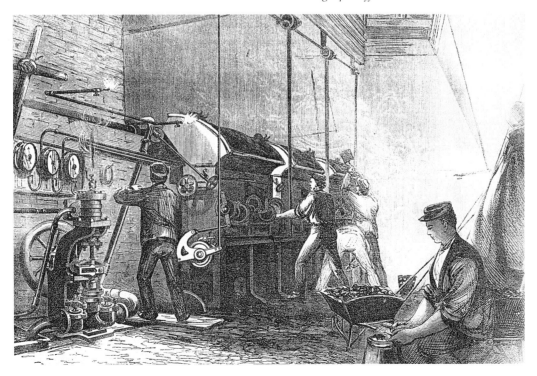

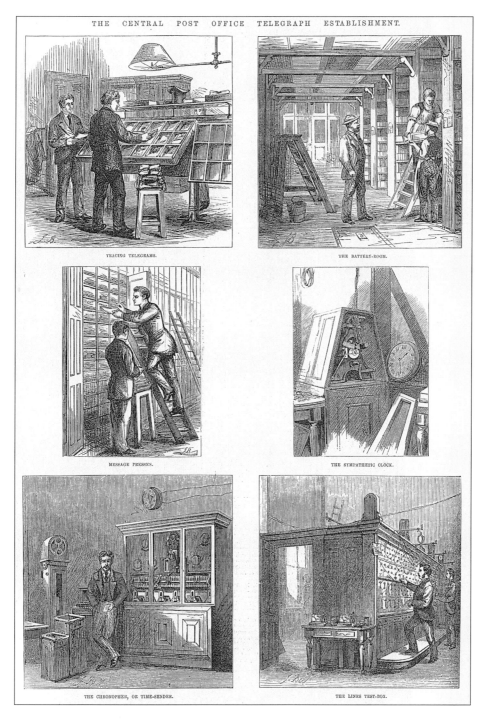

THE CENTRAL POST OFFICE TELEGRAPH ESTABLISHMENT.

TRACING TELEGRAMS.

THE BATTERY-ROOM.

MESSAGE PRESSES.

THE SYMPATHETIC CLOCK.

THE CHRONOPHER, OR TIME-SENDER.

THE LINES TEST-BOX.

73. *Various operations at the Central Telegraph Office, depicted in 1874.*

74. Dealing with messages in the Central Telegraph Office.

system also assisted in the apprehension of a murderer who was attempting to escape by train in January 1845. Thanks to the resultant publicity use of telegraphic communication spread rapidly. The Electric Telegraph Company was founded in 1846 and from 1849-1850 constructed a Central Telegraph Station at Founders' Court in Lothbury. In 1860 this moved to Little Bell Alley, Moorgate, later renamed Telegraph Street. By that time most of Britain's larger towns had been connected to the telegraph network. The majority of the early cables were placed overhead, as it was significantly cheaper than burying them underground.[13]

A number of competing telegraph companies formed in the 1860s, including the London District and the Universal Private, that helped facilitate the movement of business and financial information around London. In February 1870, all these telegraph companies were taken over by the Postal Telegraphs Department of the General Post Office. The Central Telegraph Office was transferred, in February 1874, from Telegraph Street to the General Post Office (West) in St Martin's-le-Grand. As telegraphic communication increased in popularity the Central Telegraph Office expanded until it occupied virtually the entire building; in 1884 an extra floor had to be added. It became the largest telegraph office in the world, dealing with over sixty million telegrams in 1945-46. This marked the peak of telegraph use, as superior technology was already available. Telegraph traffic gradually declined from that date, leading to the closure of the Central Telegraph Office in October 1962 and its subsequent demolition in 1967. Today the headquarters of British Telecom, the BT Centre, opened in 1984, stands on this historic site.

Close to the surface of Victorian London's streets there ran the most extensive pneumatic tube communication system in the world. Message-bearing cylinders were forced through 2¼" diameter cast-iron ducts by air pressure created by steam-driven pump engines. Used originally in conjunction with the electric telegraph system it was installed by the Post Office in 1853. The system only finally became redundant in 1962, when it was superseded by telexes (first launched in 1932), automatic teleprinters and improved telephones. The Central Telegraph Office was the control centre, dealing with an average of 50,000 messages per day during peak usage.[14]

THE TELEPHONE PIONEERS

Alexander Graham Bell (1847-1922) patented his revolutionary new telephone on 9 March 1876. The device was first demonstrated by Sir William Thomson (Lord Kelvin) before the British Association for the Advancement of Science in Glasgow on 7 September 1876. The implications of this new technology for the future of the telegraph were ominous. Progress was swift – in 1878 the National Telephone Company had been formed from a number of smaller concerns. By August 1879 the first public telephone exchange was operating in London from 36 Coleman Street. The Post Office, understandably upset by its heavy investment in increasingly outdated technology, had attempted to obstruct the growth of this new medium of communication. New companies were therefore prevented from running wires under private houses or above them without the owner's permission. Eventually, after setting up in competition with the National Telephone Company, the Post Office had, by 1892, gained control of the main telephone lines, with their rival retaining the local lines. As rivalry increased the two concerns eventually reached a compromise in 1901, whereby the Post Office would rent space underground to the National Telephone Company whilst acquiring their plant. Following the cessation of the company's charter in 1911 the entire concern (apart from Hull and the Channel Islands) was taken over by the Post Office, which was to embark on the construction of an impressive underground communications domain.[15]

The earliest telephone lines were carried overhead and converged on large derricks mounted on the roofs of exchanges. As the design of telephone cables improved these overhead webs of lines began to disappear into underground ducts. London became the first city in the world to have a substantially complete underground telephone distribution system. By 1947 the Post Office had moved more than 90% of its wires beneath the ground, carried in ducts with joint boxes or manholes where cables joined, the latter having small underground rooms accessible to engineers.

Subscriber Trunk Dialling (STD) was introduced in 1958 and International Direct Dialling (IDD) in 1973. In 1980 the replacement of the earlier analogue system by digital transmission commenced, with one of the first digital trunk and local exchanges opening at Baynard House in London. Today, following an investment of £60 billion, the BT network is completely digital.

CABLE

The cable network, the modern conduit for media, telephone and internet services, forms another important and expanding web beneath the city's streets. Three major companies – Rediffusion, Radio Rentals and British Relay Wireless and Television Limited moved into cable television in this country during the 1950s. Later, London Transport tunnels were hired to carry Mercury, Rediffusion and Visionhire cables, supplemented by the disused London Hydraulic Power Company pipes. Optical-fibre cables were first deployed in the telephone network in the early 1980s. Using these, a single pair of fibres the width of a human hair can transmit more than 10 million million bits of information a second,

75. *Installing a telephone cable between Conduit and Maddox Streets, off Regent Street, in the 1920s.*

76. *In the telephone exchange near St Paul's Churchyard, 1903. The telephone companies offered what was regarded as 'respectable' work for the daughters of middle-class families.*

equivalent to half a million two-way high definition tv channels.

The original Cable Authority established in 1984 to award specific cable franchises within geographical areas was replaced by the Independent Television Commission in 1990. The cable network expanded rapidly after 1991, when the Telecommunications Act freed the licensees from their obligations to act as agents of the national public telecommunications operators (BT or Mercury). This increased investment, but many cable operators had underestimated the cost of digging up pavements. Throughout the UK the number of telephone lines using the cable network grew from 2224 in 1991 to 3,442,196 in 1998. There were three major players in London – Cable London, which has networks including Camden, Islington, Hackney and Enfield, was the first cable operator to connect a telephone subscriber

in October 1987 in Camden Town. Telewest held the franchise for south London, and Cable and Wireless Communications covered the remainder. Cable London was originally a joint venture between Telewest and NTL, but by the end of 1999 it was wholly owned by Telewest and by March 2000 NTL had bought Cable and Wireless Communications for £8.2 billion.

Other utilities, out of their usual sphere of operation, entered the fray. British Gas announced its plan in March 2000 to construct a nationwide cable network within the next two years. A fibre-optic network would run alongside the company's gas pipes, capable of carrying internet, tv on demand and data and voice telephony services. This diversification of providers into other areas is characteristic of the present economic climate. Similarly the bids in 2000, by concerns not previously in the telecom-

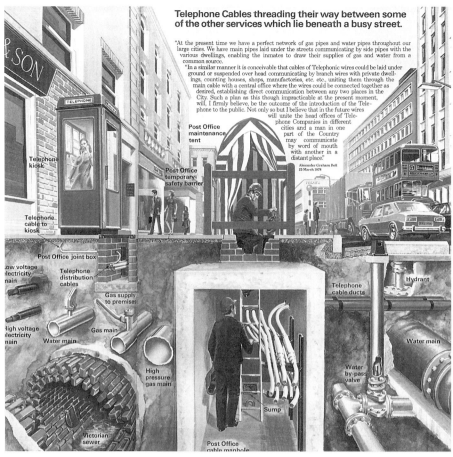

Telephone Cables threading their way between some
of the other services which lie beneath a busy street.

"At the present time we have a perfect network of gas pipes and water pipes throughout our
large cities. We have main pipes laid under the streets communicating by side pipes with the
various dwellings, enabling the inmates to draw their supplies of gas and water from a
common source.
"In a similar manner it is conceivable that cables of Telephonic wires could be laid under
ground or suspended over head communicating by branch wires with private dwellings, counting houses, shops, manufactories, etc. etc., uniting them through the
main cable with a central office where the wires could be connected together as
desired, establishing direct communication between any two places in the
City. Such a plan as this though impracticable at the present moment,
will, I firmly believe, be the outcome of the introduction of the Telephone to the public. Not only so but I believe that in the future wires
will unite the head offices of Tele-
phone Companies in different
cities and a man in one
part of the Country
may communicate
by word of mouth
with another in a
distant place."
Alexander Graham Bell
25 March 1878

Post Office
maintenance
tent

Post Office
temporary
safety barrier

Telephone
kiosk

Telephone
cable to
kiosk

Post Office joint box

Low voltage
electricity
main

Telephone
distribution
cables

Gas supply
to premises

High voltage
electricity
main

Gas main

Water main

High
pressure
gas main

Victorian
sewer

Post Office
cable manhole

Sump

Telephone
cable ducts

Hydrant

Water
by-pass
valve

Water main

*77. The workings of the 1970s Post Office telephone system showing underground
features of other utilities.*

munications business to offer free internet
access and free or very cheap telephone calls,
will have major ramifications in London.

THE LIMEHOUSE LINK
The poor transport infrastructure of
Docklands was addressed by road and rail
schemes in the 1980s and 1990s, one of the
most expensive of which was the Limehouse
Link.[16] This dual tunnel of just over a mile
was seen as an essential factor in the overall
regeneration of the area, providing rapid
access to and from the Isle of Dogs and
Canary Wharf and easing congestion on the
A13, one of the busiest roads in London.
Previously, in the heyday of the London
Docks, local people lived near their
workplace and either walked, cycled or took
the bus to work. Extensive links to central
London were not thought necessary and

fellow Londoners rarely strayed east to encounter the formidable walls surrounding large areas of the docks complex.

Following the closure of the docks and redevelopment of their vast acreage, good transport links became necessary to attract investment. After rejecting a proposal to construct a road tunnel along the side of the Thames it was decided to excavate a land-based cut-and-cover tunnel along a sinuous route to link with The Highway (A120) from the City. Descending underground to pass beneath the Limehouse Basin, curving south to skirt the side of the Thames under Lime-kiln Dock with sliproads to Westferry Road and Canary Wharf, the tunnel emerges north of the West India Dock. Despite the inevitable demolition involved in this kind of construction it was envisaged that building could continue above the tunnel once it was finished.

The London Docklands Development Corporation (LDDC), the body responsible for the overall planning of the redevelopment of the area was, however, not a highway or housing authority. It had to co-operate closely with Tower Hamlets council in a period when relations between the two bodies were strained. A number of council house blocks had to be demolished, but overall disruption was minimised by noise and vibration level agreements, which limited construction times. Work commenced in November 1989, with the top-down method being employed to construct a twin concrete box with diaphragm walls. The section beneath the Limehouse Basin was constructed behind an open cofferdam and involved the removal of 1.8 million tons of spoil by barge. At its lowest point the excavation reached 30 feet into the dense Thanet sands, making the tunnel one of the deepest major structures in this stratum of the London Basin.

As is usual with such an ambitious project a survey of pre-existing buried structures was undertaken and the congeries of exist-ing services such as cables, pipes and ducts had to be diverted. The surprising extent of these was revealed at Ropemakers Fields, where instead of uncovering the expected sixteen cables, 83 were discovered, many being forgotten remnants of the defunct Stepney Power Station. A mysterious cable found by the western portal was eventually claimed by London Underground, even though the nearest LU lines were 1¼ miles away. It had originally linked the track with the power station at Greenwich, crossing the river through Rotherhithe Tunnel, but was now dead. On the Isle of Dogs the close proximity to the tunnel of the British Telecom 48 way-ducts, built into the Westferry Road footpaths, resulted in the diaphragm walls having to be built around them.

When finally completed the Limehouse Link cost £345 million including the cost of the land and of rehousing six hundred families from council blocks in the path of the works, which made it, at that time, the most expensive stretch of road ever built in Europe. Its opening on 17 May 1993 also completed the Docklands Highway, which had cost a further £400 million. For some time after its completion it was considered a white elephant, as predicted growth in the area had stalled, Olympia & York were in receivership and 55% of the 9.6 million square feet of office space on the Isle of Dogs was empty. However, in the following years, as more companies relocated to the area around Canary Wharf the Limehouse Link gradually proved its worth. Above ground the massive postmodern entrance portals and ventilation buildings were decorated with sculptures, *Restless Dream* in painted aluminium by Zadok Ben David (b.1949) on the western side and *On Strange and Distant Lands* by Michael Kenny (b.1941), consisting of monoliths of Kilkenny limestone, on the eastern.

78. Brunel's Thames Tunnel when it opened in 1843.

BRUNEL'S THAMES TUNNEL

Within twenty years of the first enclosed docks opening in 1802 in the north of the Isle of Dogs, the East India Docks at Blackwall, London Docks at Wapping and part of the extensive Surrey Docks south of the river at Rotherhithe had all been constructed. The riverside to the north and south of the Thames was densely packed with warehouses and factories, but communication across the Thames in the port area was limited to the ancient river crossing of London Bridge and the use of ferrymen. Eventually the volume of traffic caused congestion and a number of potential solutions were given consideration. A new bridge would have to be high enough to clear the masts of ships, but the technology for a bascule bridge (such as the later Tower Bridge) was not sufficiently advanced to cope with a river as wide as the Thames. The possibility of tunnelling was then considered.

In 1798 Ralph Dodd (1756-1822), who had designed the Grand Surrey Canal, had identified a need for a river crossing in east London, principally for the movement of troops. He planned a 900-yard tunnel to connect Gravesend with Tilbury, gained sufficient money to enable a shaft to be sunk, but on encountering geological problems, failed to elicit any more. Richard Trevithick (1771-1833), pioneer of steam engine design, was brought in to collaborate with the engineer Robert Vaizey on the Thames Archway Company project to excavate a pilot tunnel five feet high from Rotherhithe to Limehouse in a narrower part of the river. A shaft was sunk at Rotherhithe to a depth of 76 feet, whence the tunnel commenced in August 1807 at an average rate of six feet per day. Work progressed well until quicksand and water broke in after the tunnel had penetrated 950 feet from the shore. The tunnel was drained and excavation continued as far as 1040 feet, when another inundation, which almost drowned Trevithick, filled the passageway. Despite his efforts at plugging the hole in the riverbed and draining the tunnel the directors of the company were having doubts about the future of the project. Trevithick's proposal for an alternative method of construction, laying a cast-iron tube into a trench excavated from within watertight coffer dams across the riverbed, was eventually rejected and the excavation effectively ceased. Trevithick's engineering prescience would be vindicated in the twentieth century when this method was used in many subaqueous engineering ventures including the construction of the Bay Area Rapid Transit tunnels in San Francisco and the Detroit river tunnel.

Marc Isambard Brunel (1769-1849), born in France and educated there as an engineer, had spent some years in the United States, before travelling to England in order to implement his successful mass-production methods for the manufacture of blocks used in the rigging of Royal Navy ships. During his time working in Chatham Dockyard he had the opportunity to study closely the destructive ship worm *teredo navalis* as it gnawed its way through wood by cutting into the material with its hard horny head and creating a coating around the resulting miniature tunnel. Having already considered excavating a tunnel under the river Neva for Alexander I of Russia, Brunel was already familiar with the technical problems inherent in underwater tunnel excavation. Inspired by the example of the ship worm, he designed and patented a tunnelling shield in 1818 for "Forming Drifts and Tunnels Under Ground", which could be used to excavate a tunnel beneath the Thames.

Rejecting the idea of an iron cylinder with rotating blades at the front, Brunel eventually devised a shield that consisted of twelve cast iron frames, each divided vertically into three cells large enough to contain a miner. The twelve frames were numbered

1-12. The odd numbers were worked first and as each board was replaced it was braced with polling screws against the adjacent cell. By this means, when all the boards had been worked down, the cell was free to move forward by 4½ inches and the polling screws re-positioned. When all the cells of the odd frames were advanced the process was repeated with the even numbered frames. Then the main frame was moved forward by means of screw jacks bracing against brickwork behind. This permanent lining would be provided by bricklayers following in the tunnel's path laying a fresh layer two and a half feet thick and adjusting the jacks accordingly. After enthusiastic lecturing and pamphleteering on Brunel's part and with the support of the Duke of Wellington, a Thames Tunnel Company was created in 1824, with Brunel as engineer. An Act for the construction of a tunnel, "convenient for the Passage of Carriages, Cattle, and Passengers" between Rotherhithe and Wapping was passed on 24 June 1824.[17]

Work started on 2 March 1825 when a shaft was sunk at Rotherhithe by the ingenious method of building the 42-ft high, 900 ton brick cylinder of the shaft at ground level and by excavating the ground beneath it, allowing it to sink under its own weight. By July the shaft had reached its intended depth of 65 feet and work on assembling the shield could commence, but not before the project had claimed its first fatal casualty, a drunken workman who fell down the shaft. Tunnelling was underway by November and Brunel's shield began to inch forward towards the river. He confidently calculated that traffic would be passing through the tunnel within three years, but the project was to become protracted and fraught with tragedy and technical difficulties.

Brunel had assembled an efficient and impressive engineering management team including Richard Beamish, appointed 7 August 1826, and William Gravett, appointed a week later as Assistant Engineers

79. *Isambard Kingdom Brunel, who worked with his father on the Thames Tunnel.*

under his son Isambard Kingdom. Initially Acting Resident Engineer in April 1826, Isambard's position was formalised on 3 January 1827 when he was only 20 years old. They were responsible for monitoring the progress of the tunnel, the performance of the miners and bricklayers, supply of materials and operation of the steam pump that attempted to maintain a reasonably dry environment. The first of five floods that afflicted the excavation occurred on 18 May 1827, a result of the tunnel being too close to the river bed, which had been deepened by dredging. Marc Brunel had a 10,000 ft² canvas sheet placed over the breach, weighted with chains around its edges. 4000 bags of clay were placed on this to fill the depression before the water could be pumped out of the tunnel. A few weeks later a miner

80. *The internal staircases of the Thames Tunnel.*

81. The entrance shaft of the Thames Tunnel.

was drowned during a subsequent inspection tour of the partially flooded excavation.

The conditions the miners worked in were, not surprisingly, extremely dangerous and unpleasant, especially as tunnelling advanced and ventilation became more difficult. Brunel had planned on installing fans, but the parsimony of the project's directors precluded this and the atmosphere at the tunnel face became polluted with foul air and the gases leaking through from the cloacal river above. The health of everyone involved in the project was suffering; Beamish lost the sight of one eye, another miner died from the appalling conditions and it has been claimed that the many hours Isambard spent in the tunnel and injuries sustained in its construction contributed to his early death. Certainly he was fortunate to survive the disastrous inundation on 12 January 1828 when the tunnel rapidly filled with water, six workers were drowned and he was swept unconscious up the shaft to be rescued by Beamish. Despite being drained and repaired, the tunnel works were abandoned as money ran out and the direc-

tors finally lost faith with the, by then, much-derided tunnel. Roughly 605 feet had been painstakingly excavated but the tunnel was only halfway complete. In August 1828 the tunnel face and shield were bricked up and covered by a mirror placed there for the benefit of paying sightseers. Public interest in this exciting project had waned and *The Times* had begun to refer to it as "the Great Bore".

Seven years then passed before the government stepped in, persuaded by Brunel's friends the Duke of Wellington and Lord Althorp, to sanction a loan of £270,000 to enable the ambitious project to be completed. The money began to arrive in December 1833, but it was not until 24 March 1835 that work on the tunnel could recommence. Fortunately Marc Brunel was still in charge, with Beamish as Resident Engineer, but his son had moved on to the career in railway engineering that was to make him probably the best known name of the Railway Age. The shield, which had been rusting in the damp tunnel all this time, required total renewal and it was rebuilt to Brunel's improved designs by the Rennie brothers. Working conditions were, however, still appalling and delays grew as the tunnel inched forward, the air quality worsened and supplies took longer to reach the face. Methane was often present in the workings and was responsible for a number of minor explosions. Many of the problems caused by gas could have been alleviated by the implementation of Brunel's plan to drive a corresponding tunnel from Wapping to meet the excavation. This was prevented by the terms of the government loan in which any expenditure apart from that of the original tunnel excavation was forbidden until the tunnel reached the low water mark on the Wapping shore. Meanwhile a third inundation of Thames water occurred on 23 August 1837 at 736 feet. A further influx on 3 November 1837 at 742 feet caused the death of a worker asleep in the shield.

Fortunately no deaths resulted from the final flood on 20 March 1838 at 763 feet.

Finally, on 22 August 1839 the tunnel reached the low-water mark on the Wapping shore. By June 1840 construction of a second shaft could begin and the brickwork for the tunnel could be completed. Funding was still insufficient and the final irony of this ill-fated project was that the original road ramps could no longer be afforded. Staircases had to be provided instead for its use as a pedestrian-only tunnel. 1200 feet long and consisting of two tunnels with interconnecting cross-passages, at its lowest point it is 76 feet below ground, but the roof is only fourteen feet below the river bed. The Thames Tunnel opened on 25 March 1843, an occasion greeted by the watermen flying black flags as they faced the inevitable diminution of their ferrying trade. Queen Victoria had knighted Marc Brunel in March 1841 and on 26 July 1843 paid a visit to the tunnel, with Prince Albert walking the entire length of the tunnel from Wapping to Rotherhithe and back.

The mortality involved in the construction of the Thames Tunnel was shocking, eleven funerals occurring in its final two years. Although the final toll was not recorded it seems to have certainly exceeded twenty men. The official number of deaths of men working on the tunnel project was seven, but it has been estimated that the figure may be closer to two hundred if related accidents and subsequent illness caused by working in the atmosphere are included. Although two million people were estimated to have passed through it within the first year it soon became the haunt of prostitutes and criminals. It was eventually decided to convert it for the use of the expanding railway network and in 1865 the tunnel was acquired by the East London Railway. On 7 December 1869 the first train ran through the tunnel, part of the service of the London, Brighton & South Coast Railway (LB&SCR) from Wapping that connected to the main railway network at

82. A banquet in the Tunnel in November 1827.

New Cross. In 1876 the line was extended from Wapping to Bishopsgate Junction on the Great Eastern Railway, enabling the LB&SCR service to be relocated at Liverpool Street. Electrified by March 1913 and taken over by the Metropolitan Line, the Thames Tunnel still today forms a part of the East London Line.[18]

This line closed on 24 March 1 1995 and reopened on 24 March 1998 after refurbishment and strengthening as it was felt that the brickwork might be in a potentially dangerous condition. Following the granting of listed status it was decided to preserve four of the original arches and to line the interior of the rest of the tunnel with an 8"-thick concrete shell incorporating the cross-passages. Brunel's original architectural features and the impressive vista along the tunnel would then be retained.[19] A mould was taken from an original arch from which steel shutters were constructed for the delicate concrete pour in order to retain the integrity of the architecture. By March 1997 the lining was completed and the stations along the line had been modernised and redecorated, that at Wapping with illustrations of the Thames Tunnel's history. In an echo of the past a banquet was held in the refurbished tunnel just as one had been on 10 November 1827 in the early stages of this impressive engineering achievement.

THE TOWER SUBWAY

Peter William Barlow (1809-1885), resident engineer for the construction of the South Eastern Railway, was another important figure in the development of tunnelling techniques. While working on the construction of his lattice-stiffened suspension bridge at Lambeth and observing the vertical cylinders being sunk into the river bed, Barlow imagined that similar structures could be propelled forward horizontally for tunnelling purposes.[20] By 1864 he had patented a cylindrical tunnelling shield that improved on Brunel's original design. It consisted of a cast-iron rim with six short spokes connecting it to a hexagonal ring mounted 3 feet from the front of an iron cyclinder, whose leading edge was sharpened. This bit into the clay as it was driven forward by hydraulic jacks. Miners excavated the clay before the shield advanced and the section behind was lined with cast-iron segments. In a pamphlet published in 1867 Barlow envisioned a network of 'omnibus subways' eight feet in diameter built to carry 12-seater carriages propelled by manpower and aided by gravity. Three levels of subways would compensate for differences of surface level and carriages would be transported from one level to another by means of hydraulic lifts. Despite his enthusiastic proselytising potential contractors recalled the difficulties in the excavation of Brunel's tunnel and withheld support.

In 1864 Barlow had acquired as an apprentice, the 20-year-old South African, James Henry Greathead (1844-1896), who after a three year pupillage with Barlow worked for a year on the construction of the Midland Railway extension from Bedford to London. It was thus as an experienced en-

83. The Tower Subway.

gineer that Greathead in 1868 made an offer to build one of Barlow's tunnels for £9400 using a shield inspired by that patented in 1864. This tunnel, with Barlow as engineer and Greathead as contractor, was to run beneath the Thames from Tower Hill to Vine Lane off Tooley Street on the south bank. Greathead's tunnelling shield of 8 feet 6 inches diameter held three men working under compressed air in a circular iron ring divided into seven segments. This working area was sealed off with a watertight bulkhead. Weighing just over two tons, it was considerably lighter than Brunel's shield. Cast iron segments of tubing were inserted every eighteen inches as the shield advanced; the gap between the tunnel and the excavation being filled with liquid cement to prevent soil settling to fill this gap. Excavations commenced on 16 February 1869 from a shaft on Tower Hill, the tunnel advancing forward 10 feet every 24 hours until work was completed an impressive five months later.

Opening on 2 August 1870 the Tower Subway, as it was now called, was 1350 feet long. At either end circular shafts ten feet in diameter, 50 to 60 feet deep, contained steam-driven lifts to convey passengers to a small 12-seat tramcar, which travelled back and forth through the tunnel by means of a cable and two steam hauling engines. The limited capacity of the tramcar failed to generate sufficient revenue and the lifts were replaced by spiral staircases. The subway was subsequently converted into a pedestrian route, handling over a million people a year until Tower Bridge opened in 1894. Thereafter the tunnel was used for carrying pipes for the London Hydraulic Power Company and more recently water mains for the Thames Water Authority, together with cables. The small circular entrance structures still exist on Tower Hill and in Vine Lane but excite little interest today. Although the Tower Subway may be largely forgotten, the Greathead shield, following more improvements, was used to excavate the City & South London Railway and the subsequent deep tunnels of the London Underground. A statue of Greathead stands today by Bank station as a memorial to this underground revolutionary.[21]

MORE TUNNELS UNDER THE THAMES

A plethora of tunnels in central London carry Underground trains, pedestrians, water, electricity and other utilities beneath the Thames or lie dormant awaiting new occupancy. The Thames Water Ring Main is one of the more recent subterranean interventions, that burrows beneath the river several times as it girdles the capital. Following the Thames from the west to the east and commencing near Hammersmith Bridge we first encounter an older, narrower water main that runs downstream from the reservoir in Barnes south of the river, to the area adjacent to the Riverside Studios. Further down river, from the long disused Battersea Power Station two tunnels dip beneath the river bed, one carrying electricity cables and now virtually disused. The other formerly conveyed water drawn from the river, which was extremely hot after having been used in the power station's boilers, across to Dolphin Square and the Churchill Gardens Estate for central heating purposes, after which the water was discharged back into the Thames. The tunnel completed in 1996, that carries the electric cable between Pimlico and Wimbledon, also burrows beneath the river near here.

From this point travelling down river London Underground tube tunnels form the majority of excavations beneath the Thames. The twin northbound and southbound tunnels of the Victoria Line extension to Brixton, which opened in 1971, run between Pimlico and Vauxhall stations. There is a very strong likelihood, as they are in such close proximity, that an under river tunnel was excavated in the late 1980s during the construction of the new MI6 building next to the south side of Vauxhall Bridge and the refurbishment of the MI5 headquarters on Millbank. The latest tube tunnels are for the Jubilee Line Extension. The first of these pass diagonally, one above the other, from the northern side of Westminster Bridge towards Waterloo. The unfinished tunnel of the putative 1865 pneumatic Waterloo & Whitehall railway stretched for a short distance below the river in the section between Westminster and Hungerford Bridges.

There then follows a heavily congested area with the northbound and southbound tunnels for the Bakerloo Line and those of the West End branch of the Northern northbound and southbound. The disused and flooded Charing Cross Loop is followed by the twin tunnels of the Waterloo & City Line. Deep-level former Post Office tunnels run from Colombo House next to Waterloo East station, one to Trafalgar Square Post Office and the other to Faraday House, one of the former 'Citadel' telephone exchanges, part of the extensive network of cable tunnels. An additional pedestrian tunnel that would link Embankment station on the north bank of the Thames with the revitalised

South Bank complex in front of the Royal Festival Hall was proposed by Paul Hyett Architects in 1995. This tunnel was never built.[22] Towards London Bridge lie the disused historic tunnels, northbound and southbound of the former City & South London Railway, abandoned when a new alignment was constructed. These are followed by the present northbound and southbound tunnels of the Northern Line on the City branch and then Greathead's Tower Subway to the west of Tower Bridge. As the Docklands area is reached the Thames Tunnel, now carrying the East London Underground line, unites Rotherhithe and Wapping, before the Rotherhithe Tunnel is encountered.

The busy single-bore tunnel linking Rotherhithe to Ratcliffe, the second road tunnel to be excavated beneath the river, was designed by Sir Maurice Fitzmaurice (1861-1924) for the London County Council. It was built between 1904 and 1908 costing £500,000 and renovated from 1979 to 1981. 6833 feet long with 3742 feet of driven tunnel, like the southbound Blackwall Tunnel it is 27 feet in diameter with a 16-ft carriageway. Fitzmaurice used the same tunnelling techniques pioneered by Brunel some eighty years earlier at the nearby Thames Tunnel. The two halves of the cutting shield have been imaginatively placed above the tunnel entrances as a height gauge, originally to prevent carts which were too high from entering the tunnel. The ventilation shaft by the Surrey Lock in Rotherhithe Street contains a staircase that leads down to the tunnel, together with four ventilation fans at a lower level. A construction shaft with a conical roof dating from 1900 can also be seen in Brunel Road.

Proceeding down river again, the site of Trevithick's ambitious but abandoned Thames Archway tunnel is followed by the new tunnels of the Jubilee Line Extension connecting Canada Water with Canary Wharf station on the Isle of Dogs peninsula. Further south in this large meander in the

Thames a tunnel carries electric cables from the remains of Deptford Power Station to the Isle of Dogs.

Another recent intervention beneath the Thames are the twin tunnels of the Docklands Light Railway Extension, carrying passengers between a new underground Island Gardens station and the brand new station on the south bank named Cutty Sark. Island Gardens, with a magnificent view of the former Royal Naval College across the Thames at Greenwich, contain in the south-western corner the red brick rotunda with its glass and steel dome which allows access to the Greenwich Foot Tunnel, 1217 feet in length. Constructed between 1896 and 1902 the passageway has an internal diameter of 12 feet 9 inches. Once a vital link for dockers and later for tourists, it will probably be less used now that the Lewisham Extension of the Docklands Light Railway has opened. After leaving the elegant wood-panelled lift (stairs are also provided) the pedestrian can follow the tunnel as it dips down towards the centre of the river in a rather claustrophobic, occasionally intimidating atmosphere.[23] On the eastern side of the peninsula the twin tunnels of the Jubilee Line Extension cross the river once more from Canary Wharf to the impressive station on another peninsula at North Greenwich.

BLACKWALL ROAD TUNNEL AND EASTWARDS
Excavation of the first road tunnel under the Thames commenced in March 1892. The northbound Blackwall Tunnel (originally designed to accommodate two lines of vehicles together with foot passengers) was opened on 22 May 1897 by the Prince of Wales. Designed by Sir Alexander Binnie (1839-1917), working for the London County Council, the tunnelled section under the Thames is 3083 feet long. Negotiating the series of sharp bends today whilst avoiding the stalactite-like protrusions hanging from the ceiling, installed as vehicle height limit

84. *The Greenwich Foot Tunnel in 1902.*

85. The southern entrance to Blackwall Tunnel in 1975.

warnings, can make driving through this tunnel a rather disquieting experience. The tunnel was dug using a shield designed by the contractors' engineer, E.W. Moir, that incorporated improvements on Greathead's prototype. The miners had to work in compressed air as the tunnel passed through water-bearing strata. This was the first time that this technique had been combined with shield excavation. The construction of the tunnel also required a temporary layer of clay to be laid as a sealant on the river bed as at one point the roof of the tunnel would have been barely five feet below the river bed.[24]

The tunnel is lined with cast-iron segments filled with concrete and faced with white glazed bricks, a prototype that was to be copied in the subsequent Greenwich, Rotherhithe and Woolwich tunnels. An additional tunnel, which took over the southbound traffic, was begun in 1960 and finished in 1967, designed by the GLC Directorate of Highways & Transportation and excavated by Mott, Hay and Anderson. It is 2870 feet in length with an internal diameter of 27 feet. Again it was carved out

under compressed air with the ground consolidated by grouting from two pilot tunnels. The twin concrete ventilation stacks, an early design by Terry Farrell, form a distinctive sculptural feature, particularly that on the Greenwich Peninsula, which has been subsumed into the structure, but fortunately not the interior, of the Millennium Dome. A new cable tunnel, excavated in 1998 to carry power to the Dome from the substation at West Ham, is one of the latest additions to the myriad Thames tunnels.

The Underground tunnels of the Jubilee Line Extension pass beneath the Thames for the last time carrying the railway from North Greenwich to Canning Town. Another masterpiece of engineering, the Thames Barrier further downstream at Woolwich Reach, constructed between 1974 and 1982, incorporates twin tunnels that carry duplicated power cables, control cables and drains between the piers and the control building on the south bank and allow staff access. Beneath the free Woolwich Ferry, introduced in 1889, runs the 1635-feet Woolwich Foot Tunnel, 12ft 8 inches in diameter, designed by Fitzmaurice for the LCC. It was constructed between 1909 and 1912 as a short cut between residential Woolwich and the docks on the north bank. Further downstream a utility tunnel once carried electricity cables between Barking Power Station and Thamesmead. Finally, outside London, the most easterly working tunnel – the toll-charging Dartford Tunnel – links Kent with Essex on the M25 for northbound traffic. Should the spectacular Queen Elizabeth II Bridge/Dartford River Crossing need to close the tunnel can revert to northbound and southbound operation. Even further towards the mouth of the Thames lies the abandoned Gravesend to Tilbury excavation, the earliest attempt at tunnelling beneath the Thames in 1798, which has been followed by so many more successful ventures in the last two hundred years.

Footnotes for Chapter Three

[1] Quoted in Ben Weinreb and Christopher Hibbert *op. cit.*, 595, from *The Monthly Magazine*.

[2] A recent history of the gas industry prior to privatisation is Hugh Barty-King *New Flame, How Gas changed the commercial domestic and industrial life of Britain between 1813 and 1984* (Graphmitre Ltd, 1984).

[3] For a detailed technical explanation see 'Watery death of electricity's rival' *New Scientist* 28 July 1977, 221-223. See also Ralph Turvey 'London lifts and Hydraulic Power' in *Newcomen Society for the study of the history of engineering and technology transactions* Vol. 65 1993-1994.

[4] Tim Smith 'Hydraulic Power' in North East London Polytechnic *Dockland - an illustrated historical survey of life and work in East London* (NELP & GLC, 1986), 159-175.

[5] For more on the early history see Brian Bowers 'The Rise of the Electricity Supply Industry' in *History Today* vol 22 March 1972, 176-183.

[6] Rob Cochrane *Pioneers of Power, the Story of the London Electricity Supply Corporation 1887-1948* (London Electricity Board, 1987). See also Antony Clayton '"Greenery - yallery, Grosvenor Gallery", avant garde outpost and electricity pioneer" in *Westminster History Review* No. 4, 2000.

[7] For general British histories see John P Wright *Vital Spark* (Heinemann, 1974) and Leslie Hannah *Electricity before Nationalisation* (Macmillan, 1979).

[8] Michael Harrison 'Five-mile electricity tunnel planned for central London' *The Independent* 23 August 1989, 5.

[9] John Camm 'Tunnel Vision' in *Electrical Review* vol. 233 no. 17, 4 July 2000.

[10] F L Stevens *Under London – a chronicle of London's underground lifelines and relics* (J M Dent, 1939), 34-37.

[11] M A C Horne *The Victoria Line, a short history* (Douglas Rose, 1988), 31.

[12] Colin Freeman 'Why the Victorians were streets ahead' *The Evening Standard* 6 April 1999, 6-7.

[13] Geoffrey Hubbard *Cooke and Wheatstone and the Invention of the Electric Telegraph* (Routledge & Kegan Paul, 1965).

[14] See D G Clow 'Pneumatic Tube Communication Systems in London' in *The Newcomen Society for the study of the history of Engineering and Technology Transactions* Vol. 66, 1994-95, 97-119.

[15] F G C Baldwin *The History of the Telephone in the United Kingdom* (Chapman & Hall, 1925).

[16] For the full construction story see the 'Limehouse Link' supplement with *New Civil Engineer* May 1993. The engineers were Sir Alexander Gibb & Partners.

[17] This major engineering achievement has been extensively documented. Marc Brunel's diaries and other reports covering the project are kept in the library of the Institution of Civil Engineers. See also Richard Beamish *Memoir of the Life of Sir Marc Isambard Brunel* (Longman, 1862) and David Lampe *The Tunnel: the Story of the World's first Tunnel under a Navigable River dug beneath the Thames 1824-42* (Harrap, 1963). The account of the tunnel's construction in Richard Trench and Ellis Hillman's *London Under London* (John Murray, 1984, rev. ed. 1993) is unreliable; for example they claim that the work proceeded from Wapping! The engine house that once accommodated the pumps for the tunnel is now open as a museum close to Rotherhithe station.

[18] John Robert Day *The Story of London's Underground* (London Transport, 1979) ch iv.

[19] *Concrete Quarterly* Winter 1998, 9.

[20] This bridge was built in 1862. It was replaced by the present five-span steel arch bridge designed by Sir George Humphreys with Sir Reginald Blomfield as architectural consultant in 1929-32.

[21] A plaque was unveiled on Greathead's home in Streatham in 2000.

[22] Paul Hyett 'South Bank Tunnel-the final piece in a jigsaw' *Architect's Journal* 30 November 1995, 26-28.

[23] Drawing on the feelings of enclosure experienced in this tunnel and the Woolwich Foot Tunnel two artists, Tanya Harris and Goldberry Broad, transformed these public thoroughfares into art installations for two weeks in the summer of 1996. They used sound and red light in Greenwich foot tunnel to evoke the sensation of walking along the interior of an artery. Blue-green light and suitable sound effects in the Woolwich Tunnel recreated the effect of being underwater.

[24] Stephen Porter ed. *Survey of London* Vol. XLIV *Poplar, Blackwall and the Isle of Dogs* (Athlone Press, 1994) 640-645.

CHAPTER FOUR
Railways beneath the city

'A true map of the London Underground shows the central complex as a shape suggestive of a swimming dolphin, its snout being Aldgate, its forehead Old Street, the crown of its head King's Cross, its spine Paddington, White City and Acton, its tail Ealing Broadway and its underbelly the stations at Kensington. The outer configurations branch out in graceful tentacles. The seal has become a medusa, a jellyfish. Its extremities touch Middlesex and Hertfordshire, Essex and Surrey. A claw penetrates Heathrow.'

Barbara Vine in *King Solomon's Carpet* (Penguin, 1991)

'He is following the Underground line northwards and as he realizes this he smiles, looks down. There is nothing to see, although he can track the direction of the tunnels with his eyes. The Tube system is like the city's bricked-over tributary rivers, he thinks; the Tyburn and Fleet, other names he has never learned. A network hidden under the surface and visible only sometimes, like the blue veins where they lie near the skin.'

Tobias Hill in *Underground* (Faber & Faber 1999)

'Underground: the title of a painting of great beauty...their sacred symbol of harmony. It is true that certain spirit names have been deciphered – angel, temple, white city, gospel oak and the legendary seven sisters - but the central purpose of the painting is still disputed.'

Peter Ackroyd in *The Plato Papers* (Chatto & Windus 1999)

The London Underground is the oldest railway network of its kind in the world and one of the most extensive rapid urban transport systems. The track runs for 259 miles, serving 278 stations with the longest single continuous journey being the 34 miles from West Ruislip to Epping on the Central Line. As 58% of the so-called Underground is actually above ground it is the 8% in cut-and-cover tunnels, running just beneath the streets and the 34% constructed in deep-level tubes that will be considered in this chapter. The complex story of the gradual spread of London's underground railway system has been admirably covered in many recent histories.[1] Initially each line was built separately by individual railway companies seeking profit, but as technology advanced and the need to electrify lines seemed unavoidable, lack of capital became a major problem. Charles Tyson Yerkes (1837-1905), who had made a fortune from electric trains and trams in Chicago, launched takeover bids for many of the lines, starting with the Charing Cross, Euston and Hampstead Railway Company in 1900. By the time of his death a mere five years later, he had established the Underground Electric Railways Company for London (UERL) that would dominate London's transport for thirty years. At the end of 1912 the City & South London and the Central London tube companies were subsumed within the UERL empire, whose managing director Albert Henry Stanley (1874-1948) oversaw many extensions to the network. In 1933 the London Passenger Transport Board (LPTB) was formed incorporating the Metropolitan Railway and unifying Underground trains, buses and trams under a single authority.

Stanley was its first chairman. When Frank Pick (1878-1941) took over the Underground Group's publicity in 1908 he went on to commission some of the finest artists and designers to produce a succession of striking and distinctive posters and was responsible for the introduction of Edward Johnston's (1872-1944) *sans serif* typeface still used in all Underground stations.[2] Pick eventually rose to become vice-chairman of the LPTB. This period also saw the appearance of the brilliantly simple and effective design for the famous Underground map first devised by Henry (Harry) C. Beck (1901-1974) in 1931.[3]

In 1948, on the nationalisation of Britain's railways, the newly created British Transport Commission (BTC) vested control of the Underground system in the London Transport Executive. On 1 January 1963 a new London Transport Board was created, reporting directly to the Minister of Transport. By the end of the 1960s, pressure had grown for London Transport to come under the control of the Greater London Council and this took effect from 1 January 1970, when a new London Transport Executive succeeded the Board. The London Transport Executive in its turn passed from Greater London Council control to that of the Secretary of State for transport on 29 June 1984 and was renamed London Regional Transport. A subsidiary company was established on 29 March 1985 called London Underground Limited (LUL) and on 1 April 1985 London Regional Transport's railway activities passed to this subsidiary company.

The tradition in London Transport of doing most things in-house was then gradually eroded as competitive tendering became a political necessity. There were ominous rumblings of privatisation of the Underground system, just as many bus routes in London had been farmed out to other operators. In 2000 proposals are being considered that would split the infrastructure – trains, track, tunnels and signalling – into three separate companies run by private consortia. Under this public-private partnership (PPP) only the train service itself would be controlled by London Underground. At present this is considered the best method of raising the estimated £7 billion required for investment over the next fifteen years to ensure that the system is modern, comfortable and efficient.

THE METROPOLITAN RAILWAY
Broughams, cabriolets, gigs, growlers, hansoms, landaus, phaetons and the ubiquitous omnibus were gradually clogging the streets of the capital by the middle of the nineteenth century, together with carts and wagons carrying produce. The population of London had more than doubled from 1,138,000 in 1811 to 2,362,000 in 1851 and commuting had become a fact of life, although many were obliged to walk to work. Newspapers and businessmen fulminated against these intolerable conditions, but one man, Charles Pearson (1794-1862) solicitor and Member of Parliament for Lambeth, became active in promoting underground railways as a solution. Since the 1830s he had been promoting a plan for a railway from King's Cross to Farringdon Street with potential for connections to other railway lines at both termini. The line itself would run at basement level, beneath a 100-foot wide new street with strategically placed openings along its length for light and ventilation. As a result of this scheme a magnificent new boulevard would be created for road traffic and the unsightly slums clustered along the Fleet valley would be obliterated.[4]

The intransigence of the Corporation of London meant that the introduction and extension of railways within the boundaries of the City was fiercely resisted. Slowly, over many years, amidst an ever worsening traffic situation, Pearson and his supporters turned the tide of opposition resulting in

86. *Construction of the Metropolitan Line at King's Cross in 1861. The distinctive clock-tower of King's Cross Great Northern station is on the mid right.*

87. *The proposed Baker Street station on the Metropolitan Line, depicted in 1860.*

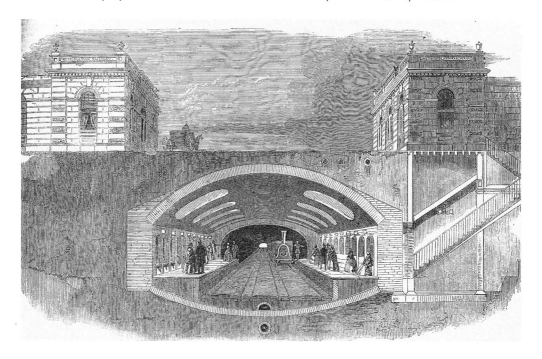

the establishment of a Royal Commission in 1846 to investigate the many proposals for new railways in London. Pearson diligently collected two thousand signatures of leading City businessmen on a petition promoting his railway, which he delivered to the Commission. When he was called before it he eloquently described the benefits of his scheme, emphasising the improved access across the chasm of the Fleet Valley, together with the social engineering effected by the eradication of the nearby slums and the movement of the poorer classes to "suburban villages". Unfortunately the Commission rejected all the new railway proposals including Pearson's. *Punch* magazine added to Pearson's humiliation by claiming "that a survey has already been made and that many of the inhabitants along the line have expressed their readiness to place their coal cellars at the disposal of the company. It is believed that much expense may be saved by taking advantage of areas, kitchens and coal holes already made, through which the trains may run without much inconvenience to the owners."[5]

In 1850 Pearson finally received approval for his plan from the Fleet Valley Improvement Committee appointed by the Court of Common Council in the City. Much wrangling ensued before the matter was decided by the passage of Bills through the House of Commons for a North Metropolitan line from Edgware Road to King's Cross, given Royal Assent in August 1853 and a further Bill for its extension to Bishop's Bridge, Paddington and to Farringdon, which received Assent a year later. By January 1860 the first shaft was sunk at Euston Square and the diversion of sewers was undertaken between there and King's Cross, the beginning of what was to become a regular occurrence in extensive excavations beneath London. The railway was constructed using the cut-and-cover method. This involved digging a deep trench for the railway, building the brick walls and roof and then covering it over once more, normally along the course of a road, for example present-day Marylebone Road and Euston Road. This caused great disruption to life above ground and resulted in a series of legal battles claiming obstruction of business premises and undermining of foundations.

A number of accidents occurred during the construction of this innovative railway. On 1 November 1860 a locomotive exploded at the junction of the Metropolitan and the Great Northern killing the driver and stoker and injuring a passing cabman when the engine's chimney landed on his head. Attempts to remove a length of the New River Company's water main near Farringdon Street almost ended tragically when the pipe burst, flooding the shaft. Fortunately all the workmen were safely hauled to the surface. A more serious setback was recorded by the *Illustrated London News* on 28 June 1862. The excavations beside the Fleet sewer near Ray Street had not been reinforced when an accumulation of water in the sewer forced the embankment to collapse in a "cracking and heaving mass". Water started to pour into the works and slowly flooded the tunnels. No lives were lost, but the destruction was severe where, "about half way down the bank the liberated sewer rushed in a black cascade; huge masses of brickwork lay strewn here and there; while on the opposite side of the railway, the water gradually creeping up its dark brown walls, stood the great burial vault containing the bodies from the old Clerkenwell pauper burial-ground."[6] Despite these vicissitudes work continued and on 9 January 1863 the directors and special guests were given an exclusive ride on the new line to be greeted by bands; the momentous day closed with a banquet at Farringdon Street station. The aged Prime Minister, Lord Palmerston, excused himself from the celebrations, explaining that he wanted to stay above ground for as long as he could. On the following day the Met-

88. The first trial trip on the Metropolitan Railway in 1862.

89. A banquet at Farringdon Station to mark the opening of the Metropolitan Railway in January 1863.

90. *Construction of Praed Street station on the Metropolitan Line, opened in 1868 as part of an extension of the original line, which eventually would be part of the Circle Line. This station was later absorbed into the Paddington Station complex.*

ropolitan Railway was opened to the general public. Massive numbers of people arrived to experience this unique mode of transport and the *Daily Telegraph* reported that "Hundreds on each occasion ... had to be left behind to take their chances on the next train."

There were intermediate stations at Edgware Road, Baker Street, Portland Road (later renamed Great Portland Street), Gower Street (Euston Square) and King's Cross. By 1864 the line was carrying 11,720,000 passengers annually which had risen to 20,770,000 ten years later. In December 1865, the first of the Metropolitan's many extensions was opened, eastwards to Moorgate.

Because the Metropolitan connected to the Great Western Railway at Paddington, it was originally built to accommodate the broad gauge trains operated by the GWR. The tunnels are wider and the tracks further

apart than on other parts of the Underground system, a feature which can be clearly seen today on that part of the Metropolitan / Circle / Hammersmith & City Lines. The emission of smoke or exhaust steam was forbidden in the tunnels for the comfort of the travelling public, but as steam was the principal form of motive power this became a significant problem.

Sir John Fowler's experiment with an engine that raised steam by piling red hot bricks around the boiler, was a failure. Eventually the Metropolitan's locomotives were fitted with condensing apparatus to convert exhaust steam into water, which was then returned to the locomotives' tanks. Nevertheless, some steam and smoke was still produced and cuttings were provided in which to release it. One such open stretch occurs in Leinster Gardens, where, in an effort to disguise the billowing smoke and to preserve the integrity of the terraced

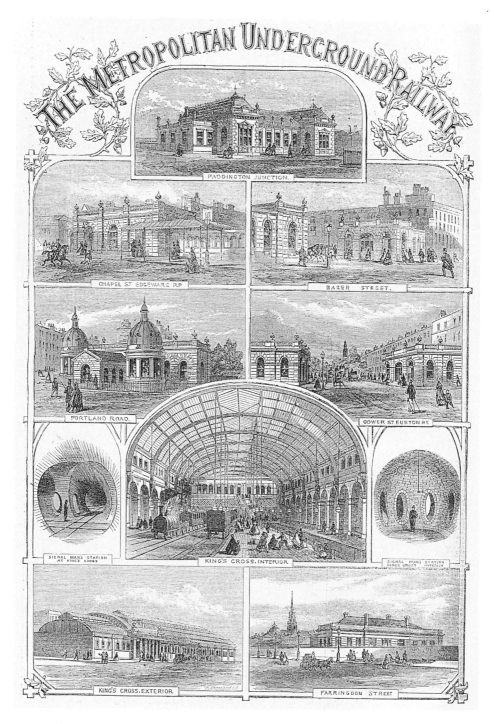

91. *The new stations built for the Metropolitan Railway, depicted in the Illustrated London News in December 1862.*

92. *A fascinating depiction of Farringdon Station, then the eastern terminus of the Metropolitan Railway, in 1863. Turnmill Street is to the right, the railway is bridged by Clerkenwell Road, and Farringdon Road is to the left.*

houses along that street, two facades were built at numbers 23 and 24 with the railway running through a cutting directly behind. The Metropolitan was supplied by Beyer, Peacock of Manchester with 4-4-0 locomotives fitted with condensing tanks, which were in regular use until electrification. The first eighteen were named after classical deities with number eight bearing the most appropriate: Pluto, god of the underworld.

An allied company, the Metropolitan & St John's Wood Railway (M&SJWR) was formed to promote a branch from Baker Street to the Finchley Road area (in fact, Swiss Cottage), a distance of 2¼ miles. Although granted permission to build in July 1864 the usual problem of insufficient finance resulted in the railway being single

93. *Dummy houses at 23 and 24 Leinster Gardens (see above), which hid the Metropolitan Railway from view and retained the symmetry of the terrace.*

94. 'Underground works at the junction of Hampstead Road, Euston Road and Tottenham Court Road', depicted in the Illustrated London News in 1864. The view looks to the east along Euston Road, with New St Pancras Church in the distance. Also shown is the Pneumatic Despatch Company's tube (see p. 130), which travelled south down Hampstead Road and Tottenham Court Road, plus, above the sewer at the bottom of the picture, a proposed railway which never got built.

track, with double track in the new stations at St John's Wood Road (later renamed Lord's), Marlborough Road and Swiss Cottage. The line was almost entirely in tunnel and opened on 13 April 1868, only running as far as Swiss Cottage. Although not particularly successful financially, this thrust northward was to continue as the M&SJWR expanded, until it was taken over by the Metropolitan in 1883. By that time the tunnel north of Baker Street had been doubled and Finchley Road station had been established. The line had already reached Harrow by 2 August 1880. Between 1936 and 1940 twin tube tunnels were excavated for the Bakerloo Line between Baker Street and Finchley Road, easing congestion on the Metropolitan, which could now run a non-stop service between those two stations. The three Metropolitan line stations at Lord's (formerly called St John's Wood), Marlborough Road and Swiss Cottage joined

the list of those abandoned and forgotten and two new deep-level Bakerloo Line stations were built as replacements.

THE DISTRICT LINE AND COMPLETION OF THE CIRCLE

A proposal by a House of Lords select committee in 1863 for an 'inner circuit' railway, principally to link the disparate railway termini, was incorporated into another scheme to construct a new road on the north bank of the Thames to relieve traffic from the overcrowded Strand. The latter became the Victoria Embankment, which contained Joseph Bazalgette's main sewer. At the same time it was hoped to include tunnels for what today forms part of the District and the southern section of the Circle Line. As the Metropolitan Railway was considered unable to raise sufficient capital or oversee the construction of the railway, a new company was formed in July 1864: the

95. The Lord Mayor of London ceremonially commencing works for the extension of the Circle Line. Despite such official encouragement the two companies involved in completing the Circle Line had their own reasons for delaying the project as long as possible.

96. What became the Circle Line began as extensions west and east from the original route of the Metropolitan Railway. In the west the line diverged in 1868 at Edgware Road running south and then east as far as Westminster. One station on this extension was Bayswater Road, pictured above.

Metropolitan District Railway to finance and build this southern portion of the proposed loop from South Kensington to Tower Hill. On 24 December 1868 the first section of the District Line opened between South Kensington and Westminster, the station initially being named Westminster Bridge.[7] The construction of this section of the loop was hampered by complex engineering work and dwindling finances. The Metropolitan Board of Works, however, wanted its sewer working and soon authority was given by Parliament to issue preference stock for the remaining money required. The railway could then proceed and it was opened to Blackfriars on 30 May 1870, passing through new stations at Charing Cross (present day Embankment) and Temple.[8] The line ran through tunnels 25 feet in width constructed by the cut-and-cover method, with the stations constructed in double-width cuttings with vertical retaining walls. Platforms were

300 feet long and their arched iron roofs had a 50' 6" span.

Unfortunately, from 1869 progress towards the completion of the 'circle' was slowed by a series of disputes between the two companies. Edward Watkin (1819-1901), known as the Railway King, became chairman of the Metropolitan in August 1872. He was already chairman of the South East Railway, which had been in dispute with the London, Chatham & Dover Railway (LC&DR). When the truculent James Staats Forbes (1823-1904) of the LC&DR became chairman and managing director of the District in November 1872 co-operation between the rival railways seemed doomed. Where previously the Metropolitan had run trains over the District's track, Forbes acquired a fleet of locomotives and coaches in order to run his own service. By 3 July 1871 the line had reached Mansion House, where three tracks and two platforms were

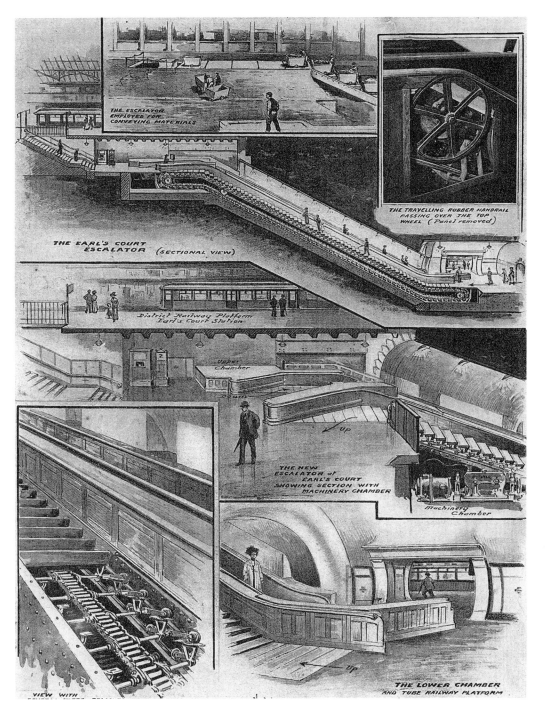

97. The first Earl's Court station was opened on the District Line in 1871 and replaced by another station in 1878. This was joined in 1906 by the Piccadilly Line and in 1911, to the admiration of the public, escalators were installed. This intricate drawing by W.B. Robinson, appeared in the Illustrated London News in October 1911.

provided. This was to be the eastern terminus for the next twenty years, much to the irritation of the authorities and the public.

Despite authorisation in the Act of 1864 to complete the line as far as Tower Hill the Metropolitan declined to do this, as it felt that revenue would decrease once the District had access to its northern section. Therefore, the Inner Circle Completion Company was independently established in 1874, in order to effect the vital connection between the two lines; this spurred the Metropolitan into action. Their northern limb of the railway was extended down to Bishopsgate (later renamed Liverpool Street) in July 1875 and on to Aldgate by 18 November 1876. Watkin parleyed with the District, a joint committee was set up and a scheme to complete the inner circle was enshrined in the Metropolitan and District Railways (City Lines and Extensions) Act of 1879. The Metropolitan crept round to Tower of London station on 25 September 1882. Finally, on 6 October 1884 the inner circle was opened to the public. New underground stations at Cannon Street, Monument and Mark Lane were opened, together with a spur off to Aldgate East and another to a station at Whitechapel.[9] The Metropolitan ran from Hammersmith via the northern half of the circle to a junction just west of Whitechapel and thence via the East London Railway to New Cross Gate. The District ran trains from Hammersmith District station over the southern side and then to the East London Railway and New Cross. In 1897 the District joined the London Tilbury & Southend Railway (LT&SR) to promote a Whitechapel & Bow Railway. Commenced in 1899 it was completed by June 1902 and ran in a tunnel from Whitechapel through Stepney Green, Mile End and Bow Road stations. From there it rose to the surface up the steepest gradient on the Underground used by passenger trains, 1 in 45, to connect with the LT&SR on its way eastwards.

An engineer who worked for many years on improvements to the London Underground tunnels and stations has written with admiration for his Victorian predecessors, "The complete Circle was a monumental work of infinite complexity and variety of structures pursued with ingenuity and courage in made ground, mud, silt, peat and between the City and Westminster along the old bed of the river. At Charing Cross the walls of the covered way had to be carried down 25ft below rail level. At places, 24 ft of the ruins of a city founded 2,000 years before [actually 1840] were cut through. There were cuttings between massive walls, bridges and elliptical brick arch tunnels, wrought iron girders, cast iron girders and a bellmouth at Praed Street, even an elliptical iron arch, 28ft wide at one end and 60ft at the other, resembling the inverted hull of a large ship."[10] Today the Circle line runs for 13 miles, serving 27 stations and on average a train will take fifty minutes to circuit the route. Prior to electrification, completed in 1905, it took seventy minutes. The sections between High Street Kensington and Gloucester Road and between Aldgate and Minories Junction to the east of Tower Hill station are only used by Circle Line trains. Otherwise the remainder of the route is covered by Metropolitan and District trains. A programme of platform lengthening was initiated in 1955 as the stations on the stretch between South Kensington and Tower Hill had difficulty accommodating eight-coach trains. The work undertaken between March 1961 and March 1962 at Blackfriars was particularly arduous, involving the demolition of the existing running tunnel, the construction of a wide covered way under the road between Blackfriars Bridge and Queen Victoria Street and the re-bridging of the Fleet sewer as it approached the Thames. The foundations of an old fort at the mouth of the Fleet were discovered together with a large number of cattle horns.[11]

PERIL IN PARLIAMENT SQUARE?

As the millennium approached the traffic island in Parliament Square became a cause for concern. It was reported that "London Underground engineers have admitted that the tunnel beneath the centre of the square is in such a precarious state that a vehicle driving over it might fall through on to the lines below."[12] The central turfed area of the square above the 1868 tunnels carrying the Circle and District lines had been fenced off for three years. A London Underground infrastructure engineer was quoted as saying that although politicians had favoured installing a fountain on the site, "we can't allow anything heavier than a mower." As New Year 1999 approached fears were expressed for millennium revellers' safety as London Underground forecast that thousands of them would congregate on Parliament Square in order to hear Big Ben chime midnight. A £1 million safety project was undertaken from October whereby the centre of the square was excavated and a load-bearing platform inserted before being grassed over once again. This was successfully completed before the end of 1999 and disaster was averted.

CITY & SOUTH LONDON RAILWAY

The first of the 'tube' railways (with circular tunnels) to be bored beneath the streets without the inconvenience of tearing up roads and the demolition of surface buildings was the City & South London Railway (C&SLR).[13] Peter Barlow (1809-1885), having successfully excavated the Tower Subway, proposed a scheme in 1870 to link Borough in Southwark with King William Street. Owing to lack of finance it was shelved until 1884, when an Act authorised the construction of a twin-tunnel subway from a point to the north of London Bridge to the Elephant and Castle. The City of London & Southwark Subway Company was formed to excavate it, with Charles Grey Mott as chairman and Barlow's pupil James

98. James Greathead.

Greathead (1844-1896) as chief engineer and designer of the tunnelling shields. From its terminus near the Monument at 46 King William Street the route curved around to the west and passed under the Thames beneath Swan Lane and Old Swan Pier, following Borough High Street on the south side and under Newington Causeway to Elephant and Castle. Work commenced on 28 October 1886 from a shaft sunk behind the Old Swan Pier just upstream from London Bridge.

Greathead's shield, based on the prototypes by Brunel and Barlow, was driven forward through the earth by hydraulic jacks, the spoil being carried away to the rear and the excavated tunnel subsequently permanently lined with cast-iron segments. The gap between the casing and the surrounding earth was filled with liquid cement. Through the efficiency of the Greathead Shield the 10' 2"-diameter tunnels beneath the river were finished within

99. *The Greathead Shield, built to tunnel the world's first underground railway.*

100. *Men working behind the shield bolting in sections of the tube.*

a remarkable fifteen weeks. However, because of the narrowness of Swan Lane, the southbound tunnel was built immediately above the northbound to avoid disturbing buildings and this, together with the sharp curve into King William Street Station, was to cause operating problems after the line was in operation. This highlights a problem that was to dog subsequent underground railway excavations, that of 'wayleaves', whereby the companies had to pay compensation to the owners of any property under which the railway passed – hence the convoluted routes of many early lines that attempted to follow roadways as much as possible. The directors applied for an extension south to Stockwell, which was granted in 1887 and further tunnels were excavated with a slightly larger diameter of 10′ 6″.

Charles Grey Mott and his directors took the important decision in January 1889 to abandon their original idea for cable-hauled carriages in favour of electric traction to be supplied by the firm of Mather & Platt Ltd of Manchester. In the 1879 Berlin Trade

Exhibition visitors could see a 150-volt locomotive pull three passenger cars around a short stretch of track. A series of electric railways followed, including Volk's Railway along the Brighton seafront in 1883. Its major advantage over steam was that it was a clean source of motive power. Mather & Platt had completed a railway electrification project in 1885 in Ireland and employed, in Dr Edward Hopkinson, an electric traction pioneer. A depot was built above ground near Stockwell station, together with a power station providing hydraulic power for the lifts and electrical energy. It was the first large-scale generating station to supply a traction load and also the largest generating plant in London. The company had changed its name to the City & South London Railway and was proud to have the Prince of Wales, later King Edward VII, inaugurate the line on 4 November 1890. The people who travelled on the official opening day on 18 December were using the first underground electric railway in the world.

This landmark railway ran entirely un-

101. Stockwell Station on the City and South London Railway.

derground for 3½ miles from King William Street to Stockwell, with intermediate stations at Borough, Elephant and Castle, Kennington and Oval. 165,000 passengers were carried in the first two weeks and it was used by over 15,000 passengers per day, who initially paid a flat fare of twopence each, with trains running every five minutes. These early tube travellers were conveyed in wooden-bodied carriages capable of seating 32 passengers on tall longitudinal upholstered seats. With an internal height of seven feet and illuminated by electric lights and emergency oil lamps these rather claustrophobic interiors were soon christened 'padded cells'. At the end of each carriage was an open platform with a gate and a member of staff who called out the names of stations and manually opened and shut the gates. The three coaches were hauled by an electric locomotive at 11½ miles an hour.[14]

In order to extend the line northwards to the Bank and eventually, via London Bridge and Moorgate, to the Angel it was necessary to abandon the original tunnel running to King William Street, since at that location it was pointing eastwards. The first section to Moorgate, using a new tunnel, opened in February 1900. Problems were encountered during the construction of the ticket hall at Bank, which was to occupy an enlargement of the crypt of Nicholas Hawksmoor's (1661-1736) St Mary Woolnoth church. Certainly the church above ground looks, in typical Hawksmoor style, formidably rugged. It proved to be of flimsy construction and widespread underpinning work had to be undertaken and £170,000 paid before the church authorities were satisfied. The remainder of the Islington extension opened on 17 November 1901. The line was also creeping southwards, with work commencing in 1898 and finishing in 1900, which saw the opening of Clapham Road (now Clapham North) and Clapham Common stations.[15]

The original under-river abandoned tun-

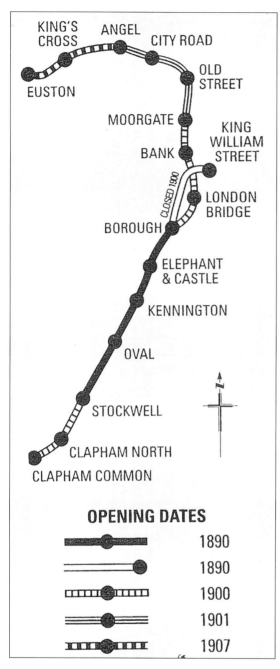

KING'S CROSS
ANGEL
CITY ROAD
EUSTON
OLD STREET
MOORGATE
KING WILLIAM STREET
BANK
CLOSED 1900
LONDON BRIDGE
BOROUGH
ELEPHANT & CASTLE
KENNINGTON
OVAL
STOCKWELL
CLAPHAM NORTH
CLAPHAM COMMON

OPENING DATES

	1890
	1890
	1900
	1901
	1907

102. The route of the City & South London Railway, later incorporated into the Northern Line. The line originally ran from Stockwell to King William Street. When extended, the original tunnel between Borough and King William Street was abandoned and a new route via London Bridge was constructed to Bank.

nels were used for gas and water mains until June 1940, when they saw service as an air raid shelter. After the closure of King William Street station from 25 February 1900 the street level buildings were used as a shop before demolition in 1933. The station tunnels and running tunnels still survive beneath the streets of the City as a decaying remnant of the earliest underground railways.[16] Thanks to the use of Greathead's tunnelling shield and the introduction of electric traction the possibility of deep-level underground train travel had become a reality. Many more subterranean lines were to follow.

WATERLOO & CITY LINE

Known colloquially as 'The Drain', the Waterloo & City Railway was the second tube line to be dug under London. Built by the London & South Western Railway (LSWR) as a fast, direct route for commuters into the heart of the City from their terminus at Waterloo, it opened on 8 August 1898.[17] Work had been authorised in 1893 and commenced in June 1894, when the first shaft was sunk from a platform in the Thames, an engineering technique that enabled spoil to be more easily removed by barge. The excavated tunnels were 12' 11½" in diameter and ran for 1½ miles. From 41 feet below Waterloo station the tunnels pass beneath Stamford Street, then diagonally under the Thames to a point near Blackfriars Bridge to continue straight under Queen Victoria Street to the City station at Bank 59 feet below street level.[18] The running tunnel segments were lined with concrete, whilst cast-iron was used for the first time in lining the station tunnels. The Waterloo & City is also unusual in that there are no intermediate stations on the line, it is physically isolated from the rest of the Underground and for many years was owned and operated by the LSWR and later British Rail. At Waterloo the platforms are connected by passenger subways and escalators to the

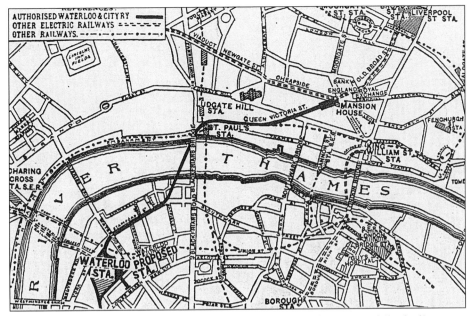

103. *The route of the Waterloo and City Railway depicted in 1896 while the line was being built. The City terminus was first called Mansion House and then City, but in 1940 it became part of the Bank station complex.*

Bakerloo, Northern and Jubilee lines and main line services. The travolator that smoothly carries passengers to the trains at Bank was the first of its type in Europe and opened on 27 September 1960.

The original wooden-bodied electric trains consisted of four coach units comprising a driving car at each end and two trailer cars in between, and survived until 1940. Their replacements, towards the end of their long life, provided a nostalgic albeit noisy and bumpy ride until 1993, when for some weeks the entire line was closed and refurbished.[19] In 1990 the powerful Armstrong hydraulic lift, that had enabled stock to be removed from and deposited onto the underground tracks from the north sidings at Waterloo, had to be dismantled to make way for the new Eurostar platform works. A temporary crane was therefore brought in to extricate the 1940 replacement stock and insert comfortable new units constructed in 1992 for the Central Line. This difficult manoeuvre took place over the Bank Holiday weekend at the end of May 1993 and was continued

during the weekend of 12 and 13 June, when Londoners were treated to the spectacle of underground stock travelling by road on the back of heavy lorries.[20] The line reopened on 19 July 1993. The track had been modified to the four-rail system standard on the London Underground and all new trains were fitted with computer-controlled Automatic Train Operation. After enjoying its splendid isolation for almost one hundred years the Waterloo & City Line passed into the ownership of London Underground in April 1994 and is at present managed by the Central Line.

CENTRAL LINE
The Central London was probably the most significant of the early tube lines in terms of its route, which passed directly east to west from the Bank of England to Shepherds Bush, beneath Cheapside, High Holborn, Oxford Street and Bayswater Road, linking residential and commercial areas. The Act to construct the 5½ mile line from Shepherds Bush to Cornhill had been passed

in 1891, but some years elapsed before the requisite capital could be raised with the aid of an Anglo-American syndicate led by the City financier Ernest Cassel (1852-1921). It was therefore not until April 1896 that work began from Chancery Lane with the sinking of a shaft to the London clay stratum, that could later act as a ventilation or lift shaft, whence a Greathead tunnelling shield excavated the running tunnels of 11' 8". Further permission had been granted in 1892 to extend the line to Liverpool Street from a station at the Bank, rather than Cornhill. Here an impressive subterranean ticket hall would also contain extensive subways to enable pedestrians to cross this busy City intersection. Having cost £260,000 per mile to build, the line was opened on 27 June 1900 by the Prince of Wales. There then followed weeks of services with empty trains to enable staff to familiarise themselves with the system prior to its opening to the public on 30 July.

This convenient route, just under six miles long, had eleven intermediate stations including Post Office (St Paul's today), British Museum (now closed), Tottenham Court Road, Oxford Circus, Marble Arch, Queens Road (renamed Queensway in 1946) and Notting Hill Gate. Another of Greathead's ideas was the hump design for track approach to the platforms, with a gradient of one in sixty up and one in thirty down to help trains decelerate on arrival and accelerate on departure. A fare of twopence for any single journey led to the *Daily Mail* christening it the 'Twopenny Tube', a nickname that even made an appearance in the 1900 revival of Gilbert and Sullivan's *Patience*. The cheap fares and a service which could provide up to thirty trains an hour resulted in high passenger numbers – around 45 million a year between 1902 and 1906. Initially the Central London was extremely popular.

There were, however, comments about the smell which greeted passengers on the platforms and trains. Sir Theodore Martin (1816-1909), giving evidence to the Royal Commission on London Traffic in February 1904 complained that, "For myself, I could not risk my health by travelling on such a railway as the Central London, with its obnoxious vapour, which I know from meeting it at the stations ... many individuals I know are giving it up."[21] Fans were installed at stations, including Bond Street and British Museum, in order to dispel the foul air, but the unpleasant situation was only alleviated by the use of a pressure system developed in 1911, which washed and ozonised the air. The early trains were drawn by locomotives, and the vibration from these heavy engines resulted in complaints from nearby property owners. Following investigations and experiments with seismographs it was discovered that electric multiple unit trains (where the drive motors were distributed along the train) caused the least problems. The Central London was to adopt this arrangement throughout the line by June 1903.

When an extensive Franco-British exhibition was announced, to be held in a new series of giant halls at Wood Lane, near Shepherds Bush, the Central London seized the opportunity to extend its line westward. The extension, finished in May 1908, ran on a loop to a new Wood Lane station close to the Central London's depot.[22] By July 1912 the railway had been extended eastwards as far as Liverpool Street and Broad Street. However, with declining passenger numbers and increasing competition from buses the line was sold on 1 January 1913 to the Underground Group, which acquired the City & South London at the same time. The Central London line was extended westward to Ealing Broadway in 1920 but few major improvements were made until the London Passenger Transport Board, with government backing, proposed the ambitious 1935-1940 New Works Programme. The Central was to have new twin tunnels running from Liverpool Street to Bethnal Green, Mile End and Stratford, where they surfaced outside the main line station. Shortly afterwards they entered tunnel once again to resurface south of Leyton to join the Ongar branch, part of the London & North Eastern Railway.[23] Outside Leytonstone a further extensive tunnel was required beneath Eastern Avenue, with stations at Wanstead, Redbridge and Gants Hill, to resurface south of Newbury Park. Given these lengthy runs away from the City and West End, with a further extension above ground to West Ruislip authorised in 1937, the line became known as the Central Line from that year. In the course of these works tunnelling was particularly difficult near Stratford where the soil around the River Lea was waterlogged.

The running tunnels 2¾ miles long east of Leytonstone were 12′ 3″ in diameter and lined with concrete segments. They were unfinished when war broke out in 1939 and they were commandeered as a secure factory in 1940. After the war the new sections were gradually unveiled, with the Eastern Avenue corridor opening in December 1947. Gants Hill, one of many influential station designs by Charles Holden (1875-1960), included a long concourse between the platforms reminiscent of the Moscow Metro.[24] The existing London & North Eastern Railway line to Epping was electrified for the Central Line by 1949. Today the line extends for 46 miles and serves 49 stations. The 1980s saw a programme of modernisation and redecoration for central London stations on the line including Bond Street, Marble Arch and Tottenham Court Road, where the latter's platform walls were encrusted with intricate mosaics designed by Eduardo Paolozzi (b.1924).[25] During the 1990s there was a complete renewal of signalling and power supplies, together with the introduction of sleek modern tube stock, made distinctive by their red finish, externally mounted doors and larger windows which continue round to the car ends for added security.

BRITISH MUSEUM STATION

British Museum Underground station was opened in July 1900 on the Central London Railway. It was situated between Tottenham Court Road and Chancery Lane stations on the north side of High Holborn, with an entrance and ticket office on the eastern corner of Bloomsbury Court. However, in 1907 a new station opened on the Great Northern, Piccadilly & Brompton Railway (Piccadilly Line) at Holborn, whose close proximity to British Museum station ultimately resulted in the Central Line station's demise. A proposal that year to link the two stations by subway was rejected and for many years passengers changing between the Central and Piccadilly Lines had to endure a 170-yard walk along the street between them. Parliamentary powers to move British Museum station were obtained in 1914, but it was only in 1930 that work began on constructing platforms to create the combined Central and Piccadilly Line station at Holborn, which was to open on 25 September 1933. The empty platforms at British Museum were dismantled.[26] Given its famous name the station was, shortly before closing, alleged to be haunted by the ghost of an Ancient Egyptian. This unlikely story probably inspired the plot of the 1935 film *Bulldog Jack* in which the lid of an Egyptian sarcophagus opens onto a secret passage leading from the British Museum to a disused underground station named Bloomsbury.[27] The remaining tunnels saw service again during the last war, when they were used as an air raid shelter. Later the station accommodated an administrative office for the Scots Guards and other regiments in the Household Division. According to Duncan Campbell, writing in 1983, "in the event of a peacetime flooding of London, the London District military command will operate from here rather than

104. British Museum station on the Central Line c. 1930. It was abandoned in 1933 when the interchange between Piccadilly and Central Lines was opened at Holborn.

from the wartime AFHQ5 at Beaconsfield."[28] By 1989 the street level building had been demolished. Although British Museum station is now almost forgotten the tiled, graffiti-covered platform walls can still be clearly seen during a tube journey between Tottenham Court Road and Holborn.

THE BAKERLOO LINE

The Bakerloo line represented the culmination of further attempts to link north and south London with a more central underground line following the failure of the Waterloo & Whitehall Railway.[29] Securing Parliamentary sanction in 1865, the Waterloo & Whitehall Company intended to construct an underground pneumatic railway from the Whitehall end of Great Scotland Yard to a point near Waterloo station. Although work commenced in October 1865, the project proved too expensive and construction ceased in 1868. The Charing Cross & Waterloo Electric Railway proposed a line beneath the Thames, carried in twin

iron caissons lowered into a river trench, running between Waterloo station and Trafalgar Square, which obtained an Act of Incorporation in 1882. Ultimately, however, this project was also stymied by lack of finance. The proposal for a Baker Street and Waterloo Railway proved more successful, with its alignment from present day Melcombe Street, near Upper Baker Street to James Street near Lower Marsh. Following incorporation in March 1893 under the revised name of the North & South London Railway, the company set about raising the necessary capital. By 1896 the proposed route had been extended to the Great Central Railway's Marylebone Station, but sufficient money was not forthcoming until November 1897 when the London & Globe Finance Corporation stepped in to enable work to commence. This was one of a number of profitable companies run by Whitaker Wright (1845-1904), an Englishman who had made a fortune in mine prospecting in the United States.

105. Construction of the Bakerloo Line at Edgware Road.

Construction work began in August 1898 on platforms on the Thames from which two vertical shafts were sunk, a strategy which avoided sites in crowded central London and enabled material to be delivered and removed efficiently by barge. By 1900 parliamentary authorisation had been obtained to extend the line still further north to Paddington station, gateway to the Great Western Railway. A southern extension to Elephant and Castle would provide an interchange with the City & South London Railway and access to South London Tramways. Unfortunately, in December that year Whitaker Wright's company finances were revealed to have been subject to extensive 'creative accounting' and he was forced to flee the country. He was extradited back to London in 1903 and whilst on trial at the Royal Courts of Justice he committed suicide with a cyanide capsule. The insolvency of Wright's venture resulted in a virtual cessation of work on the new line, which had penetrated as far north beneath Regent Street as Vigo Street. The sharp curve from Piccadilly Circus to Oxford Circus, which runs below Regent Street was necessary in order to avoid the payment of wayleaves to the owners of property above. To the rescue came the flamboyant American Charles Tyson Yerkes, who had already acquired the District Railway in 1901 and to which he added the North & South London Railway in 1902.

The line was finally opened to the public on 10 March 1906 from Baker Street to Kennington Road (now Lambeth North), with intermediate stations at Regent's Park, Oxford Circus, Piccadilly Circus, Trafalgar Square, Embankment and Waterloo. It was considered a failure initially as it was only used by 20-30,000 passengers per day. Originally a mere three miles long, the line was extended southwards to Elephant and

106. St John's Wood Road Station was opened on the northern extension of the Metropolitan Line in 1868 near Lord's cricket ground, and was renamed Lord's in June 1939 to distinguish it from the new St John's Wood station being constructed for the Bakerloo Line extension, which opened in December that year. Lord's station was then closed.

Castle in August 1906 and northwards to Edgware Road in June 1907 and Paddington in 1913. There was some disquiet about the line's American ownership and concern was expressed about the abbreviated name 'Bakerloo' bestowed upon it by the *Evening News*. *The Railway Magazine* loftily delivered its opinion that "For a railway itself to adopt its gutter title, is not what we expect from a railway company. English railway officers have more dignity than to act in this manner."[30] In 1912 authorisation was obtained for an extension of the line from Paddington to Queen's Park and tunnelling work began in the autumn of that year. The extension opened in 1915, completing the tunnelled section of the line that runs for 6.7 miles. Further extensions were effected in 1917 via the London & North Western Railway to Watford.

In February 1925 a major modernisation of the increasingly crowded and outdated Piccadilly Circus interchange was undertaken, almost twenty years after it had opened, to serve the Piccadilly and Bakerloo lines. The works occasioned the temporary

removal of Eros, as the monument occupied the site required for a service shaft. The extensive utility service mains including telephone cables, gas and water pipes, hydraulic mains and electricity cables had to be channelled into a twelve-foot diameter pipe subway, the first of its kind in Great Britain, a circular excavation around the circumference of the ticket hall. The station reopened on 10 December 1928 in an attractive Art Deco design by Charles Holden & Partners. The elliptical ticket hall featured sets of escalators that replaced the lifts from the Bakerloo and Piccadilly lines and formed the centrepiece of an attractive public area. It is difficult to appreciate its design qualities today, with the seething masses constantly surging through this centrally located ticket hall and pedestrian concourse.

From April 1936, in order to alleviate problems of overcrowding on the Metropolitan Line between Finchley Road and Baker Street, twin tube tunnels were built that plunged beneath the Metropolitan tunnels to a point near Swiss Cottage station. Here new platforms were constructed under the Metropolitan station. To the south a new station called St John's Wood was opened between the Metropolitan Line stations of Marlborough Road and St John's Wood, which was near Lord's cricket ground (these stations were closed in 1939). The new branch continued south to join the original Bakerloo line at Baker Street.[31] The new Bakerloo branch ran on the surface parallel to the Metropolitan tracks from Finchley Road to Wembley Park where, in November 1939, it took over the Stanmore branch of the Metropolitan Line to cover a total distance of 32 miles. Until the opening of the Jubilee Line in 1979 the Bakerloo operated both Stanmore and Watford services. Today the Bakerloo Line runs for fourteen miles between Elephant and Castle and Harrow and Wealdstone and serves 25 stations.

The year 1996 was a particularly frustrating one for London tube travellers as repairs costing £87 million were carried out involving many sections of line. From the end of the year the section of the Bakerloo Line between Piccadilly Circus and Elephant and Castle was closed for eight months. This was necessary in order to enable the renewal of the Bakerloo Line tunnels beneath the Thames, which were being damaged by water seepage. Even during the First World War concern had been expressed about the safety of the Bakerloo tunnels under the Thames and their susceptibility to air raid damage or terrorism, as at one point they were only three feet beneath the river-bed. The tubing of the Bakerloo Line under the river was securely encased in a waterproof concrete jacket. Engineers worked from platforms sunk into the bed of the Thames close to Hungerford Bridge, as they had done almost one hundred years earlier.

THE PICCADILLY LINE

Amidst the plethora of underground railway proposals submitted between 1892 and 1910 three were eventually to be combined into the principal central artery of the Piccadilly Line we know today.[32] In 1896 a deep level tube route, an express line with electric locomotives intended for the City commuter, was surveyed and approved by a group of Metropolitan District Railway shareholders. The line would burrow beneath the existing District Line from Earls Court and continue straight through to Mansion House beneath the 'inner circle' line with only one intermediate station, probably Charing Cross. The scheme obtained parliamentary approval in 1897, but finance was not immediately forthcoming. In that same year permission was granted for the Brompton & Piccadilly Circus tube to run from South Kensington via Brompton Road and Knightsbridge to Air Street, just west of Piccadilly Circus. Just over a year later the company was acquired by the Metropolitan District resulting in the amalgamation of the two schemes into a plan for a tube line from Earls Court to Piccadilly. In addition the Great Northern & Strand Act of 1899 envisaged a railway from Wood Green to Holborn via King's Cross. The Holborn station was to be incorporated into the London County Council plans to redevelop the notorious slum area around present-day Kingsway and Aldwych. All these railway schemes remained dormant through lack of finance until the turn of the century when many sectors of British industry became the subject of acquisition bids by American financiers.

Charles Tyson Yerkes, who already had the Northern Line in his pocket gradually swallowed the small companies that planned to build deep-level tubes. He acquired the District Railway in March 1901 and the Brompton & Piccadilly by September that year. By 1902 he had established the Underground Electric Railways Company of

107. Charles Tyson Yerkes, tramway and underground railway pioneer.

London Ltd (UERL), a consolidation of his new holdings. After his acquisition of the Great Northern & Strand Railway Company the original plan to build an extension north of Finsbury Park was abandoned. Instead it was suggested that the proposed line should run from Finsbury Park to Hammersmith, with a shuttle service on a spur from Holborn to Strand. Parliamentary approval was given in 1902, and excavations for the new line, to be called the Great Northern, Piccadilly & Brompton Railway, commenced the same year. The twin running tunnels dug with Greathead shields and a Price Rotary Excavator were each 11' 8½" in diameter and lined with flanged cast iron segments.[33]

David Lloyd George (1863-1945), then President of the Board of Trade, opened the new tube on 15 December 1906 at Hammersmith and took a ride to Finsbury Park. At nine miles it was, at that time, the longest tube railway in London, with 7¾ miles in tunnel. Three stations – South Kensington,

Down Street and Covent Garden – did not open until early the following year. The spur from Holborn to Strand (named Aldwych from 1915) opened on 30 November 1907 but attracted little custom. In an effort to entice the West End crowd a 'theatre express' was timetabled which departed from Strand station at 22.13 and terminated at Finsbury Park, but this only ran for a year before the service was withdrawn.

The stations of the Piccadilly Line were designed by Leslie W. Green (1875-1908) using a distinctive cladding of deep ruby red, *sang de boeuf*, heavily-glazed, moulded terracotta blocks. Platforms were reached from the surface either by spiral staircase or in electrically powered lifts provided by the American Otis Elevator Company. Gillespie Road (Arsenal station today) had no lifts as it was close to the surface and Finsbury Park was installed with hydraulic lifts that were taken out of use in 1921. The Piccadilly Line was the first to introduce escalators. On 4 October 1911 at Earls Court the Piccadilly and District Line platforms were linked by an escalator with a vertical rise of forty feet. Initial public fear and distrust was dispelled by the employment of 'Bumper' Harris, a man with a wooden leg, travelling constantly up and down all day, successfully inspiring confidence in this new technology. The escalators were so successful that they mostly superseded the lifts, which are today only retained in six stations on the Piccadilly Line.

The first extension to the line was not effected until September 1932, when a 4½ mile section was opened, completely in tunnel from Finsbury Park to Arnos Grove. The remaining three-mile extension to Cockfosters was unveiled on 31 July 1933, mostly above ground but including a half-mile tube tunnel section south of Southgate. Some of the new stations on the northern extension designed by Charles Holden with C.H. James and S.A. Heaps (the Underground's architect), such as Arnos Grove

108. The rebuilt underground Piccadilly Circus station.

with its drum-shaped ticket hall, have since been recognised as classics of Modernism.

After further extensions it was possible, by October 1933, to travel on the Piccadilly Line from Cockfosters to Uxbridge, a through run which was longer than any train journey previously available on London Transport. The 31¾ mile route took one hour twenty minutes to travel, immersed in tunnel from Arnos Grove to Barons Court. In the early 1930s a number of Piccadilly Line stations in central London were enlarged and improved, although these refurbishments resulted in the closure of nearby stations. Leicester Square's was the most ambitious scheme, involving the underpinning of the London Hippodrome and the installation of three escalators for the Piccadilly and three for the Northern Line amidst a new sub-surface ticket hall with shops and telephone booths.

It was not until April 1971 that work finally commenced on the long-needed extension of the Piccadilly line from Hounslow West station to Heathrow Airport. The first section was constructed in a cut-and-cover tunnel under the service road parallel to the A30. A short surface section was followed by the steep descent to Hatton Cross and then in twin 12' 6" tubes lined with concrete. Heathrow Central station

was constructed in a large trench 400 feet long, eighty feet wide and sixty feet deep, lined with concrete and later covered over, a technique used in some of the Jubilee Line Extension stations. The new extension was opened on 16 December 1977 by Queen Elizabeth II in her silver jubilee year. With a journey time of forty minutes to Piccadilly Circus the Piccadilly carries 20% of air passengers arriving or departing from Heathrow Airport. On 1 April 1986 Terminal 4 station was opened on a single tunnel loop diverging from the original line at Hatton Cross, then curving round to connect with Heathrow Central. Later plans and proposals for access to Heathrow are outlined in the final chapter. At present the Piccadilly Line is 43 miles long with 51 stations; the distance between Leicester Square and Covent Garden (0.16 miles) is the shortest between any two stations on the London Underground.

THE 'GHOST' STATIONS OF THE PICCADILLY LINE

As a number of stations on the Piccadilly Line were very closely spaced along the section between Piccadilly Circus and South Kensington some were to become less busy and eventually redundant. Following the construction of the sub-surface ticket hall at Hyde Park Corner, nearby Down Street closed to the public on 21 May 1932. Its subsequent colourful history is described in the following chapter. Dover Street station, relying on lifts, was rendered surplus to requirements by the installation of escalators at the modernised Green Park when it opened on 18 September 1933. Another Piccadilly Line station to be closed was Brompton Road, open since December 1906. Already by 1909, in order to speed up services, trains were passing through this station without stopping because of its close proximity to the busier stations at South Kensington and Knightsbridge. The shout "Passing Brompton Road" became so famil-

109. *The short-lived Brompton Road station at 206 Brompton Road. Opened in 1906, it was closed due to lack of custom in 1934.*

iar that it was used as the title of a popular West End play (by Jevan Brandon-Thomas) in 1928. This lack of custom resulted in the station finally closing in July 1934. Prior to the war it was acquired by the War Office and proved of use as the operation room of the First Anti-Aircraft Division. Two lift-shafts were converted to office space, one shaft was retained for ventilation and another as a staircase. The eastbound platform housed a teleprinter and communications centre and the westbound contained a briefing cinema. After the war the University Air Squadron used the surface building, whilst the station entrance on Brompton Road was demolished in 1972. The platforms were walled off and are not visible from the line. However, the distinctive maroon-tiled exterior by Leslie W. Green still betrays the surviving section of the station building in Cottage Place, next to the Brompton Oratory. Just before Christmas 1994 the body of a man was discovered in the station after he had apparently fallen down the lift-shaft, a sombre warning to anyone considering exploring these buildings without permission.

Shortly after York Road station opened on the Piccadilly Line between King's Cross and Caledonian Road on 15 December 1906, the *Railway Magazine* wondered whether it would attract custom in this poor area. "Much interest attaches to the experiment of planting railway stations in these districts but time will prove whether the inhabitants of the parts thus favoured rise to the occasion."[34] The experiment failed and on 4 May 1926 York Road closed for some months because of the General Strike, before reopening after parliamentary intervention. On 19 September 1932 the station closed permanently, but the distinctively designed brick surface building still stands with its name visible. Below ground a section of platform tunnel can be observed on a Piccadilly Line journey. A small signal cabin that once operated a crossover to the north east of the station survives at the north end of the eastbound platform.[35]

STRAND/ALDWYCH STATION

Strand station, connected to the Piccadilly Line by a short spur from Holborn, opened in November 1907, changing its name to Aldwych in 1915. The former Charing Cross station, on what became the Northern Line, appropriated the name Strand at that time. As noted above, Aldwych station was sparsely used because of its isolated location and from August 1917 the eastern tunnel was closed.[36] The first call for full closure came in 1933, but it remained open until the last war when it was closed and served as a shelter for up to 1500 people. Following its reopening in 1946 a variety of schemes were proposed to link it with Waterloo or the Bakerloo Line, which would probably have ensured its survival, but nothing tangible happened.

The station's chances of viability and retention seemed brighter on 4 May 1978 when the leader of the Greater London Council, Horace Cutler, appeared at a much-publicised ceremony to unveil a three-month programme of exploratory works for the second stage of the Jubilee Line, planned to run east under Fleet Street. The running tunnels built for the first stage extended well beyond Charing Cross and almost reached as far as Aldwych.[37] But the extension of the line was to have to wait for fourteen more years to get under way and by that time the route avoided Aldwych for the more politically significant Docklands. After providing a rudimentary rush-hour-only service, the last train left Aldwych station on 30 September 1994. Since then it has proved a very popular film location, as many scenes ostensibly set on the London Underground are filmed there.[38] Tours of the station are occasionally organised by the London Transport Museum.

THE NORTHERN LINE

The City section of the Northern Line was formed from the City & South London Railway tunnels which had been extended in stages since 1890. By November 1901 the line had burrowed north to Angel from Moorgate with intermediate stations at Old Street and City Road. From there it was logical to press on to King's Cross and Euston in order to pick up main line passengers; this was accomplished on 12 May 1907. The success of the C&SLR had generated a spate of proposals for further underground lines, one of the first of which was the Hampstead, St Pancras & Charing Cross Railway intended to run from Charing Cross to Hampstead. This scheme received Parliamentary approval in August 1893 by which time it had mutated into the Charing Cross, Euston & Hampstead Railway. The route was planned to run from Agar Street, north of the Strand, to High Street, Hampstead, with a branch from the main line to Euston. The project languished through lack of capital but was rescued by the intervention of Charles Tyson Yerkes, who purchased the powers for the line in October 1900 for £100,000. It became subsumed in the UERL in April 1902, part of Yerkes' vision to provide efficient electric railway services across the capital.[39]

Tunnelling finally commenced in September 1903 with the planned line now extending as far as rural Golders Green, in the hope that its presence would stimulate development. A branch to Kentish Town introduced in earlier amendments to the original plan was also extended to the foot of Highgate Hill, where a new Highgate (present day Archway) station would open. It would be the first tube to include branches and a junction – at Camden Town. In December 1906 Sir Edgar Speyer, whose international banking house had provided much of the investment in Yerkes' projects, could optimistically say that "The Charing Cross, Euston and Hampstead will, I hope, be

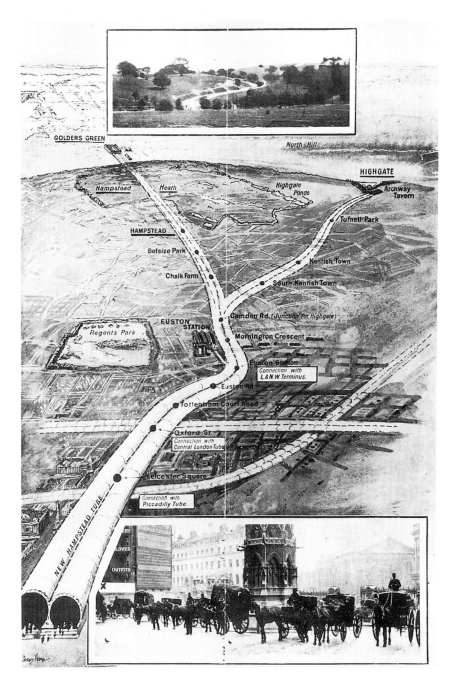

110. *A bird's-eye view of the proposed 'Hampstead Tube', which later became part of the Northern Line. The route is shown with a junction at Camden Town from which two arms go to Golders Green and to what is now Archway station. When the line opened today's Warren Street, Goodge Street and Tottenham Court Road stations were, respectively, Euston Road, Tottenham Court Road and Oxford Street. In the photograph below is part of the Eleanor Cross in the courtyard of Charing Cross station, then the terminus of the route.*

124

completed and opened in June, and we shall then have given London a system of line that will transform the traffic, render life more easy and comfortable, and enable the poorer classes more easily and comfortably to reach that happy land where houses cease, and where fields, trees, and flowers begin."[40] On 22 June 1907 the new line from Charing Cross to Golders Green, with a branch from Camden Town to Highgate was opened by David Lloyd George. On this momentous first day travel was free and over 120,000 are estimated to have taken advantage of this offer.

During the construction three new stations were added at Mornington Crescent, Castle Road (South Kentish Town) and North End, the last never opening (*see pp 158-9*). Interchange was available with the City & South London at Euston, although from a separate station. In the next few years station names were changed to those more familiar today: Euston Road to Warren Street, Tottenham Court Road to Goodge Street and Oxford Street to Tottenham Court Road. A further closed section of tunnel is recalled whilst waiting for a train on the northbound Northern Line at Embankment station, where the sharp curve of the platform is a striking feature. This is a remnant of the Charing Cross terminal loop, opened in 1914, which curved out under the Thames but became disused after 1926 when the Northern Line was extended south to Kennington.[41]

The UERL had bought the C&SLR in 1913 but its old-fashioned equipment, short platforms and incompatibility of tunnel diameter, 10' 2", narrower than the Northern's 11' 8¼", precluded full integration.[42] Tunnel enlargement became vital and in 1922 work commenced, proceeding efficiently until a dramatic collapse and gas explosion near Borough station left a crater in

111. One of the 'ghost' stations of the Northern Line - South Kentish Town, in Kentish Town Road between Camden Town and Kentish Town stations. It was closed in 1924, but the building remains, used by a retail company.

Newington Causeway and 650 tons of gravel in the tunnel.[43] The refurbished line eventually reopened in April 1924 from Moorgate to Euston, with a new tunnel connecting to Camden Town. The works provided an excuse to close City Road station, south of Angel which became an early 'ghost' station.[44] The line south of Moorgate reopened in December 1924. South Kentish Town station closed in June that year as it was never particularly busy, but the converted station building is still prominent on the corner of Kentish Town Road and Castle Place.[45]

Also from 1924 the Northern Line crawled southward via Balham and Tooting to Morden and northward to reach Edgware. A link was also to be forged from Kennington to Charing Cross. Extensive works were undertaken at Kennington to accommodate the junction of the two lines and a reversing loop was also excavated. Work was finished extremely quickly and both lines opened in September 1926, featuring attractive stations designed by Charles Holden. From 1935 to 1941 a further extension was constructed from Highgate (now named Archway) to join the LNER tracks at East Finchley, which were then electrified as far as High Barnet in 1940 and Mill Hill East in 1941.

From 1990 work began on rebuilding the congested Angel station at a cost of £70 million. The previous narrow island platform, a remnant of the City & South London Railway station designs, had become hazardous as the numbers using the station rapidly increased. The reconstruction focussed on creating two wider separate platforms. The northbound line was diverted to a completely new platform whilst the original northbound trackbed area was filled in to create a wider southbound platform. Passengers are conveyed to and from these platforms by the longest escalators on the Underground system, with a vertical rise of ninety feet. As a rebuilt station, with a ticket hall inside a new office block, was also required, this extensive project was not to be completed until spring 1993. Similarly at London Bridge the old southbound platform tunnel was converted into a central passenger concourse, as a new southbound platform was created in a fresh tunnel. Mornington Crescent station was closed for renovation and installation of new lifts in October 1992, but remained ominously shut for some years owing to the expense involved in renovating it. Just as it seemed as if the closure might be permanent, money was found for the refurbishment and the station reopened on 27 April 1998. Team members of the *I'm Sorry I haven't a Clue* radio show were present at the ceremony as the programme features an inscrutable and esoteric panel game named after the Northern Line station.

The Northern incorporates the longest train tunnel on the London Underground, over 17 miles from Morden to East Finchley via the City. It is also notable for the depth of its tunnels, the deepest point is 900 feet north of Hampstead where the line is 221 feet below Hampstead Heath. At 192 feet down Hampstead station has the deepest lift shaft on the Underground. The name Northern Line was not adopted until 1937, but since the early 1970s this much maligned tube line has been given the bitter sobriquet amongst Londoners of the 'Misery Line'. Many of the operational problems stem from the difficulties of providing a variety of routes that have to pass through the junctions at Camden Town and Kennington. In the last two decades the problems afflicting the line were seriously addressed and great improvements have been made, especially since the introduction of new rolling stock in 1998. The complete closure of the Moorgate to Kennington section during the summer of 1999 was extremely inconvenient, but resulted in the straightening of awkward curves and removal of certain speed restrictions along the former route of the City & South London Railway.

THE VICTORIA LINE

The first completely new Underground line for nearly sixty years, the Victoria's origins lay in the series of south-west to north-east London tube proposals discussed before the Second World War. During the planning period it became clear that the principal reason for a new railway was the congestion on the busy, overcrowded lines that connected north-east London with the West End. From a variety of previous plans a line was evolved in 1949 as Route C, the principal aim of which was to link King's Cross, Euston and Victoria.[46] By 1951 it had been decided that the line would run to Walthamstow in the north and Croydon via Brixton, Streatham and Norbury in the south. When the British Transport Commission Act of 1955 gave permission for the construction of the route from Walthamstow as far as Victoria, the name Victoria Line was adopted.

Tunnelling expertise had advanced considerably by then and experts favoured the use of the 'drum diggers' that had recently completed the 19-mile tunnel built by the Metropolitan Water Board between the Hampton and Lea Valley reservoirs. The leading edge of the digger's shield was equipped with a rotating cutting mechanism with a central aperture through which spoil was removed along a conveyor belt. These diggers were capable of tunnelling 400 feet a week and during the subsequent excavation a number of tunnelling records were broken. In order to test the new machines and examine developments in tunnel linings an experimental section of twin tunnel was excavated in January 1960 from Finsbury Park to South Tottenham.

In 1958 London Transport had successfully installed twenty rings of unbolted iron lining in a 14-foot diameter tunnel being driven by the Central Electricity Generating Board at Belvedere Power Station. The segments of lining were expanded against the clay and then locked together by compression of the clay acting on the completed tunnel. This method was then tested against unbolted compression-locked reinforced concrete linings, which were more difficult to install but cheaper. Inside the preliminary Victoria Line tunnels one bore was fitted with pre-cast concrete segments and the other with unbolted cast-iron segments. The tunnelling was completed in July 1961, by which time the concrete lining had been chosen at a thickness of six inches, whose smooth surface was thought to reduce air resistance on trains and save energy.[47] By May 1962 the southbound experimental tunnel had been extended to connect with the southbound Northern City Line just north of Finsbury Park station in order to enable track and stock tests to be carried out; this section was later incorporated into the route north of Finsbury Park.

On 20 August 1962 the government announced that the new tube could proceed. Those stalwarts of underground engineering, Sir William Halcrow & Partners, were chosen for the construction of the Victoria Line and work commenced in September 1962. One of the most problematic sections was expected to be around the honeycomb of tube and rail tunnels and underground structures beneath King's Cross and St Pancras, where the gravel would make tunnelling more difficult anyway. It would also have to pass beneath the Fleet sewer and avoid the Post Office Railway in that area. The entire construction of the line would be a much more complex operation owing to the tunnels and structures which had been built under central London since the last major tube works. The route through central London involved the construction of a 600-ton steel deck over Oxford Circus to carry traffic while work on the new concourse carried on beneath it.[48] It was the largest and most complex station reconstruction, intended to create an interchange between the Bakerloo, Central and Victoria lines. As with the earlier reconstruction at

Piccadilly Circus in the 1920s, considerable time was spent locating the pipes and mains of the utility services which had to be diverted around the station. Further below, the southbound tunnel roof came dangerously close to the foundations of the Peter Robinson store at Oxford Circus. From the access shaft occupying the centre of Cavendish Square during construction work an access tunnel was driven beneath the store and a pre-stressed concrete raft constructed beneath the store's basement, between it and the roof of the new tunnel. At Finsbury Park the former southbound Piccadilly platform became the northbound Victoria Line tunnel and the former Northern City Line low-level platforms were also used to facilitate same-level interchange between the Piccadilly and Victoria lines, a very useful feature of this station for which many have since been grateful.

The Victoria Line opened in stages: from Walthamstow to Highbury & Islington in September 1968, then to Victoria in March 1969. The extension of the line south of Victoria had previously occupied planners. In the event the earlier plan to reach Streatham and Croydon was abandoned in favour of a terminus at Brixton about 3½ miles from Victoria. This was the first extension of an underground line into south London since the Northern Line's expansion to Morden in the mid-1920s.

The terrain proved more difficult than in the northern sections and Greathead Shields had to be employed. A pair of new tunnels were carved out 25 feet beneath the Thames. The construction and excavation at Vauxhall was hampered by the presence of many sewers and the nearby outlet of the River Effra. These caused the ground to be waterlogged and therefore much of the station work proceeded within cofferdams. The water-bearing gravel through which the escalator shaft was sunk had to be frozen before work could proceed, a technique previously employed at Tottenham Hale

station.[49] At Stockwell some rebuilding was necessitated within the deep-level wartime shelter, where it overlapped with the new works, in order to place the Victoria Line platforms adjacent to those of the pre-existing Northern Line. Work at Brixton included the provision of twin overrun and siding tunnels, which curve south and run a considerable distance toward Herne Hill. A further extension is not possible at present owing to the signalling system, which is working at full capacity. After about four years' work the final section into south London opened on 23 July 1971. Because of late authorisation Pimlico station did not open until September 1972.

Extending for fourteen miles and serving sixteen stations, the Victoria was the first tube line designed for Automatic Train Operation. The single crew member is responsible for door operation and re-starting from stations, but acceleration, signal checks and stopping are all controlled automatically. The line, in common with many others, utilises the energy saving 'hump profile' to ease braking on a rising gradient when arriving in stations and increase acceleration down a falling gradient on departing, a feature which is clearly visible from the southbound platform at Finsbury Park. At the time of its opening the Victoria Line was an excellent example of a modern urban underground railway and the deliberate avoidance of sharp curves such as those necessitated by wayleave payments in the past. This resulted in fewer speed restrictions and faster travel. It is the only line to be immersed in tunnel for its entire route. Since its construction many new underground railways have been proposed for London. The story of the latest addition to the tube network is briefly told in the final chapter together with the projects that are shaping or are proposed to shape the city's transport infrastructure in the next ten years.

112. *Lots Road Power Station, which supplied power to the Underground system, in the early 1920s. It was dramatically sited, but a blot on the riverside view beloved of Turner. It is soon to be redeveloped for residential use.*

LOTS ROAD POWER STATION

Lots Road, the gas-fired power station which generates 180MW, was originally built in the first decade of the twentieth century by the UERL to supply electricity to its lines. Some power is also taken from the National Grid and from Greenwich Power Station producing 114MW, which was originally built for London's tramways. At present the 22kV supply from Lots Road and Greenwich is delivered to the three main traction power points at Cromwell Curve, Cobourg Street and Stockwell. From there it is stepped down to an 11kV supply distributed to 114 substations throughout the network. Each substation steps down and rectifies this AC source to the standard 630DC track voltage. The four-rail system, used throughout the Underground, with separate positive and negative conductor rails was first introduced in 1904-5. In August 1998 LUL announced that it had struck a thirty-year deal with Seeboard Powerlink to supply and distribute all power supplies on the network. As a consequence Lots Road will close as a generating station and the Underground will take all of its main supplies directly from the Grid. Recent opinion has been moving in favour of adopting an overhead power supply and the futuristic Space Train currently in development is likely to receive its power from overhead conductors.[50] In March 2000 it was announced that Lots Road had been bought by a joint venture company comprising developers Taylor Woodrow and Hutchison Whampoa. £350 million will be spent on decommissioning and decontaminating the power station and converting it into the inevitable 'loft style' apartments. According to the local council at least a third of these homes will be 'affordable', although given the present astronomical property prices in London it remains to be seen whether the average Londoner will be able to live in one of these distinctive apartments in a desirable riverside location in Chelsea.[51]

PNEUMATIC RAILWAYS

Rowland Hill (1795-1879), Secretary to the Post Office and inventor of the penny post, submitted a report in June 1855 to the Postmaster General advocating an underground tube to convey mail from the General Post Office at St Martin's-le-Grand to Little Queen Street and Holborn. The idea of two consulting engineers, (Sir) Charles Hutton Gregory and Edward Alfred Cowper (1790-1852), the 15-inch diameter tube would run beneath the line of the street and could be extended throughout London or the rest of England. Inspired by the success of pneumatic delivery systems, propulsion would be by stationary steam engines creating a vacuum in the tube. In 1853 Josiah Latimer Clark (1822-1898) had introduced a 1½"-tube for the Electric & International Telegraph Company to carry urgent messages 225 yards from their office in Telegraph Street to the Stock Exchange by atmospheric means. This prototype was to be expanded and developed by Latimer Clark over the years and many miles of such tubes were laid under London.[52]

Another contemporary engineer, Thomas Webster Rammell set about devising underground pneumatic railways for conveying mail and passengers. In his 1857 book *A New Plan for Street Railways* he advocated small overhead atmospheric railways for passengers in towns and also envisaged, in collaboration with Clark, a network of mail tubes buried just beneath the surface of city streets. The two men eventually became the engineers of the Pneumatic Despatch Company, incorporated in June 1859, with the impressive backing of the Marquess of Chandos and the MP, W. H. Smith (1792-1865).[53] After initial trials at the Soho Works in Birmingham a demonstration line 452 yards in length was laid in Battersea Fields in May 1861, where Battersea Power Station stands today. The *Illustrated London News* reported that "various irregular curves and gradients were introduced to show that hills

113. The first despatch of mail bags from Eversholt Street sorting office to Euston Station on the Pneumatic Despatch Railway in February 1863.

and valley would not prevent the effective working of the system".[54] Despatch trucks ran along the 2 foot-diameter cast-iron tubes propelled by air pressure in one direction and sub-atmospheric pressure in the other produced by a steam engine driving a ventilating fan, alternately blowing and sucking. By this method speeds of up to 40 mph were achieved and whilst the trucks were intended for freight, "Two gentlemen occupied the carriages during the first trip. They lay on their backs, on mattresses, with horsecloths for coverings, and appeared to be perfectly satisfied with their journey".[55]

Pleased with these tests the Pneumatic Despatch Company then constructed a similar line from the Arrivals Parcel Office at Euston beneath Eversholt Street to the Post Office's North Western District Office 600 yards to the north. It opened in February 1863, just one month after the Metropolitan Railway. The journey took about seventy seconds for a mail truck just over eight feet long. This was followed by a longer underground pneumatic railway completed in January 1865 that ran from Euston railway station beneath Drummond Street, Hampstead Road, Tottenham Court Road and High Holborn to a station at 245 Holborn. It was not formally opened until November, however, when the Duke of Buckingham invited several scientists to inspect this technological marvel. Some guests even travelled in the wagons although they stated that "the sensation at starting, and still more so upon arriving ... was not agreeable".[56] The horseshoe shaped tunnels through which they were conveyed were lined with cast-iron or brick, 4 feet high and 4' 6" wide. The mail was carried in four-wheeled wagons over

114. The opening of the Holborn 'station' on the Pneumatic Despatch Railway in November 1865, with human cargo.

ten feet long running on a 3' 8½" gauge track. A powerful steam engine drove a large centrifugal fan, which generated air pressure to propel the wagons that fitted closely inside the tunnels. The wagons were equipped with vulcanised rubber flaps, forming a flexible flange intended to close the gap between the outside of the cylinder-shaped carriage and the inside of the tunnel and to prevent air from passing the carriage. A cushion of air met wagons arriving in order to slow them down and both stations were on a gradient.

Construction of the next stage to the General Post Office at St Martin's-le-Grand was already underway in 1864 but the collapse of the Overend, Gurney bank in May 1866 halted finance for the work. Rammell had also been working on the Crystal Palace Pneumatic Railway in Crystal Palace Park in 1864, where a single passenger coach accommodating up to 35 people was blown and sucked back and forth in a 600-foot long 10' x 9' tunnel.[57] The success of this venture led to the passage in 1865 of the Act incorporating the Waterloo & Whitehall Railway, intended to run from

Great Scotland Yard (near Charing Cross) in a sub-Thames immersed tube to the London & South Western Railway station at Waterloo, using the same pneumatic propulsion system. Despite the considerable construction work undertaken on the tunnels the financial problems that halted the Pneumatic Despatch Company tube similarly afflicted this project.

By the end of 1868 the company managed to raise more capital. They continued the line from Holborn, beneath Holborn Viaduct but just above the River Fleet sewer, to terminate at the General Post Office by July 1869, a distance from Euston of 4738 yards. Unfortunately the Post Office was reluctant to use the line for mail and parcels and only agreed to a limited service in December 1873. The journey time of 17 minutes proved only four minutes shorter than that by horse van on the road above. As there were also problems of air pressure leakage the Post Office refused to convey any mail on the tube and the line was abandoned by October 1874; the Pneumatic Despatch Company was dissolved in 1882. Later, in 1895, the engineer George Threlfall

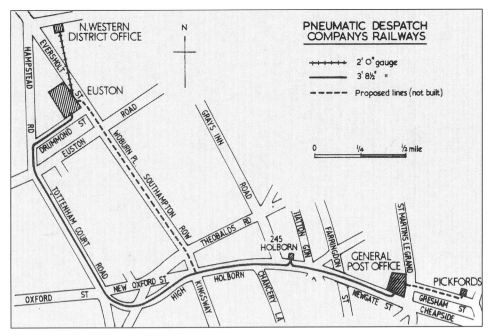

115. Map of the eventual route of the Pneumatic Despatch Railway.

proposed converting the line to electric power and revived the venture as the London Despatch Company, but its intended use for carrying mail was rejected once more by the Post Office, resulting in the company being wound up in 1905. Early in the twentieth century parts of the tunnels housed electrical cables and the Post Office used them for cable runs from the 1920s. On 20 December 1928 the long-forgotten railway made the headlines when a section of tunnel which had filled with gas was ignited by an unfortunate workman with a lighter. In the 1960s some of the original railway cars were discovered during the building of the Euston Road underpass and half of one of these can today be seen in the Victorian gallery of the Museum of London. Sections of the Pneumatic Despatch tunnels remain as telephone and electrical ducts, for example under Tottenham Court Road. Despite the system's failure it planted the seed that would germinate as the Post Office Railway.

MAIL RAIL
Mail Rail, formerly the Post Office Railway, that runs from Paddington Station to the East London Sorting Office in Whitechapel, is completely separate from the Underground system and travels devoid of passengers. Instead, each day around four million letters are conveyed below London on fully automated, computer-controlled trains at an average depth of seventy feet beneath the streets.[58] Six and a half miles long, this invaluable little railway has significantly reduced the number of mail vans on central London's overcrowded roads. A successor to the Pneumatic Despatch Railway, it was conceived as a means of bypassing the busiest areas of London. A Royal Commission on London Traffic reported in 1905 that the average speed of traffic in central London had fallen by 25% in the previous thirty years and identified the proliferating horse buses as the principal culprits.[59]

Following parliamentary approval, Harley Hugh Dalrymple-Hay (1861-1940), a major figure in London's subterranean development, was appointed joint engineer for the project with William Slingo, the Engineer-in-Chief of the Post Office. Tunnelling commenced late in 1914. Shafts were sunk into the London clay from which Greathead shields carved out the route in nine-foot diameter tunnels. Work proceeded smoothly apart from an inundation of water under Calthorpe Street near Mount Pleasant, which was soon pumped out and found to be unconnected with the nearby River Fleet. The running tunnels were completed by the end of 1917 but the remainder of the work ceased due to wartime restrictions. From January 1918 many paintings from the Tate and National Portrait Gallery collections and valuable documents from the Public Record Office were stored in the tunnels under King Edward Building. Treasures from the British Museum were stored at West Central District Office station and the King's Pictures and Wallace Collection in the tunnel beneath Paddington. Work did not recommence until December 1923 and involved installation of the two-foot gauge track, completion of stations with shafts and chutes to link them with the buildings above and delivery of rolling stock. Finally the line was opened on 3 December 1927 in time to convey the Christmas post.

Between Paddington Sorting Office, situated under the main-line station, and Whitechapel Eastern Delivery Office there were once seven intermediate stops beneath important postal buildings. These were: Bird Street Western Parcels Office, Wimpole Street Old Western Parcels Office, Rathbone Place Western Delivery Office, West Central District Office New Oxford Street, the main London Letter and Parcel Office Mount Pleasant, King Edward Building and Liverpool Street station. Today only Paddington, Rathbone Place, Mount Pleasant and Whitechapel remain. Mount Pleasant is the largest and busiest station and includes turning loops, sidings and workshops.

Possible extensions to the existing line were planned from the outset, but an Extension Study Group meeting in 1947 came to no firm conclusions and the line today remains largely as it was in 1927. Similar alignments would later be used for some of the Post Office's cable tunnels. In 1954, however, a quarter-mile deviation to the route was excavated to run beneath the newly constructed Western District Office in Rathbone Place. The tunnel left the original line near the junction of Wells Street and Eastcastle Street, rejoining it under St Giles Circus. The section came into use in 1958, but the new building and subterranean station were not opened until 1965; the former tunnel was used as a store.[60]

Although the line is designed solely for the movement of mail and parcels one notable passenger on the Post Office Railway was the broadcaster Brian Johnston (1912-1994). In December 1954 he chose to

116. *Loading a train on the Post Office Railway in 1974 at the Eastern District station.*

travel as a 'posted packet' from London to Bristol for a radio programme and was conveyed via a special container in the tunnel to Paddington. Today this efficient unpublicised railway operates for nineteen hours each day, 286 days a year but is not immune from improvement plans. In 1999 a consortium was considering linking the major department stores to rail termini by installing lift shafts directly from Mail Rail into the shops. Goods could be delivered this way, freeing up the roads. It was also considering extending Mail Rail from Paddington to the Post Office's Willesden Depot for shipment.[61]

Footnotes for Chapter Four

[1] For example T C Barker & Michael Robbins *History of London Transport* 2 vols. (Allen & Unwin, 1963, 1974), John Robert Day *The Story of London's Underground* (London Transport,1979), Alan A Jackson & Desmond Croome *Rails through the Clay* (Allen & Unwin, 1962). For the often bewildering name changes at stations and dates of construction see Douglas Rose *London Underground: a diagrammatic history* 3rd ed (Douglas Rose Publications, 1986).

[2] For Frank Pick see Christian Barman *The Man who Built London Transport* (David & Charles, 1979). See also Oliver Green *Underground Art, London Transport Posters 1908 to the Present* (Studio Vista, 1990).

[3] For the evolution of this world famous design see Ken Garland *Mr Beck's Underground Map* (Capital Transport, 1994).

[4] The most thorough history is Alan A Jackson *London's Metropolitan Railway* (David & Charles, 1986).

[5] *Punch*, vol. 11, July-December 1846.

[6] *Illustrated London News* 28 June1862, 648.

[7] For the complete history of the District Line including its many extensions above ground see Piers Connor *Going Green, the story of the District Line* (Capital Transport Publishing, 1994).

[8] A well illustrated account is 'Building the Inner Circle Railway' (reprinted from *Railway Gazette* 16 November, 7, 14, 21 and 28 December 1945).

[9] Mark Lane replaced the nearby Tower station shortly afterwards and was renamed Tower Hill on 1 September 1946. It was totally rebuilt by February 1967 on the site of the original Tower station. See Piers Connor *ibid*, 20 and J E Connor *London's Disused Underground Stations* (Connor & Butler, 1999), 54-57.

[10] H G Follenfant *Reconstructing London's Underground* (London Transport, 1974), 2. This book also contains an excellent map of Underground lines with construction dates.

[11] For technical details see H G Follenfant *ibid*, 84-85.

[12] Christian Wolmar 'Parliament Square is falling down' *The Independent* 30 November 1996, 8.

[13] T S Lascelles *The City and South London Railway* (Oakwood Press, Headington, 1987) is a useful, highly detailed account of the line's construction.

[14] Robert M Tufnell '100 Years of the "tube"' *Railway Magazine* September 1990; pp 651-655 contains more information on these early electric locomotives.

[15] The C&SLR was later integrated into the Northern Line – see Mike Horne & Bob Bayman *The Northern Line* 2nd ed. (Capital Transport, 1999).

[16] See J E Connor *London's Disused Underground Stations op. cit.*, 25-29.

[17] See Nigel Pennick *Waterloo and City Line* 2nd ed. (Electric Traction Publications, 1984).

[18] City station was renamed Bank on 28 October 1940.

[19] Colin J Marsden '£23m down the "Drain"' *Railway Magazine* April 1992, 45-49 gives an excellent history of the line and full details of the refurbishment.

[20] Colin J Marsden 'Up & Under! How they changed trains in the "Drain"' *Railway Magazine* August 1993, 42-44.

[21] Quoted in J Graeme Bruce & Desmond F Croome *The Twopenny Tube* (Capital Transport, 1996), 14.

[22] The pale plastered facades of the concrete halls led to them being known as the 'White City'. Wood Lane closed on 22 November 1947 to be replaced by the new station at White City. The abandoned station featured in an episode of the camp thriller series *Department S* entitled 'Last Train to Redbridge'. For full details see J E Connor *London's Disused Underground Stations op.cit.*, 61-66.

[23] The single-track section between Epping and Ongar finally closed in September 1994.

[24] The best book on the many fascinating buildings associated with the Underground is David Lawrence *Underground Architecture* (Capital Transport Publishing, 1994). Holden rarely had the

opportunity to penetrate below the surface in his station designs.

[25] Richard Cork ed. *Eduardo Paolozzi Underground* (Royal Academy & Weidenfeld & Nicolson, 1986).

[26] J Graeme Bruce and Desmond F Croome *The Twopenny Tube op. cit.*, 35.

[27] J E Connor *London's Disused Underground Stations op.cit.*, 10.

[28] Duncan Campbell *War Plan UK* rev. ed. (Paladin, 1993), 202.

[29] M A C Horne *The Bakerloo Line, a short history* (Douglas Rose, 1990) is an excellent detailed account.

[30] Quoted in Ben Weinreb & Christopher Hibbert *The London Encyclopedia* (Papermac, 1995 rev. ed.), 34.

[31] For details of the closed stations at St John's Wood/Lord's and Marlborough Road see J E Connor *London's Disused Underground Stations op.cit.*

[32] Desmond F Croome *The Piccadilly Line, an illustrated history* (London Transport, 1998) covers the entire history.

[33] The Excavator was similar to the Greathead shield but incorporated radial arms fitted with knives and buckets extending from a central rotating shaft worked by electric motor. Tunnelling progress was thus accelerated.

[34] *Railway Magazine* February 1907. This thoroughfare has since been renamed York Way.

[35] For Brompton Road, York Road and Aldwych see J E Connor *London's Disused Underground Stations op. cit.*

[36] See J E Connor *London's Disused Underground Stations op. cit.*, 5-8 and Nigel Welbourn *Lost Lines – London* (Ian Allan, 1999) 28-31.

[37] Mike Horne *The Jubilee Line* (Capital Transport, 2000), 42.

[38] Simon Calder 'No return to the Aldwych' *The Independent* 5 February 1997, 10.

[39] Mike Horne & Bob Bayman *The Northern Line, an Illustrated History* (Capital Transport, 1999).

[40] Quoted in Hugh Douglas *The Underground Story* (Robert Hale, 1963), 157.

[41] Jackson & Croome *op cit.*, 141-2 with a plan on 180.

[42] In 1892 a Lords and Commons Joint Committee decided on a standard 11' 6" tunnel diameter but the eventual dimensions used were 11' 8ˇ" internal diameter, with an external diameter of 12' 6"

and 12' 8" to the edge of the tunnelling shield.

[43] H G Follenfant *Reconstructing London's Underground op.cit.*, 13.

[44] City Road closed permanently on 9 August 1922. It was converted to an air raid shelter in 1941.

[45] Covered in J T Connor *op. cit.*, it plays a prominent part in the recent novel by Tobias Hill *Underground*, (Faber & Faber, 1999).

[46] The full convoluted planning story of the Victoria Line is told in M A C Horne *The Victoria Line, a short history* (Douglas Rose, 1988) – an extremely thorough account.

[47] The Victoria Line does, however, have some sections lined with cast-iron. See Nigel Pennick *Tunnels Under London* 3rd ed. (Electric Traction Publications, 1981), 22-23.

[48] The building of the deck was accomplished in 65 hours from 3 to 6 August 1963; it was finally removed during the Easter weekend of 1968. See John R Day *The Story of the Victoria Line* (London Transport, 1969) ch vii. Also M A C Horne *op.cit.*, 34.

[49] *The Brixton Extension of the Victoria Line* (London Transport, 1971), 26.

[50] Roger Bradley 'Revitalisation of the London Underground' *Electrical Review* Vol 232 No 6, 16 March 1999, 22-24.

[51] *Planning* 17 March 2000.

[52] See D G Clow 'Pneumatic Tube Communication Systems in London' in *The Newcomen Society for the study of the history of Engineering and Technology Transactions* Vol. 66 1994-95, 97-119.

[53] For the Pneumatic Despatch Company see Derek A Bayliss *The Post Office Railway London* (Turntable Publications, 1978) Ch.1.

[54] *Illustrated London News* 24 August 1861.

[55] *ibid.*

[56] *Illustrated London News* 18 November 1865.

[57] Francis H Clayton *Atmospheric Railways* (The Author, Lichfield, 1966), 126-127.

[58] See Derek A Bayliss *op. cit.* and Peter Johnson *Mail by Rail: the history of the TPO and Post Office Railway* (Ian Allan, 1995).

[59] Cmd. 2597.

[60] Bayliss *op. cit.*, 53 & 59. According to Pennick *Tunnels under London,* 9 this building stands above a cable tunnel running between Leicester Square tube station and the Telecom Tower.

[61] *The Guardian* 'Space' supplement 19 February 1999, 10-11.

CHAPTER FIVE

Secret Places
Bunkers, Citadels, Shelters and Tunnels

*'I have seen much unmeant for mortal eyes in my wanderings beneath that dark and forgotten city
... Great was my fear of this place, but greater was the strange sleep-like fascination that gripped
my mind and guided my feet ever downwards through realms unknown.'*
The R'lyeh Text, researched, transcribed and annotated by Robert Turner (Skoob Books 1995).

*'Glance at the map of the Thames, at all the territory along its banks, within the alembic, between
Hungerford and Vauxhall Bridges – the ministries, military/political architecture with memorials
to war heroes; Treasury, Foreign Office; historic and contemporary bunkers and tunnels; abbeys,
cathedrals, church palaces, Parliament, private and official residences of party functionaries; enclosed
gardens, police surveillance, counter terror.'*
Lights Out for the Territory by Iain Sinclair (Granta Books, 1997)

The heart of modern London contains a vast clandestine underworld of tunnels, telephone exchanges, nuclear bunkers and control centres, many of which were constructed in the years leading up to the Second World War, throughout the Blitz, or during the period of the Cold War, when nuclear war paranoia was at its height.[1] Some are well documented, but the existence of others can be surmised only from careful scrutiny of government reports and accounts and occasional accidental disclosures reported in the news media. Rumours abound and the dearth of official information makes precise identification of sites difficult. However, many sources agree on the location of some of these defensive hideaways. In the late 1930s the threat of high explosive dropping on London initiated an intensive period of tunnelling and construction to protect senior politicians and officials. Many of the resulting structures and converted underground stations survive today. Protection for the royal family and officialdom took precedence during the whole of this period, resulting in many of the shelters being constructed beneath the already overcrowded central London streets. Even today the close proximity of Buckingham Palace, the Houses of Parliament, Whitehall and the Ministry of Defence and the headquarters of MI5 and MI6 would clearly require some form of subterranean protection and interconnection.

During the last thirty years a number of books and articles have been published which confirm the existence of many of these structures and contain suppositions about less publicised tunnels and bunkers, the more probable of which are summarised in this chapter.[2] As much of this information has therefore been in the public domain for many years its description as truly 'secret' is no longer justified. Some of the former Cold War bunkers outside London have since been decommissioned and opened up to the public by enthusiastic entrepreneurs, so that a good idea of their original purpose and design can be gained from a visit.[3]

Beneath an inconspicuous bungalow at Kelvedon Hatch, deep in the Essex countryside, lies a massive three-storey underground bunker with concrete walls and roof 10 feet thick and strengthened with tungsten rods. The 27,000 square foot bunker was constructed in the early 1950s as part of the Rotor defence network.[4] The entire structure rests in a deep layer of gravel designed to absorb the shock of a nuclear blast. It is built inside a Faraday Cage, wire mesh netting, surrounded by earth, that creates a space in which there is no electrical field that might damage vital computer or telecommunications equipment should they be exposed to the electromagnetic pulse generated by such a powerful explosion.[5] The bunker contains dormitories, kitchens with supplies to feed 600 people for eight weeks, a broadcasting studio, offices with desks for government departments and a separate room, possibly once intended to accommodate the prime minister. Sophisticated structures such as the Kelvedon Hatch bunker are a culmination of years of civil defence measures and secretive official excavations beneath London, that began as a result of the First World War.

SUBTERRANEAN LIFE DURING WARTIME[6]

Although the appalling carnage of the First World War was largely confined to the battlefields of Northern Europe, London was to experience for the first time the terrifying effects of aerial bombardment. The first Zeppelin raid occurred on 31 May 1915 when a ton of bombs was dropped, apparently randomly, causing seven deaths. By the time that the sporadic attacks from Zeppelins and bombers had ceased, in mid-1918, 670 Londoners had been killed. The psychological effect on the populace was marked and in response many sought refuge in the stations of the Underground system. During one air raid on 18 February 1918 a third of a million Londoners spent the night underground. This experience engendered the later government fear that a 'deep shelter mentality' might develop, which would

hamper any future civil defence plans. By way of contrast, King George V was protected onboard the royal train, which was shunted into a tunnel for the duration of the air raids. Treasures such as the Elgin Marbles from the British Museum were also stored in a tunnel intended for the future Post Office Railway and members of the Cabinet and War Office sheltered in the tunnel between Holborn and Aldwych stations. There were, however, no purpose-built shelters or government hideaways constructed in London, in marked contrast to the flurry of activity during the next conflict.

Blitzkrieg tactics had been used to devastating effect during the Spanish Civil War and as the Munich Crisis escalated in 1938 the threat of the effects of future air raids over London on public morale and urban infrastructure began to be taken extremely seriously; experts predicted massive casualties. The first sign of official action, at the behest of the Home Office and the London County Council, was the digging of trenches in many public parks and open spaces. They were shortly afterwards made more permanent with steel and concrete roofs and linings and protected with airlocks in the event of possible gas attacks. Although the trenches were initially dug in straight lines, it was soon realised that a zig-zag configuration would be safer. This was soon adopted in the one million feet of trench (about 7 feet deep) that had been excavated by September 1938. Many famous London squares and parks were affected including Hampstead Heath, Hyde Park, Russell Square, Woburn Square and Lincoln's Inn Fields.

With war increasingly inevitable the government began to construct secure shelters for important personnel.[7] The public, however, were expected to use such domestic protection as the Anderson shelter, named after Sir John Anderson, who played a major role in civil defence early in the war, but who had nothing to do with its design. A typical Anderson shelter consisted of two curved sections of corrugated steel bolted together at the top and sunk three feet into the ground, with a protected entrance and a recommended layer of at least eighteen inches of soil piled on top. It was cheap and easy to build and could resist most bomb damage apart from a direct hit, but could only be installed in private gardens. Later, the government took over a number of solid buildings, together with crypts, vaults and cellars, which could be used to protect the public. Local authorities were encouraged to construct surface shelters that could individually accommodate up to fifty people.[8] Underground stations, however, were considered to be strictly off-limits as it was felt that shelterers would interfere with the operation of trains. However, one disused part of the early Underground system which was converted into a shelter was an old tunnel of the City & South London Railway, which led north from Borough Station to King William Street that had been abandoned since 1900, when the line was extended to Moorgate on a different alignment. The under-river section was sealed off and concrete staircases were installed at Borough in new shafts. On 26 June 1940 the shelter was opened, with the capacity to house 14,000 people.

A series of minor air raids on the London region commencing in June 1940 had not unduly troubled the population but on 7 September a heavy raid on the London Docks turned many areas of the East End into blazing infernos and killed 430 people. With the return of the bombers on the following night another 400 died and as a result the large hastily-provided local shelters were to be filled with frightened East Enders, who soon became critical of the overcrowded and unhygienic living conditions. At the 'Tilbury' shelter, part of the Liverpool Street goods station under the Commercial Road and Cable Street, the officially designated area rapidly became full and an adjacent

warehouse was taken over. This damp complex eventually accommodated up to 14,000 people crammed beneath the railway arches in appalling conditions. As one employee of the government-backed Mass Observation project described it, "There were thousands and thousands of people lying head to toe, all along the bays and with no facilities. At the beginning there were only four earth buckets down the far end, behind screens, for toilets ... The place was a hell hole, it was an outrage that people had to live in these conditions."[9] In those early days, assailed by the terrible stench and wading through the effluvia of overflowing latrines, many refuge-seekers could not stand the primitive conditions in the shelters and preferred to return home.

Despite their fears of a reclusive 'deep shelter mentality' developing, the government's opposition to public occupation of Underground stations became increasingly untenable. Widespread civil disobedience and flouting of regulations resulted in people travelling for hours on tube trains or settling themselves on the platforms at night in order to avoid danger. Fortunately for British morale the *Railway Gazette* could report that "We are happy to be able to record that the vast majority of offenders are members of alien races or at least of alien extraction." On 8 September a huge crowd gained entrance to Liverpool Street Underground station despite the efforts of troops and officials to keep them out. Unable to fight against the tide of public opinion, the government relented and opened up the Underground, with fifteen miles of platforms and tunnels eventually becoming available. For example, at Liverpool Street a mile of tunnel and unopened sidings to the east of the station could accommodate up to 10,000 people. During the worst nights of the Blitz up to 177,000 spent the night underground, their recumbent forms being recorded memorably by Henry Moore in his sketchbooks and in many evocative photographs.

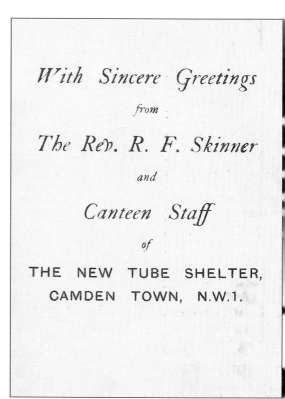

With Sincere Greetings

from

The Rev. R. F. Skinner

and

Canteen Staff

of

THE NEW TUBE SHELTER,
CAMDEN TOWN, N.W.1.

117. A sombre greetings card issued by the organisers of the Camden Town tube shelter.

The Underground stations and tunnels, never designed for this use, became unhygienic, with some having plagues of mosquitoes that thrived in the foetid atmosphere. Neither was safety assured, as evinced at Trafalgar Square on 12 October 1940, where seven civilians were killed after a bomb penetrated the surface and exploded at the top of the escalator causing an avalanche of wet earth to descend onto the platforms. Much more serious was the incident on 14 October at Balham, where six hundred were sheltering. Following a direct hit on the street above, the roadway collapsed and masses of ballast and earth slid into the tunnel, whilst the flood from the shattered mains carried all before it. From the resulting pile of sludge 68 bodies were eventually recovered.[10] On 11 January 1941 at Bank station 56 people were killed after a bomb plunged into the station concourse, exploding in the escalator machine room and damaging trains at the platforms below. A huge crater remained at this busy junction, which was soon crossed by a temporary road bridge. Unfortunately the greatest loss of life at a London Underground station during the Second World War did not occur through enemy action. At Bethnal Green on 3 March 1943 an alert was sounded and people poured into the station down a poorly lit staircase. After a woman with a child tripped and fell at the foot of this staircase panic ensued, with more people falling and being crushed by the relentless push from those behind. When the mass of humanity had been cleared from the scene 173 victims were found to have died from suffocation.

To relieve the squalid conditions in the stations bunks and first-aid posts were provided and some tube trains converted into

118. *Shelterers at Aldwych station in October 1940, being entertained by a concert party.*

119. On 14 October 1940, 68 people were killed when Balham Underground station sustained a direct hit.

mobile canteens. Progress was slow, but by early 1941 22,000 bunk beds had been installed and basic amenities were available. By way of contrast, there was more sophistication in Chislehurst caves, where thousands had been sheltering since the onset of the bombing: subterranean facilities included canteens, a dance hall, cinema, hospital and chapel. The government also realised that special deep-level shelters would eventually be required for both public and official use.

DEEP-LEVEL SHELTERS

In October 1940 the government grudgingly agreed to construct eight purpose-built deep-level shelters with sleeping accommodation for 64,000.[11] Eventually the number was to be expanded to ten, with five shelters planned south of the Thames, to be built beneath the existing Northern Line stations at Clapham South, Clapham Common, Clapham North, Stockwell and Oval and five to the north beneath St Paul's, Chancery Lane, Goodge Street, Camden Town and Belsize Park stations. The consulting engineers for the construction work were the firm of Mott, Hay and Anderson for the shelters south of the Thames and William Halcrow and Partners for those to the north. All works were to be carried out in secret.

The design of these shelters adhered to a similar pattern of two parallel tunnels of 16' 6" in diameter and 1200 to 1400 feet in length, lined with cast iron and concrete and divided into upper and lower levels for bunk accommodation and linked by cross passages. Access to the shelters was gained from the street by the use of a shaft at either end of the tunnels, containing two separate steel and concrete spiral staircases. These connected to both levels and were encased on the surface in grim looking block-houses. Solidly constructed from reinforced concrete and intended to prevent the bomb penetration that had caused such devasta-

120. *During the night of 11/12 January 1941, one of intense bombing, a bomb penetrated Bank station in the City. There were 35 deaths.*

tion at Bank and Balham, these edifices can still be seen close to their respective Underground stations, sturdy reminders of the still extant shelters beneath. Entrance was also possible from the stations via stairways and access shafts, although these are all now sealed. The average depth below ground of these shelters was 85 feet and the deepest, at Goodge Street, was 105 feet. As an added precaution gas and smoke filters were installed in the ventilation system, which included four powerful fans. The vital toilet facilities were housed in eight lavatory tunnels, with Elsans connected to a special ejector system as they were situated below sewer level. Water was available from the mains or from an auxiliary supply tank and electricity was either supplied by London Transport or from the local supply authority.

Each installation was intended to shelter about 8000 people and included an electric lift in the staircase shaft to convey food and drink to the canteens provided for the shelterers' refreshment. In November 1940 work began on the first shelter beneath Chancery Lane Underground station, but according to Charles Graves, "When faced with the realities of the job, the engineers found it necessary to vary considerably from the original scheme."[12] Indeed, as it was already favourably placed for telecommunication links, Chancery Lane shelter was to become a major communication centre, which was expanded after the war and was never opened to the public (see Kingsway Telephone Exchange below). In the construction of the other shelters the prototype was soon altered to accommodate extra important features such as improved ventilation and fire-extinguishing plant and offices for wardens and medical staff. Finally, it was reported in *The Engineer* of 18 September 1942 that "Eight new tube shelters in the London area, it was announced last week, are now so nearly completed that they could be brought into use without

delay. Actually it is not intended to throw them open for the use of tube shelterers unless and until there is a need for the extra accommodation they will provide."

Although ten had been intended to be built, two were not completed, as work on them was reported to have been abandoned owing to technical difficulties. Work on the Oval shelter started at the end of 1940, but stopped in August 1941, allegedly after excavators encountered springs and water-bearing ground. It would appear, however, that during that time a 300-foot section of standard shelter tunnel was driven from a shaft in Camberwell New Road and another section from a shaft in Church Street, which included a cross-shaft and a ladies' lavatory tunnel.[13] Interestingly, one can still see today that fences on a nearby housing estate on Kennington Park Road consist of a series of welded-together stretchers probably reused from the South London deep-level bunkers and nearby air raid shelters.[14] Similarly, work on the prospective shelter at St Paul's was halted, as it was asserted that an Act of Parliament forbade underground works that might threaten Wren's cathedral. However, just before the war, shafts had been driven at this station for escalators, without any complaint. These works were in close proximity to the Chancery Lane shelter and more importantly the Faraday House telephone exchange. Unusually, the shelter tunnels at St Paul's had been intended to lie next to the existing railway tunnels, not beneath them.

The apparent cessation of work at the Oval and St Paul's resulted in the capacity of the other shelters having to be expanded. Ironically, by the time the deep-level shelters were completed in August 1942 the intensive Luftwaffe bombing had ceased and the bunkers at Chancery Lane, Clapham Common and Goodge Street found an alternative use as telecommunications centres. The remaining shelters were used to billet troops and Ministry of Works staff responsible for urgent repairs to government buildings. It was not until July 1944, after flying bombs had begun to fall on London, that Clapham North, Clapham South, Camden Town and Belsize Park became available as public shelters. However, by October, two of them had been closed and with the diminution of air attacks the others soon followed. By the end of the war only four of the deep-level shelters had ever been occupied by the public.

The previously mentioned announcement in *The Engineer* went on to state that "These shelters, the design of all of which is practically the same, have been constructed in such positions that they can become parts of new tube railways that may be driven below London when the war is over." It was originally claimed that following the conclusion of the war the deep tunnels would be joined together to constitute an express line beneath the congested Northern line offering speedy access to the West End and City, but as Londoners are fully aware, this has never transpired.[15] It does seem strange, however, that these shelters should be constructed separately and apparently without connecting tunnels as many of them, especially those in South London, are in such close proximity and alignment. In the years after the war some of the shelters served a variety of purposes, initially being used as hostels for troops travelling through London and in recent years as secure storage for private companies. It is said that a clause in the contract allows the government to regain possession of these buildings at any time. In 1948 the shelter at Clapham South was reopened temporarily to accommodate some of the first of the Afro-Caribbean community who were soon to settle in nearby Brixton and it later saw service as a youth hostel throughout the Festival of Britain.[16]

GOODGE STREET BUNKER AND THE TUBEWAY ARMIES

In his official history of civil defence during the last war, Terence O'Brien wrote that "At the end of 1942, part of the Goodge Street deep-level shelter was made available for General Eisenhower's London headquarters, and later two others were adapted for use by the operational staffs of Government Departments".[17] The shelter was requisitioned by Eisenhower in his role as Chief of Staff, Supreme Allied Command (COSSAC) and the "two others" referred to were the shelters beneath Clapham Common and Chancery Lane. Inside the Goodge Street shelter, 105 feet down, the upper level of the standard twin tunnels was used for office and telecommunications facilities and the lower for bunks and canteens. Eisenhower had it converted into the signal centre for SHAEF (Special Headquarters Allied Expeditionary Force) during the Normandy Landings in 1944. He also stayed in the more comfortable surroundings of the Dorchester, as it had sturdily constructed reinforced concrete and gas-proof basements. At Goodge Street telephone communication was supplemented by connec-

121. The deep level tube shelter at Belsize Park in 2000.

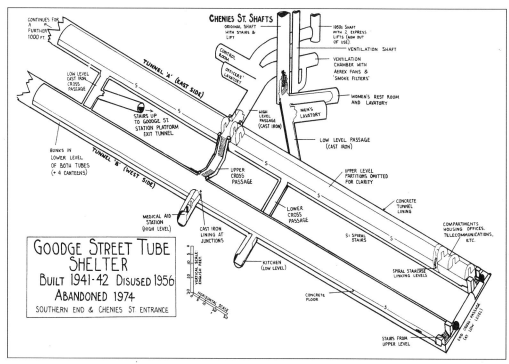

122. *Plan of the Goodge Street deep level shelter, reproduced from Nigel Pennick's 'Bunkers Under London' (1985 edition).*

tion to the GPO 1½"-diameter pneumatic tube message carriers, which were linked to Churchill's Cabinet War Rooms.[18]

After the war Goodge Street was used as an overnight hostel that could accommodate up to 8000 British troops on their way to Cyprus, Gibraltar, Aden and Singapore. Separate toilets were provided for officers and men and graffiti left by these transient soldiers is still visible on the walls and ceilings of the shelter. One example reads, "I pray to God I never come here again." Following a serious fire in the easternmost tunnel on the night of 21 May 1956, which caused considerable damage, it was abandoned. In 1986 it was leased for £40,000 per year to the Security Archives company, which also leased the shelters at Camden Town and Belsize Park. In 1992 the Goodge Street bunker was reported to hold 350,000 master tapes for recording artists, 1.5 million videos including the entire output of Channel 4, whose offices were then nearby,

computer discs and thousands of mortgage deeds and company records.[19] Though the original bunks had been removed, some original features remained such as the glass mercury arc rectifier, which converted AC to DC. This had once provided emergency lighting and powered the express lifts requested by Eisenhower during his occupancy. Its eerie glow earned it immortality as an alien brain in an early episode of the *Dr Who* television series. Today the entrance, with staircases from Goodge Street underground station, is sealed, but the blockhouse in Whitefield Gardens and the colourfully painted cylindrical entrance in Chenies Street are highly visible.

THE UNDERGROUND AT WAR

The platforms of the old maroon-tiled Underground station in Down Street, off Piccadilly have been mostly abandoned since the station's closure in 1932 apart from a brief, but important, period of government occupancy during the last war. Shortly after the closure the construction of an 835-foot siding between the eastbound and westbound lines, for reversing and servicing, commenced. The siding was connected to the east end of Hyde Park Station by a passageway. The Down Street complex was to prove extremely useful and was refitted and used as the deep-level headquarters of the Railway Executive Committee and was also the occasional home of Winston Churchill and the War Cabinet in 1940.[20]   In his account of wartime operations Churchill describes his occupancy of the "considerable underground office in Piccadilly", stating that "from the middle of October till the end of the year I used to go there once the firing had started, to transact my evening business and sleep undisturbed."[21]

This emergency headquarters, protected by gas-proof steel doors, included a telephone exchange, sleeping accommodation and basic amenities for the shelterers. On the platforms a reinforced wall divided the shelter from the tube lines. A control room contained a switch that activated a red light that could halt a passing underground train to allow, "executive men onto the driver's platform without the passengers having any inkling that the stop was for anything other than operational reasons."[22] After the war Down Street returned to its abandoned state, but some of the toilets and bathrooms still survive today and can be seen on one of the occasional visits that may be arranged to this ghost station.[23] There have also been rumours of a tunnel linking this station to Whitehall, but no evidence has ever come to light.[24] In 1996 the station was used as a location for the poorly-received BBC television fantasy series *Neverwhere*, set in a hidden world existing beneath London. Peering from within a Piccadilly Line train carriage today a change in tunnel brickwork and small openings onto the platforms are still discernible between Hyde Park Corner and Green Park stations.

Not far from Down Street, Dover Street (now Green Park) station housed some of the wartime London Transport senior staff, who were also accommodated in Knightsbridge and Hyde Park Corner stations. At South Kensington two deep-level tunnels originally intended for an express District Line were used by London Transport emergency engineering staff. These tunnels were linked, via the pedestrian tunnel that passes beneath Exhibition Road, to a Civil Defence headquarters under the Natural History and Geological Museums. Brompton Road station, which had been closed since 1934, was used as the control room for the 1st Anti-Aircraft Division. On the eastern edge of London 2½ miles of unfinished twin tube extensions to the Central Line, running beneath Whipps Cross, Wanstead and Gants Hill, were utilised as an aviation component and military equipment factory. Conversion work started late in 1940 and was finished by March 1942. Access was gained via the unfinished station buildings or by lift shafts sunk in Cambridge Park and Danehurst Gardens. Inside this complex, comprising 300,000 square feet of floor space, Plessey employed day and night shifts of 2000 workers who manufactured wiring sets for Halifax and Lancaster bombers, gear levers, shell fuses, wireless equipment and field telephones. The employees worked on a false floor with air conditioning ducts beneath, which allowed 9' 3" headroom to the apex of the tunnel roof. Battery locomotives ran along each tunnel on an 18-inch gauge railway to transport materials through this elongated underground factory.[25] As a further wartime precaution, emergency underground studios were built at Maida Vale for the BBC, so that broad-

*123. A wartime telephone exchange underneath
Whitehall.*

casting could continue should the main studios be destroyed.[26]

Before the war it had been realised that a single bomb dropped in the Thames in the proximity of the Charing Cross-Waterloo tunnels could have swamped half London's Underground system. Flooding would occur from Shepherds Bush to Liverpool Street, from Hammersmith to King's Cross, from Clapham Common to Euston, and from Elephant and Castle to Marylebone.[27] In order to prevent this disaster a number of tube tunnels that passed under the river were temporarily plugged with concrete whilst formidable steel flood-gates were installed at strategic points in close proximity. The platforms at Charing Cross could be isolated by means of electrically-operated sector flood-gates, which was fortunate as the abandoned loop line from that station, that passed under the Thames was struck by a bomb and flooded. £1 million was spent on protecting the Underground network and major water mains and sewers, whilst hydrophones were installed on the river bed to detect the impact of delayed-action bombs and mines, the signals being relayed to the Chief Engineer at South Kensington. Leicester Square station housed a control room to warn stations of any impending bomb or rocket attack. The six-ton floodgates could either be closed electrically or manually and were constantly manned in order to prevent a potentially disastrous inundation.[28]

THE GOVERNMENT PREPARES FOR WAR

Harley Hugh Dalrymple-Hay (1861-1940) played a major role in the civil engineering history of London's underground railways. He had already been responsible for over sixty miles of tube tunnels in London, including those on the Piccadilly and Bakerloo lines and for extensive works at Piccadilly Circus, Leicester Square, King's Cross and Elephant and Castle stations as well as having been consulting engineer on the Post Office Railway. He was given a knighthood in 1933. According to his entry in the *Dictionary of National Biography,* his last major work was "a secret system of deep-level tunnels beneath Whitehall to preserve from aerial bombardment intercommunication between government offices." In the autumn of 1939 a tunnel twelve feet in diameter was excavated from a point just south of Trafalgar Square as far as the Cenotaph to carry telephone and telegraph cables between government departments and war rooms. This was to be the first section of what was to become a huge complex of 'secret' tunnels that still exists beneath Whitehall and central London. A shaft eight feet in diameter connected the north end of this fledgling government tunnel with the Whitehall Post Office telephone exchange in Craig's Court. Another telephone exchange was situated in the basement of the Old War Office in Whitehall and known as Federal, connected to the public network, but restricted to ministers and top civil servants.

At the same time a series of fortified underground buildings or citadels, for military and government use, were constructed away from the centre of the city. The first were located in the suburbs of north-west London and were intended for the Admiralty at Cricklewood, the Air Ministry at Harrow and the Cabinet Office at Dollis Hill (known as Paddock, see below). In addition a series of citadels in central London were built that were to be completed by the end of 1941 and which together were capable of accommodating three thousand staff.[29] One of these, the Admiralty citadel and operations centre, an ivy-covered colossus in Pall Mall, was referred to by Churchill as "the vast monstrosity which weighs on the Horse Guards Parade". Another citadel, which is still visible above ground, consists of three rotundas constructed within the disused bases of the Horseferry Road gasometers and later incorporated into the ground floor of the former Department of the Environment buildings in Marsham Street. Long considered amongst the ugliest buildings in London, the three crumbling slabs of office blocks completed in 1961 and resting on the rotundas are too expensive to repair and are expected to be demolished.[30] Churchill had the original Whitehall tunnel extended from the Cenotaph through Parliament Square in order to terminate at the Marsham Street citadel, with an emergency exit in the basement of the nearby Westminster Hospital.[31] Part of this tunnel was widened beneath Broad Sanctuary to fourteen feet in order to house a teleprinter centre. This extension south had been difficult to excavate, owing to the presence of the buried River Tyburn and by 1983 the derelict tunnel had flooded, although the remainder of the system was protected by floodgates. Eventually the Department of the Environment accepted responsibility for draining this remnant of wartime security.[32] As the war continued members of the royal family were provided with a protected suite of rooms beneath Curzon Street, intended to replace their gas-proof shelter that extended for five hundred yards beneath the north terrace of Buckingham Palace.

CABINET WAR ROOMS

The Cabinet War Rooms are the most widely-known of Winston Churchill's various wartime shelters in London.[33] Visitors to this fascinating warren see only a small section of the underground offices and corridors that extend under Whitehall. It operated 24 hours a day under Royal Marine guard and its location, beneath today's Treasury building, was one of the best kept secrets of the war. This was fortunate as a well-aimed bomb would have been likely to destroy Churchill, his War Cabinet, the chiefs of staff of the air, naval and land forces and the top echelons of military intelligence and planning who regularly sheltered there.

The site chosen, conveniently situated between Parliament and Downing Street, was beneath the Office of Works' building which had the strongest structure in Whitehall. The cellars ten feet below ground were converted into a military information centre from June 1938 and were fully operational by 27 August 1939, shortly before Britain's declaration of war. By late 1940 protection was strengthened by a three-feet thick reinforced concrete slab inserted at ground floor level. Despite this work it is unlikely that the shelter would have been able to withstand a direct hit on the building above and doubts were expressed during wartime as to whether it were indeed bomb-proof. Walking along the underground corridor today the visitor can see the heavy steel doors giving access to the Cabinet Room and the rooms used to house 'C', the anonymous head of British Intelligence, Hastings Ismay, Chief of Staff to Churchill and Deputy Secretary to the Cabinet and Sir Edward Bridges, Secretary to the Cabinet. The subterranean complex also includes a room containing outside broadcasting equipment, a telephone exchange and the vital Map Room situated next door to Churchill's own quarters. Disguised as Churchill's personal toilet, the Transatlantic Telephone Room gave him a direct untapped connection to President Roosevelt. This employed the 'Sigsaly' code technology, which required a large and complex enciphering machine, housed in an annexe basement of Selfridge's store in Oxford Street, through which messages were conveyed to and from the Cabinet War Rooms.

124. Officers on duty in the Map Room beneath Whitehall in May 1945.

PADDOCK AND RAF UXBRIDGE

'Paddock' was another secret underground citadel located in Dollis Hill in the grounds of the Post Office Research Station at Brook Road. It was intended to form a last bastion of defence in the event of a German invasion in the last war and from its position built into the northern heights commanded a panoramic view above ground over the rest of London. Two levels of protected basement were separated by reinforced concrete floors ten feet thick. With accommodation for the War Cabinet and 200 staff the bunker was hidden beneath the Post Office research laboratories and covered in camouflage netting. The laboratories played a role in the development of the 'Ultra' code-breaking system. Churchill described Paddock as the "citadel for the War Cabinet ... with offices and bedrooms and wire and fortified telephone communication." He also suggested a "dress rehearsal (for) ... if it got too hot" on 3 October 1940. On that day a Cabinet meeting was held "far from the light of day" where "each minister was requested to inspect and satisfy himself about his sleeping and working apartments." This was followed by a "vivacious luncheon" and a return to Whitehall.[34] A telephone exchange was provided, together with a broadcasting studio in which it was claimed that David Niven would impersonate Churchill for a series of rallying speeches should the Wehrmacht start besieging Neasden. Meanwhile the real Prime Minister, Cabinet and members of the royal family would have been picked up by a flying boat from a nearby reservoir and taken to Canada. Fortunately the aeroplane was never required and Paddock was later sold by the Ministry of Defence in the 1970s to a property company, which has since had problems finding a suitably attractive use for it. In 1995 there were suggestions of refurbishing this increasingly damp and dilapidated bunker and opening it as a companion to the Cabinet War Rooms.[35]

In the course of the war Britain's air space was divided up into a system of Sectors and Groups. Each Sector Control was in charge of three or four airfields and reported to a Group Control directing a number of Sectors, which in turn reported to Fighter Command at Bentley Priory, Stanmore. In 1940 seven radial Sectors around London constituted 11 Group, whose headquarters were in a bunker beneath RAF Uxbridge. The operations room, from which the Battle of Britain was directed, still exists 70 feet underground. Visitors today can see the operations room perfectly preserved, with its central plotting table showing the whole of southern England and Europe and the telephone headsets and 'croupiers rakes' familiar from countless war films.[36]

TELEPHONE EXCHANGES AND CABLE TUNNELS

The Post Office was also responsible for a great deal of burrowing beneath London's streets in order to provide secure cable runs in times of emergency. During the Second World War and subsequent Cold War period its aims and those of the government largely ran in tandem with the result that its cable tunnels link together with those beneath Whitehall. William Halcrow (1883-1958), veteran of many prestigious engineering projects in London was also enlisted to extend the Post Office and government tunnel network.[37]

In 1939 a 1½-mile telephone cable tunnel was dug linking Whitehall with the important telephone exchange of Holborn in High Holborn and continued eastwards to the Faraday International Exchange, which constituted "the bottleneck through which virtually all overseas communications passed".[38] Faraday was also a citadel, with four blast and flood-proofed shafts connecting to this tunnel, together with cross tunnels into the Waterloo & City line. Similarly at St Martin's-le-Grand, the Post Office headquarters, already a station on the Post

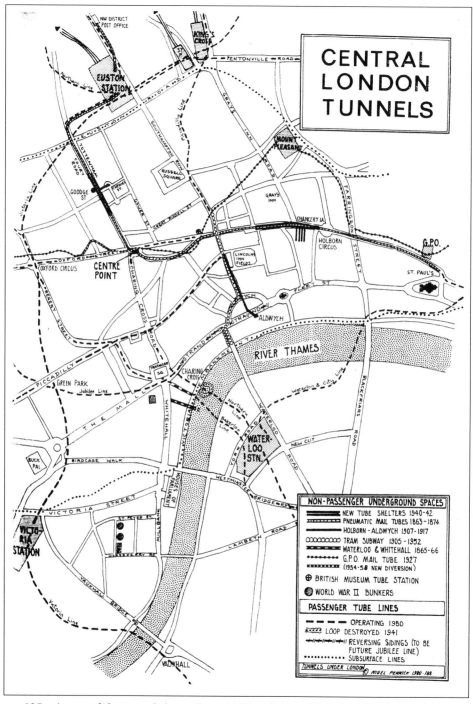

125. *A map of the tunnels beneath central London, published in Nigel Pennick's Bunkers Under London (1985). It does not include the later tunnels made for the Jubilee Line Extension, but it does show the Jubilee tunnel made as far as the Aldwych that was part of the originally proposed route.*

Office Railway, had connecting shafts to the nearby Central Line tube tunnels. This interconnection between the Post Office's deep-level shafts and the Underground railway tunnels ensured secure cable runs under London. In the event of damage "a circumferential cable network was constructed, with provision for rerouting any damaged cables around the outskirts of London."[39] After the war and the detonation of the atomic bomb in 1945 an even deeper series of tunnels to protect communications was ordered and Halcrow's expertise was enlisted once more. Throughout the early 1950s these concrete-lined tunnels, one hundred feet deep and stretching for eight miles, mostly with a diameter of seven feet, but including some with a diameter of 16½ feet, snaked their way beneath Central London, intended for telephone cables. Extended yet further in the 1960s, they now run for twelve miles from Bethnal Green to Maida Vale and from Euston station to Waterloo. Excavation of the deep London Post Office tunnels began in 1951 and one of the first priorities was to connect them with the huge underground trunk exchange known as Kingsway.

KINGSWAY TELEPHONE EXCHANGE
Look through the shabby, mottled doorway of 31 High Holborn and you are confronted by a steel door concealing a lift. If you were to descend from here you would encounter the remains of perhaps the most extensive and fascinating of central London's secret subterranean structures. This is the huge former telephone exchange, confusingly named Kingsway, which extends beneath Chancery Lane underground station, Furnival Street and Red Lion Street. Originally built from 1940-42 as a pair of standard parallel deep-level tunnels, it was a typical example of the deep-level shelter project. 100 feet below High Holborn, it was used as one of the government's telecommunications centres during the last war.[40]

The tunnels contained power plant and emergency power supply, medical aid stations, a kitchen and dining area and some sleeping accommodation. Kingsway was taken over by the GPO in 1949 and equipped in the early 1950s with a further four tunnels of larger diameter running at right angles from the eastern end of the southern tunnel beneath the Patent Office. These housed a secret international telephone exchange, which opened in October 1954 and could handle up to two million calls a week. The complex had its own artesian well, room for eighty telephone engineers in self-contained living accommodation and six months' supply of food. At this time, further underground connections were made with the parallel GPO cable tunnel to the south, effecting access to the Faraday House Continental Exchange and Wood Street International Exchange and via the GPO tunnel beneath Red Lion Street to the telephone exchange at Tavistock Place, near St Pancras.

The sheer size of this installation is evident from a visit to Furnival Street, where another grimy entrance is provided with a freight lift. A short distance around the corner in Took's Court the tall ventilation filter towers, built during the 1951-2 works programme, stand like sinister sentinels. The Post Office Works Act of 1959 provided official authorisation of these extensive works, even though they had long been completed. It mentions "certain underground works situated partly in the metropolitan borough of Holborn and partly in the City of London and connected with the underground railway station at Chancery Lane", which were later extended and "consist of a system of tunnels, together with shafts and other means of access thereto from the surface and other ancillary works." As an important telecommunications centre it became, in 1956, the London terminal for TAT1, the first transatlantic telephone cable. Although its existence was finally revealed publicly in an article in the *Post*

Office Courier in 1972, Kingsway is alleged to have still been in use in the 1980s. A bunker was said to have been housed in the easternmost north-south tunnels, but this has apparently now been decommissioned and the entire complex abandoned. According to the Research Study Group, "British Telecom used another part of these tunnels for the Kingsway Computer Centre between 1986 and 1990. This housed a secure backup for ICARUS (International Circuit Allocation Record Update System) located in central London."[41] Presumably care had to be taken with deep foundations on two recent construction sites at either end of this installation, the site of the former *Daily Mirror* building on Holborn Circus at the eastern extremity of Kingsway Exchange and the Midcity Place development to the west at the Red Lion Street/High Holborn junction.

Kingsway was connected to the network of citadels by the Post Office deep cable tunnel system, whose basic network was, by 1954, nearing completion. From the nearby Wood Street telephone exchange a new tunnel was driven on the same alignment as the Post Office Railway to the Houndsditch Exchange, passing beneath the Moorgate Exchange, which was a citadel code-named Fortress, and continuing to Bishopsgate and Bethnal Green. A section of this tunnel was brought to light again recently when the site of the exchange at 88 Wood Street was earmarked for redevelopment by the Daiwa Europe finance house. For a while it looked as though English Heritage were intending to list the building as "the most outstanding example of an inter-war telephone exchange", but the listing was changed in favour of Faraday House by the same architect, A.W. Myers. In its place Richard Rogers Partnership has designed a dramatic new office building on the site. However, beneath this sophisticated heavily-glazed edifice, British Telecom's modern hi-tech telecommunications equipment lies buried in a giant vault.[42] According to *The Architects' Journal*, "An old basement fills the site. This contains an operational telephone exchange. A series of cable and Mailrail tunnels underlie the site and connect to the basement chambers via shafts. These installations were to remain operational during construction and were to be structurally independent of the new building."[43]

Faraday Exchange was itself rather confusingly code-named Citadel and was linked to the subterranean network by a new tunnel passing beneath the Thames to Colombo House, code-named Rampart, on Blackfriars Road, which housed the South Bank Exchange. Extensions were also made from the cable tunnels beneath Holborn, one as far west as Paddington District Post Office and another via the Covent Garden Exchange, code-named Bastion, to Trafalgar Square Post Office and thence to the warren of tunnels beneath Whitehall. The Museum telephone exchange which occupied the site of the present British Telecom Tower was also connected to this growing network of cable tunnels and exchanges.

A SECRET SUBTERRANEAN CHRISTMAS

In December 1980 the *New Statesman* treated its readers to a tour of these cable tunnels courtesy of the intrepid journalist Duncan Campbell who undertook a fascinating and disturbing journey which revealed the massive extent of this hidden network. In the course of his subterranean researches he discovered that "Over 30 shafts and a dozen lifts connect these catacombs with the surface – most of them emerging unobtrusively in government buildings or telephone exchanges."[44] Campbell claims that these tunnels would have been used as part of a secret government network in the event of a national emergency or nuclear attack and, certainly in the Whitehall area they could have been used for this purpose. Entering, without permission, from an access shaft situated on a traffic island in Bethnal Green Road he descended one hundred feet to meet a tunnel, designated L, stretching into the distance and strung with cables and lights. From here he cycled, in order to cover the distance to Whitehall at speed.

The first major interchange he encountered was beneath St Martin's-le-Grand, close to St Paul's Cathedral, where tunnels diverge to meet those of the Central Line and Mail Rail. Two further tunnels designated R and A travel to the nearby Citadel telephone exchange south of St Paul's at Faraday House. Campbell was aided on his journey by conveniently placed signposts giving distances to various important destinations such as Whitehall, Holborn, The Mall and Lord's cricket ground! He also passed a group of stationary electric cars and trailers for hauling cables as he cycled along Tunnel G under Holborn. From Tunnel G, Tunnel M leads to Fleet Street and P travels under Leicester Square to the then Post Office Tower, with Tunnel S crossing beneath the river to Waterloo. It was recently reported that when the IMAX cinema inside the roundabout outside Waterloo station was being constructed the contractor's requests to deep-pile the foundations were refused, probably owing to the continued presence of this tunnel.[45] This was the last of these conduits to be dug and connects Trafalgar Square Post Office and the Whitehall tunnels with Colombo House (Rampart) and must run very close to the newly constructed Jubilee Line Extension and its impressive new station at Southwark.

From Holborn, travelling in eerie silence beneath the crowds of Covent Garden, Campbell soon arrived at the subterranean Whitehall complex of bunkers and war rooms. At this point and with remarkable ease, he reached the James Bond-style Q Whitehall telephone exchange about 40 yards south of Nelson's Column. The main tunnel at this point is twenty feet wide and forms a central spine from which further tunnels eight feet wide containing spiral staircases and lifts lead to the Ministry of Defence, the Treasury, the Admiralty and No.10 Downing Street. This is the same tunnel that leads ultimately to the former Department of the Environment buildings at Marsham Street, built above an abandoned citadel. Campbell re-emerged in Holborn Telephone Exchange, close to the *New Stateman's* headquarters in High Holborn, noting on his way the huge Kingsway subterranean telephone exchange. The Post Office tunnels are now only used for cables. The explosion of the first Soviet atomic bomb in 1949 and their successful detonation of a hydrogen bomb in 1955 rendered most of these underground installations in London redundant in the event of nuclear war.[46] It would appear, however, that before the Soviet H-bomb test the British government intended to accommodate thousands of essential staff in the bunkers and citadels around Whitehall, with the Post Office tunnels being used in the event of a nuclear war.

Apart from the tunnels explored by Campbell, yet another branch tunnel is believed to run from the Whitehall spine to the Admiralty citadel in Pall Mall and then to Buckingham Palace, with an entrance at the base of the Duke of York's steps. This is probably the same tunnel referred to by Peter Laurie[47] that sparked an interesting correspondence in *The Guardian's* 'Notes & Queries' column in 1997.[48] The respondent to an enquiry regarding secret tunnels beneath Buckingham Palace and Parliament outlined some of the rumoured tunnels in the vicinity, such as those linking the Palace to the nearby Piccadilly and Victoria Lines, together with a foot-tunnel to Wellington Barracks. Evidence for the Whitehall to Buckingham Palace tunnel includes an extractor fan outside the gents' toilet at the Institute of Contemporary Arts, which has no obvious connection to the building. At the foot of the Duke of York's Steps there is certainly a mysterious door on the ICA side, which supposedly leads underground. By standing on the seat and peering through a louvered window in one of the cubicles in the gents' toilet a short series of steps down to the alleged tunnel entrance can be seen.[49] It would seem that if the need arose the Prime Minister and the Queen could walk between each other's residences without having to be seen in public. Certainly, in October 1951 a shaft was sunk in Horseguards Parade and large numbers of workmen were engaged in a tunnelling project in the vicinity.[50] This already elaborate subterrannean network of tunnels and bunkers beneath Whitehall has recently been joined by a deep and costly neighbour.

PINDAR AND COBRA
One of the Second World War network of citadels was situated beneath Montagu House, the former War Office, now an annexe of the Ministry of Defence building. Evidence for the modernisation and extension of two existing bunkers deep underground at this site was disclosed by *The Guardian* in 1993. After close scrutiny of the annual Defence Works Services budget the existence of the so-called Pindar Project was revealed, a plan for a nuclear bomb-proof bunker, that had cost £66 million to excavate. The final bill, after expensive satellite-link communications equipment was installed, was £126 million with an overspend of £30 million. MPs initially were kept in ignorance of these costly blunders. Part of the extra expenditure was due to the many changes of plan as to the capacity of the installation. Severe structural faults entailed expensive strengthening and rebuilding before sensitive electronic equipment could be installed, resulting in a four-year delay.[51] Pindar was first authorised by Margaret Thatcher as a military command centre during the Falklands War, at an

original estimate of £42 million and with space for 40 to 50 officials, but by 1988 the number of occupants had been revised upwards to between 400 and 500. The bunker, once home of the Joint Operations Centre, intended to control events resulting from a Russian nuclear attack, is also connected to the warren of underground corridors that run from Downing Street along the whole of Whitehall and through central Westminster. One Whitehall source was quoted as complaining that cost had gone through the floor and in this instance it was literally true. *The Observer* noted in 1994 that:

> "Access to the site was through a hole measuring 12ft by 6ft. As much of the plant and equipment was larger than this, most of it had to be dismantled above ground, lowered into the hole, then reassembled. The obvious solution of digging a bigger hole would not have worked, because there was an existing network of tunnels underground that were also too narrow for the equipment."[52]

In 1999 another facet of this expensive and wasteful project was revealed when it was reported that the elaborate top-secret computer system named Trawlerman, designed to supply information to Pindar, approved in 1988, but not delivered until 1993, had similarly needed to be disassembled, lowered into the bunker and rebuilt. Added to this inconvenience was the difficulty that "because of the high classification of the information it handled, its security facilities made it incompatible with other computers to which it had to be linked."[53] In 1995, after a series of technical problems, Trawlerman was abandoned, dismantled and removed from Pindar at considerable cost. A report by the Committee of Public Accounts concluded that "When procuring computer systems it is essential that the complexity of the requirement is properly recognised at the outset" and that "the Department failed to do this in the case of Trawlerman, and that this was a key factor in the eventual decision to abandon the project and write off some £40 million."[54] It was superseded by a replacement system called Touchstone, which cost around £4 million.

A recent description of the interior of Pindar was furnished in a newspaper story on the Kosovo conflict, which informs us that:

"Deep below the Ministry of Defence building in Whitehall, past red, steel-reinforced doors, two computerised glass checkpoints and surveillance cameras lies the Crisis Management Centre: 'The Bunker' ... It is an air-pressurised network of low-ceilinged corridors leading to a large and dimly-lit room. At its centre is a broad ash table capable of seating 18. The bunker is serviced by one of the most sophisticated communication centres in the western world, including a video conference screen capable of simultaneously linking the crisis centre to Nato Headquarters, Permanent Joint Headquarters at Northwood, RAF Strike Command at High Wycombe and Army Command at Wilton."[55]

At this time Foreign Secretary Robin Cook, Defence Secretary George Robertson and Sir Charles Guthrie, the chief of the Defence staff, were descending into Pindar every morning to discuss military stategy. Later they would pass beneath Whitehall and through bullet-proof doors into the Cobra (Cabinet Office Briefing) Room under the Cabinet office. This office, intended for occupation in times of national crisis, was used to discuss the even more significant media strategy and propaganda campaign covering events in Kosovo.[56] Cobra is a secretive Cabinet group, initially set up by Michael Mates to combat terrorism during the term of the Heath government in 1972. It controls the Civil Contingency Unit, which can assemble the heads of the Army, Navy, Royal Air Force, security services and the SAS for emergency strategy meetings to deal with major civil emergencies and disasters.

Mobilised in 1994 for a training exercise to prepare for a possible terrorist nuclear attack, this unit was also on hand to deal with the potential chaos and civil unrest that was expected to result from the Millennium Bug's malign effects, which we now know to have been negligible.[57]

More disturbingly, it was reported in March 1998 that ministers had donned nylon suits and gas masks for a full-scale 'Doomsday' exercise in Downing Street, in order to test out the Government's defences against biological and chemical weapons attacks. This practice was rumoured to have involved the Queen and Tony Blair and to have taken place in a "Downing Street bunker" but would be more likely to have occurred in Pindar, which presumably includes many anti-biological and chemical attack features. This exercise coincided with a fresh wave of stories in the media regarding Iraq's chemical weapons cache and the ease with which deadly chemical weapons, including anthrax, mustard gas and sarin could be smuggled into Britain.[58] In April 2000 it was revealed that basements along the Whitehall tunnels were being "turned into high-security offices for the Government". The central tunnel which connects the Old Admiralty Buildings with the Cabinet Office and the Ministry of Defence is to be retiled and fitted with new fire doors. Offices placed every two hundred yards along this corridor will have computers and video surveillance cameras installed. Workers on the project had to sign the Official Secrets Act and any maps and plans used had to be handed in at the end of each day. Access to the site was gained from the telephone exchange in Craig's Court close to Q Whitehall. It was also reported that "although several MPs have asked for full details of the work, the Government has refused to supply them on security grounds".[59] During the same period a military parade down Whitehall, intended to feature the army's new Mark II Challenger tanks, had to be cancelled as it was claimed that the 62-ton tanks would damage the road surface and drop into London Underground tunnels, although the presence of the mass of security tunnels in the vicinity was undoubtedly the chief reason for the cancellation.

NORTHWOOD BUNKER

This vital element in Britain's contemporary defence strategy was formerly Group Headquarters, 18 Group (Coastal Command) during the last war, later to find another role during the Falklands War in 1982. The Operations room at the heart of the bunker was reactivated in 1996, after having been abandoned by NATO staff at the end of the Cold War. Buried 300 feet, Northwood near Ruislip now houses the Permanent Joint Headquarters with command of the armed forces and a massive array of sophisticated computer and telecommunications technology. During the course of the 1998 Defence Review it was revealed that the Army required six deployable armoured or mechanised brigades, which could be despatched and commanded, along with any naval or air forces on the same mission, from the tri-service Permanent Joint Headquarters.[60]

Northwood can also deploy a 200-strong flexible team, drawn from all the armed services and known as JFHQ (Joint Forces Headquarters). First established in 1998 JFHQ has carried out operations in Indonesia, Sierra Leone, Albania and East Timor.[61] In that same year a journalist gained access to the bunker and described the impressive hardware installed in the Operations Room and the twenty feet-high screen showing television footage. The Chief of Joint Operations, General Christopher Wallace, could observe events from a gallery overlooking this room. When seated at the head of a conference table he could view a bank of television screens which connect, via video conferencing links, to the other bunkers that would be activated should any conflict occur, including Pindar, beneath the Ministry of Defence and Strike Command in High Wycombe. These links also allowed him face-to-face contact with General Anthony Zinni, his American counterpart at that time, at US Central Command in Tampa, Florida.[62] During the Kosovo campaign in 1999 operational decisions were made by government officials via the video link between Pindar and Northwood, but Tony Blair, unlike Margaret Thatcher, did not visit either bunker, preferring to conduct business from his study in Downing Street.

TUBE ODDITIES AND ANOMALIES

A further series of hydraulic flood-gates was built into tunnels from 1953 to 1957, between stations on the deep tube lines such as the Northern, Piccadilly and Central lines which forms a protective circle about three or four miles in diameter beneath central London. These were controlled from an unfinished remnant of the Northern Line built in the vicinity of the Bull and Bush at North End, Hampstead Heath at a time when a tube station at that site was part of the line's original plan. Construction of this was underway by 1903, but after concerted local opposition it became increasingly obvious that if the Heath was to be preserved as a public open space then no tube station, whose presence would encourage development, could open there. Work on platforms, cross passages and lower stairs had already commenced, but when the provision of lift shafts and stairs to the surface was under consideration in 1906 it was finally decided to abandon the project. The station was never completed and was not accessible from the surface. If opened it would have been London's deepest station, 200 feet beneath Hampstead Heath, with an entrance building intended to stand on Hampstead Way opposite Wylde's Farm. Used for archival storage during the last war, North End took on a more important role in the 1950s as a control centre for the underground system's flood-gates. To facilitate access from ground level a 100 foot shaft housing a spiral staircase and a lift was sunk from an anonymous concrete block-house to the newly-constructed blast-protected control room, which was in turn connected to the earlier station works below. This control room would have enabled the flood-gates to be closed individually or all together from a single master control. It was intended to be London Transport's emergency headquarters in the event of nuclear attack. North End station is now reported to be abandoned.[63]

A plan for a proposed extension of the Bakerloo line to Camberwell was renewed in 1949, a logical and extremely useful connection that would have enhanced the notoriously limited tube access to South London. Originally authorised in 1931 and postponed in 1933, an estimate for it was included in the New Works programme of 1934. Although it did not survive to reach the Treasury stage in 1935, powers to excavate it were kept alive and two short sidings and a crossover were built in 1940 at Elephant and Castle, the Bakerloo Line's terminus. After much local encouragement the plan for the 1½ mile extension was reactivated in 1948 with the inclusion of a station between Elephant and Castle and Camberwell Green for a total cost estimated at £4.5 million. By January 1950 five working shafts had been sunk and the extension was expected to be completed by 1953. However, in September 1950 it was announced that "with regret it has been found necessary to defer the proposed extension." Fifty years later it is still deferred and one wonders what has happened to any excavations that occurred during 1950.[64]

The routes chosen for the Victoria and Jubilee lines have been the subject of speculation as to whether parts of the alignments were already in existence as cable tunnels that could have been widened to accommodate tube trains. Peter Laurie wondered whether the Victoria Line tunnels originally formed part of a cable tunnel running beneath the important Museum telephone exchange on the site of the Telecom Tower that was later released to London Transport. When the then Post Office Tower was being constructed it rested on a concrete raft, as pre-existing tunnels below prevented piles being driven. Perhaps coincidentally the Victoria Line passes directly beneath a number of important government buildings in Westminster and runs very close to Buckingham Palace.[65]

THE SECRET SERVICES AND MODERN SECURITY PRECAUTIONS

The former MI5 building at 1 Curzon Street was visited by a journalist from *The Independent* in July 1995, after it had been deserted in favour of the new headquarters in Thames House, Millbank. The nine-storey building, covering 3,930 square metres, featured steel shuttered windows, transparent light switches and wire casings, a reinforced concrete windowless bomb-proof room built to hold 200 people and, on the sixth floor, the Pig and Eye bar, an alternative to 'insecure' hostelries in Mayfair.[66] Thames House was acquired in 1988 for £100 million and it is hardly surprising to learn that there are many rumours about a tunnel linking Thames House with the lavish new post-modern MI6 building on the Lambeth riverside, Vauxhall Cross, designed by Terry Farrell.

The threat of terrorist bomb attacks has undoubtedly influenced the architecture of modern London and the choice of materials, particularly glass, used in a building's construction. As a 1993 article in *The Independent* stated, "some buildings in London are already designed to be bomb proof. The Queen Elizabeth Conference Centre in Westminster has an underground bunker and steps out from the third floor to protect the upper floors against damage from bombs

126. *The new MI6 building at Vauxhall Cross, designed by Terry Farrell. The picture was taken on 21 September 2000, the day after the building suffered a supposedly terrorist missile attack.*

placed at ground level."[67] According to Duncan Campbell this bunker was origi-nally occupied by the Palace of Westminster telephone exchange, which was replaced in the 1980s by a secret communications project.[68] When the nearby Westminster un-derground station was being rebuilt for the Jubilee Line Extension security advisers insisted that a thick concrete platform be inserted between the station and the contro-versial £250 million Portcullis House, an overflow office block for 200 MPs, built directly above, in order to minimise the threat from a modern-day Guy Fawkes.

For many months a pair of canary yellow tower cranes straddled the massive box sunk 131 feet into the ground, containing a be-wilderingly elaborate 'diagrid structure' and surrounding the skeleton of Westminster Station, soon to be surmounted by the Michael Hopkins-designed office block. This was the last of the impressive new stations to open, on 22 December 1999, as it was situated on the most technically challeng-ing section of the project. The reasons for the delay cannot be explained solely by difficult soil conditions, for the station stands

amidst one of the most politically sensitive and heavily tunnelled areas of London. As well as the presence of the District and Circle tube lines, gas and water pipes and electric-ity cables, there was the added complica-tion of the government tunnels that connect Whitehall and the Palace of Westminster. It was reported that in the planning stage of the Jubilee Line Extension official resistance had been encountered, when several pro-jected routes through Westminster were rejected without an explanation, although no potential subterranean obstructions were indicated on the planners' maps. Accord-ing to one source, "the situation around Parliament Square is still very uncertain. There is a lot going on, but we don't really know what it is … the rumour is that there is a vast bunker down there, which the gov-ernment has kept secret, which is the granddaddy of them all."[69]

Many of the major office buildings and potential terrorist targets in the City of London are fortunate in not having under-ground car parks in which explosives might be planted. Key institutions and companies today prefer to create separate sites for data and communication networks that can be housed in high security 'black box parks', packed with sophisticated computer equipment, remotely operated and therefore largely bereft of human presence. The redevelopment of the Docklands area provided the opportunity to construct a number of these retiring structures. The Reuters building, standing at Blackwall on the opposite side of the Thames to the Millennium Dome was also designed by Richard Rogers and Partners, but has deliberately kept a much lower profile than its distinctive neighbour. Despite some telltale external Rogers features the building seeks anonymity for its vital task of supplying up-to-the-minute financial information to the City. From behind tinted glass windows, which can swiftly be replaced with aluminium cladding, electronic information is processed and transmitted. The restaurant and sporting facilities for the small number of human operators the building requires are relegated to a bunker beneath this hi-tech block.[70] The gleaming London Telehouse nearby, which acts as a junction box on the Internet, is Japanese-owned and is another structure dominated by computer technology, where few if any human personnel are required.

THE EPSOM BUNKER

Late in 1999 it was revealed that a long-forgotten deep air raid shelter on the outskirts of Epsom had been sold to an anonymous buyer for £90,000. Amidst a beechwood copse at the end of a path and behind sturdy steel entrance doors a series of underground tunnels, eight feet wide and nine feet high, run for three quarters of a mile at a depth of fifty feet. Floor space amounts to 17,000 square feet and a large number of toilets had been installed. Mystery surrounds the history of the installation, as no government records relating to the bunker have been discovered. Local rumours suggest that the shelter was built

to house the royal family in an emergency or that it was a secret underground hospital. It would seem unlikely that it would have been a royal refuge as it was built to hold about 1500 people. One report on the bunker was discovered in Epsom Borough Council's museum, commissioned by the Property Services Agency in 1989 and stating that the land above the tunnels was requisitioned in February 1941 and that the total cost of construction was £26,658. A floor plan discovered in Surrey County Council's archives indicates food stores, a shelter marshal's post and a field kitchen and rest centre.[71] No doubt many more bunkers, tunnels and secret underground structures will be 'discovered' beneath London in the future.

Footnotes for Chapter Five

[1] For a post-nuclear scenario see O. Greene, B. Rubin et al *London after the Bomb: What a nuclear attack really means* (O.U.P. 1982).

[2] One of the earliest and most important speculative works was Peter Laurie's *Beneath the City Streets*, available in a number of revised editions, but now rather outdated. References here are to the 1983 Granada paperback edition. Nigel Pennick's booklets *Tunnels under London* and *Bunkers under London* (both Electric Traction Publications, 1981 & 1985) are extremely useful summaries with sourced information and well-founded supposition. Journalist Duncan Campbell has devoted many years to exposing this secret world and its often ludicrous expense and wastage. His *War Plan UK* (Paladin, rev. ed. 1983), although rapidly becoming a work of history, is essential reading, both for the information on London tunnels, bunkers and citadels and for an overview of the government's national plans in the event of nuclear war.

[3] Kelvedon Hatch Cold War Bunker was intended to be a Regional Seat of Government in the event of a nuclear attack on the South East. It is now open to the public and is accessible from the A128 Ongar

to Brentwood Road. Telephone 01277 364883. Also in Essex and open to the public is the Mistley Cold War Bunker. Telephone 01206 392271.

[4] See Campbell *op. cit.*, 181-185.

[5] The MI6 building in Lambeth incorporates a Faraday Cage to prevent external monitoring of communications.

[6] Two of the best recent studies, that also dispel some of the myths about wartime London, are Philip Ziegler *London at War 1939-1945* (Sinclair-Stevenson, 1995) and Joanna Mack & Steve Humphries *The Making of Modern London 1939-1945, London at War* (Sidgwick & Jackson, 1985) Also Campbell *op. cit.*, ch.3.

[7] A good general account of the variety of buildings generated by warfare in the last century is Keith Mallory & Arvid Ottar *Architecture of Aggression, a history of military architecture in North West Europe 1900-1945* (Architectural Press, 1973)

[8] Many of these surface shelters were shoddily built and offered inadequate protection. In some cases a nearby blast would suck the brick walls outwards, causing the thick concrete roof to collapse on to the occupants, leading Londoners to refer to them as 'Morrison Sandwiches'. Herbert Morrison was Minister for Home Security. See Ziegler *op. cit.*, 71.

[9] Mack & Humphries *op. cit.*, 59.

[10] *ibid.*, 70-72.

[11] The articles on these deep-level shelters published in *The Engineer* on 27 November and 4 and 11 December 1942 are very detailed. One of the best descriptions of the interior of the shelters is in Pennick *Bunkers under London op. cit.*, 11-25.

[12] Charles Graves *London Transport Carried On* (LPTB, 1947), 60.

[13] Pennick *Bunkers under London op. cit*, 18-19 who claims that the ground was stable.

[14] Information gleaned from Patrick Keiller's fascinating 1994 film *London*.

[15] The deep-level or New Tube shelters were included in a series of new Underground route proposals in the late 1940s under the Inglis Plan, one of whose priorities was the removal of the "unsightly" rail bridges over the Thames in central London. Although the shelter routes were not utilised the Victoria and Jubilee lines follow some of the plan's proposed alignments. See Pennick *Tunnels under London op. cit.*, 17 & 21-23.

[16] Francis Sheppard *London, a History* (Oxford University Press, 1998), 346.

[17] Terence H. O'Brien *Civil Defence (History of the Second World War, United Kingdom Civil Series)* (HMSO, 1955), 545.

[18] Pennick *Bunkers Under London op. cit.*, 21-23, also includes a diagram of the shelter.

[19] David Hencke 'Wartime bunker has security taped' *The Guardian* 26 August 1992, 5.

[20] On 1 September 1939 all railways, including the tubes, passed into government control under the Railway Executive Committee.

[21] Winston Churchill *Second World War* Vol.II *Their Finest Hour* (Cassell & Co, 1949), 331.

[22] Pennick *Bunkers under London op. cit.*, 9-10 contains a detailed description of the shelter's interior. See also *After the Battle* magazine No. 12, 36-41 and J E Connor *London's Disused Underground Stations* (Connor & Butler Specialist Publications, 1999), 15-16.

[23] Visits can be arranged through the London Transport Museum. Otherwise it can be visited 'virtually' on their website at http://www.ltmuseum.co.uk.

[24] Maev Kennedy 'Phantoms of Underground's dead stations come to life', *The Guardian* 27 August 1992, 4. See also Duncan *op. cit.*, 47.

[25] J Graeme Bruce & Desmond F Croome *The Twopenny Tube* (Capital Transport, 1996), 44.

[26] Laurie *Beneath the City Streets op. cit.*, 203.

[27] Graves *London Transport Carried On op. cit.*, 10.

[28] Pennick *Bunkers under London op. cit.*, 12-13.

[29] O'Brien *Civil Defence op. cit.*, 532. Campbell *War Plan UK op. cit.* lists them 170-171.

[30] Deyan Sudjic 'They don't make them like that any more' in *The Guardian* ''Space' supplement 11 September 1998, 6.

[31] Campbell *op. cit.*, 172.

[32] Trench and Hillman *London Under London, a subterranean guide* (John Murray, 1984), 199.

[33] *The Cabinet War Rooms* (Imperial War Museum, 1996). Opened to the public as a museum since 1984.

[34] Winston Churchill *Second World War* Vol II: *Their Finest Hour op. cit.*, 323-325.

[35] Christy Campbell 'If the Nazis had reached Neasden ... Churchill's suburban bunker to become a museum' *Sunday Telegraph* 16 April 1995.

[36] Individuals and groups can visit the former No. 11 (Fighter) Group Operations Rooms by appointment only.

[37] See his entry in the *Dictionary of National Biography*. He became Sir William Halcrow in 1944. The firm of Sir William Halcrow and Partners is still involved in civil engineering.

[38] Gareth Gardner '3-2-1 win for Rogers' *Building Design* 14 May1999, 20-21.

[39] Kenneth Powell 'Capital Gain' in *The Architects' Journal* 13 January 2000, 22-29.

[40] Trench & Hillman *op. cit.*, 184.

[41] Campbell *op. cit.*, 173.

[42] See Laurie (1983 ed.), 208-211 including a plan with entrance points. Also Nigel Pennick *Bunkers Under London op. cit.*, 26-27. Kingsway is also mentioned in C.M. Kohan *Works and Buildings: History of the Second World War, United Kingdom Civil Series* (HMSO, 1952), 386.

[43] The RSG has an interesting internet site at http://www.subbrit.org.uk/rsg/ which covers Kingsway and other wartime and Cold War installations.

[44] Duncan Campbell 'A Christmas party for the moles' *New Statesman* 19/26 December 1980, 4-5. According to Campbell the Post Office suggested that the photographs of the cable tunnels accompanying his article had been produced in a studio.

[45] Andrew Smith 'Tubeway Armies' in *The Observer* 7 November 1999, 28-39.

[46] For nuclear war preparations outside London see Laurie *op.cit.* and Campbell *op.cit.* N J McCamley's *Secret Underground Cities* (Leo Cooper, 1998) describes in detail the huge underground ammunition depots and factories built in England and Wales before and during the Second World War.

[47] Laurie (1983 ed.) *op. cit.*, 208.

[48] *The Guardian* 'Notes & Queries' 2 April, 23 April, 7 May and 4 June 1997.

[49] Andrew Duncan *Secret London* (New Holland, 1995), 45. See also Trench & Hillman *op. cit.*, 161.

[50] Campbell *War Plan UK op. cit.*, 191.

[51] David Hencke 'Inquiry launched into blunder over PM's war bunker' *The Guardian* 28 October 1993, 26.

[52] Andy McSmith 'Millions disappear down Whitehall spy hole' *The Observer* 3 July 1994, 4.

[53] Duncan Campbell 'Computing that doesn't compute' *The Guardian* 22 June 1999, 15.

[54] *Treasury Minutes on the Eighteenth to Twenty-second Reports from the Committee of Public Accounts 1998-99* Cm4456, 1.

[55] Peter Beaumont & Patrick Wintour *et al* 'Kosovo; the untold story: How the war was won' Part One, *The Observer* 18 July 1999, 13.

[56] Rachel Sylvester 'War in Europe, Labour turns up the spin' *Independent on Sunday* 4 April 1999.

[57] Marie Woolf 'Disaster Alert for 2000 bug' *Independent on Sunday* 8 November 1998.

[58] Jason Bennetto, Colin Brown and David Usborne 'Ministers in "Doomsday" exercise after anthrax alert' *The Independent* 25 March 1998.

[59] Rajeev Syal 'No. 10's secrets go underground', the *Sunday Telegraph* 30 April 2000, 7. The article is illustrated with an artist's impression of the tunnels and basements, which unfortunately includes another tunnel labelled 'Post Office underground railway' that in fact runs some distance to the north of Whitehall.

[60] David Fairhall 'The Defence Review: your flexible foe' *The Guardian* 24 March 1998, 15.

[61] Richard Lloyd Parry 'Crack British Force braces for Timor role' *The Independent* 16 September 1999.

[62] Ian Burrell 'Bunker Mentality as UK prepares for Gulf War II' *The Independent* 3 February 1998, 14.

[63] See Connor *op cit*, 40 and Trench & Hillman *op cit.*, 198.

[64] Nigel Pennick *Tunnels under London op. cit.*, 20. Also Alan A Jackson & Desmond Croome *Rails Through the Clay* (Allen & Unwin, 1962), 329-330. M A C Horne's *The Bakerloo Line, a short History* (Douglas Rose, 1990), 48 claims that the extension was abandoned because of financial difficulties, combined with the stabilising of the huge increase in post-war underground traffic and that "there was little other crucial need for the extension." He makes no mention of the shafts.

[65] This theory is mentioned in Laurie, 204-207, and Pennick *Bunkers Under London op. cit.*, 30.

[66] Mary Braid 'For sale: des res for the owner with an eye on security' *The Independent* 28 July 1995, 3. Sold for an undisclosed sum in October 1995 it was replaced by an office and retail building. Amongst a number of bland Security Service buildings 140 Gower Street (now demolished) was a former MI5 office. See Roy Berkeley *A Spy's London* (Leo Cooper, 1994). MI5 employs around 1900 staff of whom 47% are women. See *MI5 The Security Service* Third Edition (HMSO, 1998).

[67] Amanda Baillieu 'Bombings? We're off to the bunker' *The Independent* 5 May 1993, 15.

[68] Duncan Campbell 'Admission Impossible' *Time Out* 10-17 August 1994, 14-15.

[69] Andrew Smith 'Tubeway Armies' *op. cit.*, 34.

[70] See Baillieu *op. cit.* also Samantha Hardingham *London, a guide to recent architecture* (Ellipsis Konemann, 1996 ed.), 284.

[71] Peter Birkett 'Mystery of tunnels that could have been wartime royal refuge' *Evening Standard* 26 November 1999.

CHAPTER SIX

The Jubilee Line Extension
and Future Projects

'The Jubilee Line extension is incredibly interesting in terms of the historic fabric that it goes through. It links up with every other line. At Canada Water, we connect with the East London line, which still runs through Brunel's original Thames Tunnel. We were working in the grounds of abbeys at either end, the old Benedictine one at Westminster and a Cistercian community at Stratford Depot. London Bridge stands at the junction of Roman roads going north and back to Rome – we were digging up all sorts of artifacts there ... We had to go very deep with this line, down to 35 metres, even 40 ... It's chaotic down there – you can't believe what's going on.'
    Roland Paoletti, Architect-in-Chief of the Jubilee Line Extension, quoted in Andrew Smith's
    'Tubeway Armies' in the *Observer Life Magazine* 7 November 1999.

'A fag-end to the blandest of Underground lines, planned in an age not of paternalism but consumerism, during the heyday of the free market and at the nadir in repute and morale of the whole London Transport system; its route manipulated for the sake of the buccaneering Docklands experiment; its funding alternately promised and withheld by grudging governments; its execution mired in cost overruns and engineering entanglements.'
    Andrew Saint writing about the Jubilee Line Extension in the *London Review of Books* 20 January 2000.

The first phase of the Jubilee Line Extension (JLE) to be surreptitiously opened was the three-mile stretch between Stratford and North Greenwich on 14 May 1999. After this tantalising glimpse of the future the travelling public had to wait until Monday 18 October 1999 when the section between North Greenwich and Waterloo was unveiled. Trains only ran from Monday to Friday between the hours of 0630 and 1945 and were not stopping at Southwark station. The full route from Stanmore to Stratford was operational on Saturday 20 November 1999, although Westminster station did not open until 22 December. A swift underground connection between suburban north-west London, the consumer paradise of the West End, stately Westminster, sorely neglected south London and a regenerated Docklands had finally been established. Its completion had been promised "well in time

for the millennium" in order to transport the millions of projected visitors to the much-hyped Dome at North Greenwich and to extend another tendril across London's increasingly busy Underground network. Nevertheless it was a close run thing. Coming in twenty months overdue at a final cost of £3.5 billion and amidst increasing controversy and exasperation, the Jubilee Line Extension was finished as London prepared to enter a new century. Its troubled history was, however, inextricably tied up with the political and economic developments which had impacted on the capital during the previous fifteen years.[1]

THE FLEET/JUBILEE LINE
The Jubilee Line's origins lay in the putative Fleet Line project first mooted amongst a series of pre-Second World War and wartime railway plans. The section of the

Bakerloo line to the south of Baker Street was becoming increasingly overcrowded and services on the northern branches that converged on that busy interchange were judged inadequate. In 1946 plans for new Underground lines were published, containing a proposal for a line from north-east to south-west London, eventually built in the 1960s as the Victoria Line. Another suggested alignment in this scheme, later featured in the 1965 Railway Plan for London, was for a diagonal line running from north-west to south-east London – connecting Baker Street with New Cross and Lewisham. Intended to relieve congested sections of the Underground on the Central and District lines it would also provide a passenger connection with the Southern Region of British Rail. As part of the proposed route ran beneath Fleet Street it was named the Fleet Line, a welcome reference to one of the lost rivers in the area.

In early 1969 London Transport obtained Parliamentary powers to commence tunnelling for the Fleet Line and the go-ahead was given in August 1971, with the GLC providing 25% of the capital cost and central government the remaining 75%. Work on the first stage began in February 1972 initiating the excavation of the three miles of 12½-ft diameter tunnels that were to follow a route through the heart of the West End, from Baker Street via Bond Street and Green Park to terminate beneath Charing Cross station. To the north of Baker Street the Fleet took over the existing Stanmore branch of the Bakerloo Line, in operation since 1939. A further stage would extend the line from Charing Cross eastwards to stations at Aldwych, Ludgate Circus, Cannon Street, Fenchurch Street and thence to poorly-served south London via Surrey Docks East London Line station and Lewisham.[2] As the Queen's Silver Jubilee in 1977 was celebrated during work on the tunnelling it was decided to rename it the Jubilee Line. After considerable delays this section of the line

opened to the public on 1 May 1979.

At Baker Street a new station tunnel was built to allow same-level interchange between Bakerloo and Jubilee Line trains. The opportunity to provide a low level interchange at Green Park between the Jubilee and Piccadilly Lines had to be abandoned for financial reasons, but was eventually addressed as part of the Jubilee Line Extension station works. Strand station on the Northern and Trafalgar Square station on the Bakerloo Line were subsumed within the new Charing Cross Underground station in a massive complex beneath the Square with a subway link to the edge of Covent Garden. At the same time, the former Charing Cross station close to the Thames was renamed Embankment. Despite officially terminating at Charing Cross it was decided to continue the Jubilee Line tunnels almost as far as Aldwych in the expectation that the planned extension to Fenchurch Street and south-east London would be built. However the spiralling costs of safeguarding the line onwards through the City, at a time when an increasing number of buildings required deep-piled foundations, proved prohibitive to any advance directly eastward.

DECLINE AND REGENERATION IN DOCKLANDS

By the late 1960s containerisation, mechanisation, the relocation of port facilities to Tilbury in order to accommodate larger ships on a tidal river and increased competition from air transport and European ports had taken their toll on the once thriving London docks. Although the Royal Docks still appeared viable, much of the 8.5 square miles of docks and warehousing was becoming derelict and in need of redevelopment. The Royal Docks finally closed in 1981. As various planning bodies tentatively investigated alternative usage, the 1974 London Rail Study outlined the possibility of a new River Line with a northern route above ground from Fenchurch Street through Stepney East and Poplar, Custom House and Beckton. A section beneath the Thames would connect from here to the modernist utopia of Thamesmead, then considered an important destination.[3] The southern alignment would run underground from Fenchurch Street through the Surrey Docks, Isle of Dogs, North Greenwich and Custom House to Woolwich Arsenal, similarly terminating at Thamesmead. This forward-looking proposal could not be justified at the time on a social cost-benefit basis, but was intended to help stimulate new development to the east of the City. 25 years later, with the exception of Thamesmead and Woolwich Arsenal, many of these areas have now been connected with the Underground system and Docklands Light Railway.

The Docklands Strategic Plan of 1976 recommended the construction of the southern River Line extension from Fenchurch Street as a catalyst for redevelopment, leaving options open for the line east of Custom House. In 1978 London Transport, with the Greater London Council's backing, obtained parliamentary powers to construct an extension from the Jubilee Line to Woolwich Arsenal. At the time that authorisation for this second stage was being sought in 1979 the election of a Conservative government resulted in the necessary money being refused. By 1980 the project had been shelved. The government did, however, approve of the regeneration of the former docks and established the London Docklands Development Corporation (LDDC) in 1981 to organise this massive task. Unlike previous planners the LDDC believed in market-led development, whereby free rein was given to developers in the controversial Isle of Dogs Enterprise Zone. The cranes alongside the docks, once handling exotic cargoes, were to be replaced by those on proliferating building sites. The most serious potential obstacle to redevelopment, that the LDDC did not have the powers to address, was the woeful lack of public transport facilities. The choice of a cheap light railway to solve this was to have important consequences in the area.

THE DOCKLANDS LIGHT RAILWAY AND ITS CITY EXTENSION

With its relatively small budget of £77 million the Docklands Light Railway (DLR) was initially a short-term, quick-fix solution, constructed between 1984-87 and running from Tower Gateway, not far from Fenchurch Street, to Stratford and Island Gardens. Shortly after its opening 27,000 passengers were travelling each day on the DLR, as compared with the forecast of 22,000 and it soon became clear that the service would need upgrading. Concern about the capacity of the DLR was exacerbated by the announcement in 1985 of the proposed development at Canary Wharf at the heart of the Enterprise Zone. In this vast new scheme, the developers originally intended to create one million square metres of office space, some of it in what would be Britain's tallest building, with a potential working population of 50,000. Unfortunately, owing to cost-cutting in the construction of the DLR (for example, only Tower Gateway was provided with escalators), it soon became clear that two coach trains stopping at short platforms would be wholly inadequate for this workforce. Eventually £276 million had to be spent on lengthening platforms, improving signalling and, most importantly, providing a connection with the Underground in the centre of the City at Bank. About 40% of the capital cost was to be provided by the developers of Canary Wharf, Olympia & York, who needed vastly improved transport links. They demanded that the extension to the heart of the City be built as a condition of their development.

Another vital link in the transport network to Docklands was therefore forged in 1991 when the Docklands Light Railway

127. The brave new world of Docklands. The Docklands Light Railway is a scenic route once it is out of the tunnel into Bank station.

tunnel to Bank was completed, allowing access to the Central and Northern lines with the existing travolator connection to the Waterloo & City line.[4] The station was also linked with Monument on the Circle and District lines. Elaborate precautions had to be taken before tunnelling permission was granted by the City Corporation. Diverging from a viaduct near Royal Mint Street the DLR extension descends steeply into two running tunnels 16 feet in diameter for one mile to reach the station tunnels 23 feet wide. Sections of the walls on the north side of the Tower of London had to be shored up whilst the extension was burrowing away nearby.

Anyone who has had to walk between the ticket hall at Bank, the deepest station in central London, and the DLR platforms soon appreciates the extent of these excavtions.[5] The extension of the DLR lies 140 feet down and beneath the Circle and District Line tunnels for much of its length. According

to *Railway Magazine*, "One particular feature of historical interest is provided in the maintenance of the original Greathead shield used for driving of the Waterloo & City line running tunnels in 1894-96. The shield will be retained in its current position at the end of that line's overrun tunnel to become part of the passageway connection to the DLR."[6] Access from the street is through the existing ticket hall at Bank and via a completely reconstructed hall at Monument. The trains on the DLR are fully automatic and driverless, with an override capability from the control room and within the train. Many of the initial computer problems that had plagued the line had, by this time, been ironed out. From planning to opening this important project took only five years to complete. By Spring 1994 a further extension costing £280 million connected the DLR with the Royal Docks and Beckton and an extra £200 million was required for the later southerly extension to Lewisham (see below).[7]

THE JUBILEE LINE EXTENSION

The Texan developer Gooch Ware Travelstead and the consortium originally behind Canary Wharf were promised by the Conservative government that transport links between their proposed office city and the West End would be improved. Pressure increased when Travelstead and his backers pulled out, to be replaced by the Canadian developer Olympia & York, headed by the ambitious Reichmann brothers, confident following their lucrative and showy developments in North America. Despite potential improvements to the DLR it was realised that the workforce of Canary Wharf would need something more substantial to get them there. By the late 1980s both London Transport and Olympia & York concluded that a second link between Docklands and the centre of London would be required. Olympia & York's proposals focussed on a connection from Waterloo to Canary Wharf, either as an extension to the Bakerloo line or as a dedicated stand-alone railway. Although this would have eased commuting from the south of England into Canary Wharf it would have provided few benefits for the rest of London. London Transport favoured an extension to the Jubilee Line that would ultimately link up with Underground and main line services at Stratford. The East London Rail Study, commissioned by the Department of Transport in 1989, concluded that this option was viable, following a route from Green Park (avoiding Charing Cross) via Waterloo, London Bridge and Canary Wharf to Stratford, with a possible alignment across the Greenwich peninsula.

Olympia & York were still heavily involved in the planning process and even helped to finance the preparation of the Bill to obtain the powers to construct this extension. The company also promised an investment of £400 million in the line's construction and, given the enthusiasm of the government for privately funded public ventures at the time, other pressing schemes, such as the Chelsea to Hackney line and the CrossRail project, were given a lower priority than the line to Docklands. The Bill gained Royal Assent in March 1992 and the plan to extend the Jubilee Line was underway.[8] The final chosen alignment ran in tunnel from Green Park through Waterloo, London Bridge, Bermondsey and Canada Water, across the North Greenwich peninsula and through the Isle of Dogs to Canary Wharf and then above ground, parallel to the North London Line, to Stratford.[9] Given the circumstances of the Jubilee Line Extension's origins it was certainly true that "Never before had an Underground line been such a key issue in maintaining confidence in economic regeneration."[10]

By April 1992, however, the first of the many serious problems that were to dog the project occurred, when the overstretched Olympia & York went into administration in the USA and Canada. Alternative finance for the JLE was provided by an international syndicate led by Lloyds Bank in association with the European Investment Bank. Despite this setback the project went ahead regardless as London Transport planners continued frantically organising this massive undertaking and commenced hiring architects for the eleven stations. An impressive roster of leading UK civil engineers such as McAlpine, Balfour Beatty, Amec and John Laing was also brought onboard, together with Aoki from Japan and Soletanche from France. A new fleet of 59 trains was to be constructed by GEC Alsthom and signalling was to be provided by Westinghouse Signals. This fragmentation and spreading of responsibility over a group of companies was, however, to result in lack of synchronisation and co-operation in crucial areas of railway engineering and infrastructure. By 1994 banks had invested £98 million and the government had paid £1.5 billion. The opening date for the JLE was the apparently unproblematic Spring 1998.

In December 1993 the first piles for the project were sunk at the site of the future Canary Wharf station. During the subsequent excavation and building the JLE was claimed to be the largest construction project in Europe and the most complicated tunnelling operation ever carried out beneath London. Work proceeded well until 21 October 1994, when excavation of an unrelated tunnel for the Heathrow Express beneath the airport was dramatically halted by a collapse. Although nobody was injured, a large crater appeared between two runways near Terminal 3, leading to the cancellation of hundreds of flights. This event had serious implications for the JLE as the same New Austrian Tunnelling Method (NATM) was being used in its excavations at Waterloo and London Bridge.[11] An enquiry had to be held, necessitating a cessation of work on these stations and a delay of three months. Eventually tunnelling resumed in January 1995 using the same method, but reinforcing the walls with massive iron sections. The legal battle resulting from the incident at Heathrow was finally resolved in February 1999, when Balfour Beatty, the building company responsible for the tunnel, was fined a record £1.2 million and Geoconsult, an Austrian engineering consultancy, was fined £500,000 for failing to ensure the safety of the public and of workers on the project.[12]

The JLE tunnels were excavated at the rate of up to 185 yards per week. Over three quarters, 7.7 miles, of the route required tunnelling, with twin bore tunnels being excavated from six sites. The tunnels beneath the Thames and the Blackwall Tunnel from North Greenwich to Canary Wharf were carved out by a pair of 220 tonnes earth-pressure tunnelling machines nicknamed Tracey and Sharon, ferocious beasts with revolving cutting faces guided by laser that crush the ground as they move forward. The resulting spoil is passed back through the innards on a conveyor belt to waiting containers. One description of the tunnels and caverns under construction at Waterloo, using a variety of tunnelling methods, gives some of the atmosphere of working deep beneath London.

"Climbing up a mixture of ladders and temporary steps along what will eventually become a bank of escalators we reach the upper level concourse. Here, on either side of the densely propped cavern, hand tunnellers are hacking through the thick, sticky London Clay. On one side an escalator shaft rises, while on the other a tunnel shield pushes towards the Northern and Bakerloo lines ... Here beneath the shield and tight up against the dark green-grey wall of clay, a twinge of claustrophobia and a sense of the massive weight of earth above makes itself felt for the first time."[13]

Throughout the work on the Westminster section much publicity was given to the alleged threat to the stability of Big Ben. It was claimed its shallow foundations were being undermined by the new tunnels. Tests revealed that a 3mm shift on the clock's east face had been detected and remedial action was taken. In this instance a series of shafts was dug in and around Parliament Square to enable vast quantities of grout to be pumped into the gravel subsoil, in order to prevent ground movement and any collapse. At the same time concern was also expressed by members of the palatial Royal Automobile Club in Pall Mall, whose Art Deco swimming pool is sixteen feet above the new tunnels. A spokesman was quoted as saying, "the prospect of members diving into the swimming pool and ending up in Neasden is not one I relish."[14]

SIGNAL FAILURES

As the competitively priced offices at Canary Wharf attracted increasingly important clients including a large part of London Underground's administration and influential newspapers, its fortunes were turned around. In October 1995 Paul Reichmann returned to the fray heading up a consortium of investors that bought the development for £800 million. March 1996 proved to be another significant month for the JLE, as it was then that the North Greenwich peninsula was chosen as the site for the Millennium Dome. Suddenly the need to complete the line on time became paramount as the JLE was expected to carry 60 per cent of the anticipated 12 million visitors to the Dome. Failure to provide an efficient underground rail link to this planned cynosure of travellers would result in even more traffic chaos in London and would have dire consequences for traffic through the Blackwall Tunnel.

Once tunnelling was completed by October 1996 the installation of an innovative signalling system proved to be the next problem. In the Underground system as a whole the traditional 'fixed block' system of signalling is used: the railway line is divided into sections that keep trains at a fixed minimum distance. A train cannot enter a new section of track until the previous train has left it. London Underground intended, however, that on the Jubilee line the 'moving block' system was to be used. Already installed successfully on the Docklands Light Railway 'moving block' has the train contained within a protective electronic envelope in which no other train can operate as it travels along the track. The train's position is constantly monitored so that if the computerised system senses another train or an obstruction or if it moves outside its envelope, it is slowed or stopped automatically. The major reason for using 'moving block' is that it would allow more trains to be run. On the JLE it was envisaged that 36 trains per hour would run each way at peak times thanks to this signalling system. Unfortunately, after repeated technical difficulties Westinghouse could only promise a maximum of 17 trains each hour, an embarrassing prospect as the older Jubilee Line already ran 24. Eventually after

much prevarication and the early retirement of Westinghouse's managing director, it was decided to opt for the familiar 'fixed block' system.[15]

By March 1997 after more delays with signalling and electrical work London Underground regretted to announce that the JLE would be six months late and would not open until September 1998. During the summer the recently-elected Labour government became apprehensive, as the lack of an efficient rail link to the Dome could not be countenanced. February 1998 saw the apologetic announcement that the troubled line would not now open until Spring 1999. By September 1998 Deputy Prime Minister John Prescott had taken control of the project away from London Transport and had passed it to Bechtel, a troubleshooting US construction company, previously employed to ensure completion of the Channel Tunnel in 1990. Bechtel's role was to knock heads together and establish a timetable for progressive opening of the line in three stages, although by that time it seemed likely that the JLE would be further delayed until October 1999. Two months after Bechtel assumed control another crisis hit the troubled project as all five hundred electricians working on the extension took unofficial industrial action following months of deteriorating industrial relations and increasing pressure to work longer hours. Even with the resolution of this dispute at the end of November 1998 the JLE was still many months overdue and costs had risen dramatically to £2.85 billion. Fortunately by this time light was visible at the end of the tunnel; in May 1999 the first passenger trains ran between Stratford and North Greenwich and the entire JLE was operational by late November.

The Jubilee Line Extension was the subject of much controversy during its protracted construction. Certainly the project exposed the lack of continuity in the planning of London's transport infrastructure and the uncertainty created by using a mixture of public and private finance. On the western edge of Paris the developers of the gleaming office city at La Défense took the precaution of installing the transport infrastructure *before* building commenced. Political vacillation and the lack of long term planning has also meant that after the opening of the JLE the highly skilled teams assembled for excavation, construction and services have dispersed and will not move on to another project such as CrossRail. The millennial deadline exacerbated unrealistic expectations of untried technology and the overall fragmentation of the project resulted in unnecessary delays. Furthermore, the colossal expense may increase politicians' reluctance to sanction new underground projects and allow private sector finance to take over.

In the final reckoning the Jubilee Line Extension cost £3.5 billion to build, with each of the ten miles costing £350 million, making it probably the most expensive piece of railway ever built. This can be compared with the huge Channel Tunnel project that cost £320 million per mile or Line 14 on the Paris Metro which opened in October 1998 with fast driverless trains at £120 million per mile. As completed the Jubilee Line Extension is just under ten miles long with 7.75 of those in tunnel at depths of between 48 to 100 feet. This now makes the entire length of the Jubilee Line 22½ miles. The twin-bore tunnels, 14¼ feet in diameter, pass beneath the Thames four times. The journey from Stratford to Green Park should take 22 minutes with each station having interchange facilities with the Underground, buses, mainline services or Docklands Light Railway. In spite of the long wait and vast expense this *grand projet* should be seen as a great achievement and a step forward for the city where underground rail travel was first introduced. It has also provided London with eleven magnificent new stations, that have revolutionised the experience of underground travel.[16]

THE JUBILEE LINE EXTENSION STATIONS

Roland Paoletti has been dubbed the 'Medici of the Underground' in recognition of his significant role as commissioning architect for the eleven new Jubilee Line Extension stations. Born in London, Paoletti had been trained as an architect in Manchester in the late 1950s alongside Norman Foster, worked for a time for Basil Spence and relocated to Rome, spending a formative period with the eminent Italian architect-engineer Pier Luigi Nervi. From 1975 he worked for the Hong Kong Mass Transit Authority at a time when it was installing a new subway system from scratch, where he oversaw the design and construction of 36 stations. The accountant in charge of this massive project, Wilfred Newton, was called to London by Margaret Thatcher in 1990, to shake up London Transport and mastermind the Jubilee Line Extension. He requested that Paoletti accompany him and in the subsequent project the architect was given a relatively free hand. It was his intention to commission some of the best British architects to design nine of the stations, the other two being handled by an in-house team. Six of the stations are brand new, five substantially redesigned.[17]

The most recent Underground projects had been undistinguished aesthetically. Although swift, efficient and highly-automated the Victoria Line is rather uninspiring in its decoration and the original Jubilee Line austere and lacking identity. Uniformity was to be avoided in the new station designs; each station was to look radically different as an individual entity. Another hope was that each of these landmark stations would act as a focus for local communities and as a symbol of regeneration in the more blighted areas of London, especially around Stratford, West Ham and Canning Town. This commission seemed to mark a return to the confidence of Frank Pick whose enlightened patronage welded a powerful image from the disparate collection of lines unified by the creation of London Transport in 1933. Pick commissioned architect Charles Holden to design such distinctive stations as Arnos Grove or Sudbury Town and the headquarters building at 55 Broadway, decorated externally with sculpture by Henry Moore, Eric Gill and Jacob Epstein.[18] Holden's influence on Jubilee Line Extension design is manifest in individual stations such as Southwark and Canada Water that emulate his drum-shaped halls, but also in the space afforded travellers in Gants Hill, Holden's homage to the Moscow Metro.[19]

As a result of Paoletti's influence architects used to doing only the 'fitting out' were given the freedom to design the station above and below ground in partnership with civil engineers, but with the requirement to include a number of design priorities. Most unusually for deep-level stations natural light was, where possible, to be allowed to penetrate to platform level. For the first time since the early days of the London Underground the cut-and-cover technique was favoured in the excavation of some of the stations. Large subterranean chambers were to be created containing generous spaces for easy access and numerous escape exits. This makes a welcome change when compared with the comparative claustrophobia of the older deep tube stations, particularly the narrow platforms on much of the Northern Line. Passenger routing was to be clear and direct. The provision of banks of silvery escalators was another essential feature – 116 in the new stations compared with 295 on the remainder of the Underground network – together with lifts for the disabled. Unfortunately many of the lifts have not been in service owing to over-strict safety rules.

Integration with other public transport has allowed access to an elegant bus station at North Greenwich, the Docklands Light Railway at Canning Town and the Silverlink Metro North London Line on the eastern section. Probably the most unexpected visual features are the glass safety screens lining the platform edges, prominent in all the subterranean stations. At an extra cost of £9.5 million they were installed to prevent suicides, currently attempted three times each week on London Underground.[20] The precisely straight platforms of the new stations were ideal for this safety measure. As the train stops, correctly aligned with the screens, the two sets of doors on train and platform slide open simultaneously, controlled by an onboard computer.

The JLE stations embody an aesthetic at odds with the 'heritage' decoration of stations such as Baker Street with its Sherlock Holmes motifs and proclaim a belief in postmodernity and the technology that shaped the twentieth century. This rigorous industrial architecture has produced, in many of the buildings, a stark but attractive brutalism: roughcast concrete walls contrasting with smooth concrete pillars and roofs. According to the *Architectural Review*, "the stations share a common language of sleek hard-edged functionalism that synthesises architecture and engineering to generate its own austere elegance."[21] Many of the platform walls display their cast iron construction, the coffers neatly infilled with dark blue metal inserts. Despite the inevitable addition of posters and chocolate machines, the stark simplicity of many of the platforms and concourses is impressive. The tarnished metal plates beside the tracks, future advertising hoardings, initially resembled the minimal sculptures of Carl André or Richard Serra. The sheer scale of some of these concrete caverns recalls the theatrical space of a film set or the subterranean lair of a Bond villain as designed by Ken Adam.[22]

Stratford, West Ham and Canning Town

These three stations, all situated above ground, link the JLE to many vital transport links in east London, with Stratford and its nearby train depot forming the eastern terminus of the project. Stratford station is a complex interchange between main line services to and from Liverpool Street, Essex and the east of England, the Central Line, the Docklands Light Railway and the North London Line. Futuristic in appearance and prominent in plans to connect it with fast services to North Kent via a river crossing at Woolwich, Stratford's importance will increase with the completion of the Channel Tunnel Rail Link. If that were not enough, space has also had to be allowed for the potential CrossRail service if it ever transpires. The same architects, Wilkinson Eyre, also designed the new bus station. One of the most striking features of the station is the sweeping roof that also acts as a convection mechanism to control the internal climate. As the sun warms the outer envelope cooler air is drawn up from outside the building and through the subways to lower the internal temperature. This elegant wave of glass and metal allows the large internal public space to be flooded with light, so that the concourse resembles an aircraft terminal more than a station.[23]

West Ham provides connections with the District, Hammersmith and City lines, North London Line and the Tilbury and Southend line. It is probably the most traditional of the stations, involving extensive rebuilding of the existing structure. Brick built, but also incorporating glass blocks that glow luminously after dark, it is a plain functional building and was the first of the stations to be completed. Charles Holden's influence can be discerned in the lofty ticket hall, similar to his design for Oakwood station near the northern tip of the Piccadilly Line.[24] The construction of Canning Town station entailed the closure of this section of the North London Line for eight-

een months to allow its platforms to be relocated south of the A13. Similarly the DLR track alignments were modified in order to accommodate the new Jubilee Line platforms directly below. Powerful V-shaped precast concrete struts support the DLR platforms. The sandwich effect continues downward with the ticket hall and concourse situated below ground, illuminated by rooflights consisting of large glass sheets suspended from cast stainless-steel brackets. A bus station provided for London Transport buses also serves the nearby London City Airport.[25]

North Greenwich

Constructed on a Herculean scale and one of the largest underground stations in Europe, North Greenwich is arguably the most spectacular of the new Jubilee Line Extension stations. Designed by Alsop, Lyall and Störmer this robust structure is decorated in a distinctive cobalt blue, similar to that of the Hôtel du Departement des Bouder-du-Rhone or 'Big Blue' in Marseilles, one of their earlier works. A light-filled bus station designed by Norman Foster and Partners stands directly above, concealing the entrance. The principal spectacle and drama have been saved for the journey underground. North Greenwich is the gateway to the Millennium Dome and will also be the nearest station to the rather optimistically named Millennium Village. The Dome and Alsop's station are architectural masterpieces placed amongst what was formerly a scarred, hideous and polluted landscape.[26] This bleak peninsula once housed the gasworks of the South Metropolitan Gas Company built in 1886, one of the most extensive in the country, together with its now vanished network of railways.[27]

The legacy of industrial decay was an advantage in the construction of North Greenwich as the ground was not encumbered with buildings and the task of excavating the huge trench in which the station

128. One of the splendid vistas in the new stations of the Jubilee Line Extension. This view is of North Greenwich station, designed by Alsop, Lyall and Störmer. (Photo: Roderick Coyne)

sits was therefore made easier. The cut-and-cover construction method was adopted; the initial plan for a landscaped walkway across the open station later abandoned in favour of an enclosed underground station. 100,000m³ of contaminated spoil had to be removed from the site; an indication of the depth to which the ground has been polluted in certain industrial areas of London.[28]

Amidst this tainted land a stunning Underground station has been inserted. It contains a pair of parallel rows of elegant aerofoil shaped concrete columns about 43 feet high which add a Piranesian quality to the design and also support the roof slab, their surfaces encrusted with soothing blue mosaic tiles. The concourse is suspended between the ground and platforms with one side wall of backlit blue glass enhancing the overall colour of this busy grotto. The station has nine escalators and four lifts to cope with what were originally expected to be large numbers of visitors to the Millennium Dome. But it is difficult to envisage North Greenwich as a major destination after the closure of this attraction. After visiting North Greenwich station it is possible to agree with architect Will Alsop's assertion that, "great architecture lifts people's spirit; it creates a place of delight and fascination."[29]

129. Canary Wharf station, designed by Foster and Partners.

Canary Wharf Station

Originally the focal point for the whole project, before the arrival of the Dome, Norman Foster and Partners' Canary Wharf station is as ambitious and colossal as Alsop's North Greenwich, albeit starker and more ascetic. It stands within a section of the former West India Dock that, prior to any excavation work, had to be drained for the installation of cofferdams, inside which a concrete box 919' x 105' x 79' deep was constructed. From the platforms reinforced-concrete columns reach to the roof, where elliptical bearings allow the station to move in response to any geological pressure. One of the most stunning facts about this station is that is large enough to accommodate the monolithic Canary Wharf Tower (No. 1 Canada Square) laid on its side. The struc-

ture includes an emergency escape stairway and a crossover box which allows trains to switch lines.[30] It is unfortunate that because of its position there is no direct interchange with the nearby Docklands Light Railway.

The image of a secular cathedral was evoked in many of the descriptions of the concourse when the station opened. Similarly, because of the sweeping concrete ribs of the roof, standing in it was compared with being trapped inside a whale or the stomach of a very large fly![31] Bereft of the serene veneer of the mosaics at North Greenwich, Foster's station is the harshest in its exposure of concrete, stainless steel and glass. These relate it appropriately to the rather dehumanising Alphaville architecture gradually engulfing the centre of the former Enterprise Zone, some of which will be designed by the same practice. The vast

130. The main hall at Canary Wharf station. (Photo by Dennis Gilbert)

Canary Wharf development incorporates that other essential post-modern feature, a large shopping mall, underground in this case and within easy reach of the station.

The entrance is impressive. Passing beneath a delicate elliptical glass canopy and immediately onto a phalanx of escalators the traveller is given a leisurely and awe-inspiring view of the entire station. The glazing of the canopy is comprised of 48 different shapes of glass to maximise light penetration and diffusion, manufactured by the same company that produces wind-screens for Ferraris.[32] As recent estimates claim that the Canary Wharf development's workforce of 25,000 would rise to 50,000 in 2002 and possibly 90,000 by 2006 it is expected that by 2010 this Underground station will be the second busiest in London, handling 35,000 people per hour during peak periods.

Canada Water
Canada Water stands within a short distance of Surrey Quays shopping mall and amid the rapidly increasing residential and working population of the former Surrey Docks. 6700 passengers per hour are expected to use this station in peak periods, many of them connecting with the East London Line, passing to the north through Brunel's historic tunnel. Most of the station was constructed using the bottom-up construction method, building the slabs and walls extending upwards towards the roof of the ticket hall. 75 feet down, the vast underground cavern occupies the same volume of space as St Paul's Cathedral. Illuminated by daylight pouring through the glass drum on the surface, Canada Water is reminiscent of the station buildings at Arnos Grove or Southgate designed by Holden. Eight escalators and four lifts ferry

travellers to the ticket hall, East London Line platforms and, at the deepest level, the Jubilee Line. A bus station with its steel and glass spine, designed by Eva Jiricna, complements the graceful drum and at night both glow with an eerie blue light.

Bermondsey

Located in a residential area that had previously been fairly isolated from the Underground network, Bermondsey station's presence has certainly helped to accelerate the rising property prices in south London that have accompanied the building of the new line. A gently curving glass roof allows natural light to penetrate down to the ticket hall, escalators and platforms. The station design manages to insert a deceptively complex engineering structure into the most compact site on the project, measuring 150 ft x 158 ft with a maximum depth of 72 feet. Modest but impressive, the surface ticket hall features a brave and extensive use of glass, which might become prone to the attacks of vandals. Should the need arise, however, panels can be easily replaced thanks to a unique fixing device that utilises clamps, designed by the station's architects, Ian Ritchie Associates. As they descend on one of the three escalators to the platforms, passengers face a beautifully finished concrete wall and an interlocking set of massive v-shaped concrete trusses that dramatically break up the subterranean void. The smooth concrete textures were achieved by incorporating ground granulated blast furnace slag and sand aggregates.[33] A peak usage of 4000 people per hour is expected at Bermondsey and provision has been made for the future construction of a six-storey office block above the ticket hall.

London Bridge

The excavation of the new underground platforms beneath the bus garage at the front of the busy commuter station at London Bridge has exposed the attractive brick construction of the earliest railway terminus in London. A new pedestrian thoroughfare, formerly a road, now passes through these Victorian undercrofts, connecting Tooley Street with St Thomas Street and allowing access to the Jubilee Line station. Lighting, telecommunications and safety systems are carried in a futuristic overhead boom that runs through these vaults and tunnels. The new underground tunnels have a purpose-built cast-iron cladding system, supposedly resistant to vandalism and dirt. This covering also lines the sides of the escalator shafts, a welcome alternative to the plethora of serial advertising elsewhere. At the same time as work on the Jubilee Line platforms was underway the Northern Line station was completely upgraded with a larger platform tunnel, in an attempt to avoid the cramped conditions of many stations on that line. A new ticket hall was provided under Borough High Street, together with extensive subway connections. During the excavation for these works huge caverns were created using the New Austrian Tunnelling Method and a number of important archaeological finds were made.[34] A third-century Roman amphora and fourth-century mosaic are imaginatively displayed at the top of the main escalators.

Southwark

Parts of the station have been integrated into the spaces beneath the brick viaducts carrying the busy railway from Charing Cross to London Bridge. During construction work these viaducts were given extra support, a precaution particularly necessary during excavation of the escalator shaft. Southwark station reveals its treasures slowly as passengers move through a series of logical but diverse spaces downwards to the Jubilee Line or upwards to Waterloo East. The traditional rotunda entrance on the corner of The Cut and Blackfriars Road shows the influence of Charles Holden once

131. Glass triangles at the top of the escalators at Southwark station.

more and leads to a second drum and an intermediate concourse. From here escalators drop at right angles to the Jubilee Line platforms, with escalator links further along to Waterloo East.

This space with its large concrete beams and exposed masonry is dominated by the cerulean glass wall on one side, created by the artist Alexander Beleschenko. In the form of an elongated ellipse 130 feet long and 52 feet high, the computer-configured design consists of 630 triangular panes of shimmering glass, patterned by firing them with blue enamel containing crystal bubbles. Each pane is held in place by specially-designed stainless steel spiders.[35] The wall is even more striking when approached from the concealed escalators, giving the brief impression of staring up into the vault of the Planetarium or perhaps recalling the original subterranean splendour of the Golden House of Nero in Rome. Expected to cope with 7000 passengers at peak times Southwark has eight escalators and two lifts

and is intended to be the main station for visitors to the Tate Modern gallery that opened in May 2000 in the converted Bankside power station.

Waterloo
At about 100 feet below ground Waterloo is one of the deepest stations on the Jubilee Line, situated beneath all the other lines at this crowded interchange. Travolators assist on the lengthy walk from the Northern and Bakerloo platforms, two of the Underground's oldest lines, to this modern addition which is designed to deal with 15,400 travellers at peak times. Nicholas Grimshaw's stunning Eurostar terminus for international travel can also be reached, as can the much older Waterloo & City Line. Platforms and tunnels were excavated through the London clay using the New Austrian Tunnelling Method. A short length of tunnel is excavated, then a concrete lining is sprayed onto a steel reinforcement cage, with permanent linings installed later. The JLE ticket hall with its double-height glass wall is located in the Colonnades, formerly a road lined with bus stops, a neat solution to the problems of integrating the station within existing nineteenth century structures.

Westminster
Westminster was the last of the Jubilee Line stations to open, on 22 December 1999; it is also the deepest, sunk 130 feet into the ground. It was at this delicate site, directly opposite the Palace of Westminster, that some of the most publicised problems occurred. The previous station building had to be totally demolished to accommodate the complex construction site opposite Big Ben. On-site difficulties were exacerbated by the need to keep the District and Circle lines operating throughout the extended construction period. These lines were lowered 12 inches and supported by a bridge 50 feet below ground which carried the

platforms and tracks above the deeper excavations. The station box is 246 feet long by 89 feet wide, formed by a diaphragm wall extending below the existing Underground lines.

Because of the mass of previous subterranean activity in this central area and subsidence threats to Big Ben and Westminster Bridge the station tunnels, 14¼ feet in diameter, had to be placed one above the other, hence the necessity of descending further by escalator in order to travel westwards. The stark central concourse and Jubilee Line platforms are served by seventeen escalators and five lifts. The escalators are clad with highly finished perforated panels for improved acoustics. From the station the tunnels pass beneath the Thames and run north-east, appropriately beneath Jubilee Gardens on the South Bank. Westwards they head towards Green Park beneath St James's Park. Emergency escape shafts can be seen at either end of the station platforms and are also visible in Canon Row and also on the corner of Horse Guards Road and Birdcage Walk, built into a fenced-off yard behind the police station. New and refurbished subways have improved access to the ticket hall and run beneath bustling Bridge Street and Whitehall. Above the station looms Portcullis House constructed concurrently and sitting on a thick layer of reinforced concrete as a shield against bomb blasts from the station below. This Parliamentary building is as tall as the station is deep, but is kept separate from the publicly accessible station. In such a heavily visited area thick with tourists Westminster JLE station will be dealing with 15,400 passengers during rush hours. As with London Bridge this station stands on a site of prime archaeological importance, close to Thorney Island and the River Tyburn and finds stretching back to the neolithic period were made.[36]

PRESENT AND FUTURE RAIL PROJECTS FOR LONDON

In 1987/88 there were 798 million passenger journeys on London Underground; by 1997/98 this figure had risen to 832 million. After decades of decline London's population is growing again; in 1997 at over 7.1 million, it was 5.3 % higher than the low of 1983. The number of passengers using London's airports increased by 63% between 1987 and 1997 and by more than 7% between 1996 and 1997.[37] Given these statistics and the present booming London economy it is clear that passenger demand is set to increase throughout the south-east region in the foreseeable future. The Channel Tunnel Rail Link, which is planned to run via Stratford into St Pancras, is currently under construction and the decision regarding the next major transport infrastructure projects affecting the capital, CrossRail or the Chelsea-Hackney line, could be decided by London's Mayor, Ken Livingstone, elected in May 2000. One of the mayor's influential roles will be the creation of an integrated public transport strategy at a time when many exciting developments are taking place or are at the planning stage. These recently completed, ongoing or future long-term schemes are summarised in the following section.

THAMESLINK – PAST AND FUTURE

London does not possess a Central Station or Hauptbahnhof, as the encroachment of the burgeoning railway network into the heart of the city was prevented by a ruling of the Royal Commission on Railway Termini in 1846. As a result each major railway station is a terminus placed in a chain around the centre and long journeys often involve time-consuming and irritating interchanges onto the tube network, or some other form of transport. In recent years the few railway lines that cross London have been rescued from neglect and rapidly expanded. The most potentially important of these lines, given the prospect of a Channel Tunnel Rail Link station under King's Cross & St Pancras, is the north-south Thameslink line. Thameslink services through the City of London, soon to be massively upgraded, follow some of the earliest underground railway alignments.

In 1859 the East Kent Railway attempted to establish itself in central London but was prevented by competition from using the London, Brighton & South Coast Railway station at London Bridge. By November that year the company had changed its name to the London, Chatham & Dover Railway (LC&DR). It had also deposited plans to build a new line 4½ miles long from Herne Hill in the south with a bridge over the Thames and a viaduct above the traffic of Ludgate Hill. This new railway would then descend into a tunnel to join up with the Metropolitan Railway, under construction at the time, at Farringdon. A spur, the Smithfield Junction line, would later link it with the Metropolitan station at Moorgate. The new line would gain passengers from the increasing number of City commuters and would carry goods to and from the nearby markets at Newgate and Smithfield, at that time the largest meat market in the country. There were also potentially lucrative connections to the Great Northern Railway at King's Cross. The new line was given the green light when the LC&DR's Metropolitan Extension Act was passed on 6 August 1860.

Dogged by financial problems, the line reached the south side of the Thames near Blackfriars Bridge on 1 June 1864 at a temporary station. By December, the Thames had been bridged by the railway and the line was extended to Ludgate Hill, where another station opened on 1 June 1865.[38] With the completion of the line to Farringdon on 1 January 1866 a connection was established that allowed through traffic on a vital artery, enabling trains from the north to access the south London rail network.[39] In July, however, the LC&DR was declared bankrupt and a web of corruption was eventually revealed which involved the eminent contractor Sir Samuel Morton Peto. These financial complexities took five years to sort out. By February 1868 a pair of extra tracks, the so-called 'City Widened Lines' had been laid between King's Cross and Moorgate to provide other railways with a route to the City. The City Widened Lines began in the tunnels leading to the Great Northern and the Midland under King's Cross and St Pancras, then ran parallel to the existing Metropolitan line until approaching Farringdon Street, where the new tunnel dived under the old one to emerge just outside the station.[40] Also, the Metropolitan Railway agreed to construct the curve into Moorgate Station under Smithfield, which opened in September 1871, with extensive goods yards being created beneath Smithfield Market.

From its inception the line was heavily used by both freight and passenger services from a variety of rail companies; by 1873 between 300 and 400 trains were passing daily through Ludgate Hill. An intermediate station between Farringdon Street and Ludgate Hill called Snow Hill was opened on 1 August 1874. Holborn Viaduct station had been constructed on a spur at a higher level and had opened a few months earlier on 2 March 1874 in order to handle main line trains and to ease increasing congestion. Suburban services used the Smithfield line, stopping at Snow Hill, which was renamed Holborn Viaduct Low Level on 1 May 1912. As traffic was growing rapidly, improvements to the line south of Holborn Viaduct were undertaken, together with the construction of another new station built in 1886 just north of the Thames and named St Paul's. This was part through-station, part terminus and renamed Blackfriars on 1 February 1937.[41] Compared with today's service a surprising number of destinations and journeys were available along this line through the City, including Woolwich to Hendon, fifty trains a day between Moorgate and Victoria and a through service to New Barnet and Enfield as well as trains to Crystal Palace and Clapham Junction. The working timetable for 1888 detailing the numerous services ran to 94 pages. Given all this steam train activity Snow Hill acquired a reputation as a "smoky and sulphurous cavern".[42]

Eventually, however, short distance traffic through the City was hit by the spread of underground railways and the introduction of trams. Through services to the GNR ceased in 1907 and to the Midland in 1908, those to Moorgate followed in 1916. Holborn Viaduct Low Level services stopped on 1 June that year, effectively ending the passenger traffic on the through line. Underground goods services to Smithfield ceased in July 1962, but freight continued to be carried on the Farringdon to Snow Hill tracks until 23 March 1969. Following the withdrawal of trains this potentially invaluable connection slipped into desuetude and dereliction. Alan Jackson gives an evocative description of an earlier unofficial visit to the abandoned station at Snow Hill from Holborn Viaduct. "To the initiated, a sly push on an unlocked door on the concourse offered a special treat. Descending dark steps, one would arrive in the smoky cavern that was once Snow Hill. Here the ghosts of the nineteenth century still lingered. Daylight somehow penetrated through the ever-present smoke and the deep shadows cast by the high buildings all around, feebly illuminating the station walls, on which soot had become encrusted..."[43]

Fortunately, with the huge growth in transport demands throughout the south-east region and the dearth of direct rail links across the Thames through central London, plans were made to reopen the line, with British Rail unveiling a £54 million scheme in 1985. Finally in May 1988 the railway reopened between Farringdon and Blackfriars through the Snow Hill tunnel. In order to realise the redevelopment potential of the Holborn Viaduct station site, a major engineering project was undertaken to remove the station and the unsightly bridge across Ludgate Hill. Constructed by the cut-and-cover method the new subterranean station, initially named St Paul's and now City Thameslink opened in 1990. The track realignment necessary in burying the station beneath the street has resulted in an extremely steep gradient between the almost contiguous Blackfriars and City Thameslink stations of 1 in 29, although previously the gradient between Farringdon and Ludgate Hill stations had been 1 in 39. It has also resulted in the raising of the levels of the lower end of Ludgate Hill and of Ludgate Circus.

Journeys along the Blackfriars to Farringdon section have increased by 300% since 1988 and overcrowding is becoming a major problem during busy periods – Thameslink says it is running at peak capacity. It also provides a direct connection between Gatwick and Luton airports. There are now further plans for a major upgrade of the service, Thameslink 2000, which, at the earliest, will not be finished until 2006. This considerable enhancement of the existing Bedford and Luton to Sutton and Brighton services will require large-scale engineering works. At Blackfriars station covered platforms will traverse the river, with entrances on both banks, probably with an added track and platform. London Bridge station will be substantially remodelled with a new concourse and extra tracks leading to a controversial new viaduct across Borough Market, that will entail the demolition of some of the historic buildings in its path.

The Moorgate-Farringdon branch will have to close and Farringdon station platforms extended to accommodate twelve coach trains. The frequently overcrowded and drab King's Cross Thameslink station will also close to be replaced by a new low-level station at St Pancras. A tunnel will connect the track from here with the East Coast Main Line just north of King's Cross. This densely packed railway interchange will also need to accommodate the tracks of the Channel Tunnel Rail Link. Construction of the new works, presently budgeted at £800 million could begin in 2002 following a public inquiry in 2000. The only other direct north-south link is the previously underused West London Line whose potential is finally being exploited.[44] Both Thameslink and the West London Line run parallel respectively with the vanished rivers Fleet and Counter's Creek to the north of the Thames.

CROSSRAIL

A project to introduce an effective link through the centre of London from east to west was proposed by the Central London Rail Study in 1989, compiled by the Department of Transport, British Railways Board, London Regional Transport and London Underground Ltd. Their plans were based on an expected increase in central London passenger figures of 15% by 2001. The CrossRail route emerged as the most promising of the various proposals and by November 1991 it was expected that a Bill would be put before Parliament containing powers to build the line. The project was costed at £1.5 billion although present estimates are closer to £2.5 billion.[45]

In its eastern section the route will run over existing suburban tracks from Shenfield via Romford and Ilford to Stratford. Near Bethnal Green new twin-bore 20-foot diameter tunnels would plunge underground to Liverpool Street and emerge near Royal Oak outside Paddington. The tunnels are wider than the usual 12 feet in order to accommodate larger trains, overhead electrification equipment and emergency passenger walkways. Boring through the London Clay for six miles at an average depth of 70 feet, they will have to pass beneath the tube lines at

Liverpool Street at a depth of 100 feet and further east through the top of the Woolwich and Reading beds. Services could proceed in the west to Reading or Aylesbury, but to be economically viable must also serve Heathrow airport.

Five new stations on existing Underground sites in central London would be required at Paddington, Bond Street, Tottenham Court Road, Farringdon and Liverpool Street, providing interchanges to eight underground lines as well as overground rail routes. Stratford would offer a connection with the Jubilee Line Extension, Docklands Light Railway and the future Channel Tunnel Rail Link. A further station at Holborn was also envisaged. London Underground would have to be directly involved in any work at these vital stations and there would be implications for the future running of the Metropolitan Line in the west. Stations are intended to be spacious, allowing twice the height of average tube stations, with platforms nearly 1000 feet in length. Building Design Partnership (BDP) and Ralph Erskine of London Ark fame have collaborated "to create a series of civic spaces below ground – an extension of the city beneath the streets, with a high domed roof lined in copper." Seeking inspiration they studied similar subterranean structures such as the vaults of Robert Adam's Royal Society of Arts, a crypt in Delft and Stockholm's cellar restaurants.[46] Farringdon, in particular would become a huge interchange with the Underground, CrossRail and Thameslink at the station that formed the original terminus of the world's first underground railway.

If CrossRail goes ahead and Thameslink 2000 is given the green light London will finally have high-capacity, fast railway routes across the entire city that will speed up cross-country journeys considerably.

THE CHELSEA-HACKNEY LINE

In March 1999 a spokesman for London Underground confirmed that "LT's first choice was to build the Chelsea to Hackney line ... we were quite confident we could manage that without any difficulties, and Hackney is very deprived of public transport. It was a political decision by Mrs Thatcher to go for the Jubilee Line extension."[47] Apart from serving two areas of London difficult to reach by Underground, the route would relieve congested lines such as the Victoria and District. Its construction would involve an 11-mile tunnel beneath central London, linking key stations such as Victoria, Piccadilly Circus, Tottenham Court Road, King's Cross and the Angel. Current estimates of cost run at £3 billion. The decision whether to go ahead with the Chelsea-Hackney line is in the hands of the Mayor of London.

EAST LONDON EXTENSION

The East London Line runs from Whitechapel to New Cross and New Cross Gate, a mere four miles serving and seven stations. More of a shuttle service through Brunel's old Thames Tunnel, it was virtually self-contained with one underground connection at Whitechapel, until the DLR and Jubilee Line Extension recently forged stronger links with the rest of the network. Plans are now underway for an extension of this much-maligned line, which has been subject to long closures in recent years owing to a complete refurbishment of the Thames Tunnel. A 2½ mile extension to the existing track would continue the line north from Whitechapel with a new station at Bishopsgate, replacing that at Shoreditch, then passing over the disused Broad Street railway viaduct proceeding north to new stations at Hoxton and Haggerston. It would terminate at the former Dalston Junction station, with possible future connections to Canonbury and Highbury & Islington along the North London Line.

The area around Shoreditch and Hoxton is currently furiously fashionable but lacks a decent train service. The vast atmospheric series of caverns beneath the Bishopsgate Goods Yard north of Spitalfields will be transformed, after years of neglect, into a shopping mall. Here, amongst the brick-built accretions of the Victorian age, runs John Braithwaite's (1797-1870) original viaduct, one of the oldest railway structures in the country. To the south of the Thames the line may well be extended on existing Railtrack infrastructure, through Peckham, Tulse Hill and Streatham to Wimbledon. It would also be possible to extend the line from New Cross Gate, perhaps to West Croydon to connect with the recently installed Croydon Tramlink. The cost of the proposals at present is estimated at £500 million and construction could begin in 2002.[48]

THE DOCKLANDS LIGHT RAILWAY EXTENDS TO LEWISHAM AND BEYOND?

Unlike the more ambitious and highly publicised Jubilee Line Extension the continuation beneath the Thames of the Docklands Light Railway to Lewisham opened ahead of schedule and within budget. Costing £200 million the extension leaves the previous alignment just outside Crossharbour and London Arena station and descends to a replacement Mudchute station built in a cutting. From there it continues in a cut-and-cover tunnel under Millwall Park to the new Island Gardens underground station. In its previous elevated location this terminus station always seemed rather isolated. Within a few months all traces of this ephemeral structure had been obliterated and the viaduct which used to carry the railway now ends abruptly on the north side of Manchester Road. Carried under the river in twin bored tunnels to the west of the Greenwich foot tunnel the line reaches the brand new station at Cutty Sark situated close to the historic clipper. In the concourse a section of the shield used in the excavation of the tunnels is displayed on the wall. From here the extension passes underneath Greenwich railway station just to the east before rising steeply to reach adjacent platforms. In its final stretch the line follows a viaduct across Deptford Creek which it has to cross five times, so meandering is this watercourse, to an elevated station at Deptford Broadway.

Interestingly, in the context of this book, the route then descends to run along the former concrete culvert of the River Ravensbourne, which has been diverted through a re-landscaped Brookmill Park. Calling at Elverson Road, it follows the Ravensbourne once more to Lewisham and enters another new tunnel beneath the mainline platforms to emerge between the existing rail and bus stations. According to the *Architect's Journal*, "the short tunnel under platforms 3 and 4 ... comprises an open-ended concrete box through a former car park which was then jacked through the embankment behind a tunnelling frame through which workers excavated the ground metre by metre; the method Brunel used in the first Thames tunnel at Rotherhithe."[49]

Work began in October 1996 and the line was actually opened earlier than expected in November 1999. From Lewisham both Stratford and Bank can now be reached within thirty minutes. The whole project is financed by a Private Finance Initiative (PFI) provided by City, Greenwich, Lewisham Rail Link plc (CGL) which won a 24-year concession to construct and maintain the extension.[50] It is also planned to extend the Docklands Light Railway further, from the existing line south of Canning Town to London City Airport with stations at Thames Wharf, West Silvertown and Pontoon Dock. Replacement of the existing Silverlink North London line to North Woolwich and a river crossing from there to Woolwich Arsenal are amongst long-term future plans.[51]

TRAINS TO HEATHROW

The long-awaited underground extension of the Piccadilly Line to Terminals 1, 2 and 3 at Heathrow was finished in 1977 and that to Terminal 4 in 1986. The tube journey can still, however, seem agonisingly slow. A direct rail link was first planned in 1956. Inquiries in 1981 to 1983 and a government study in 1987 again recommended a high-speed rail link, but a joint venture between BAA and British Rail in 1991 failed through lack of funds. Finally, with the British Airports Authority having agreed to construct the line at a cost of £450 million the Heathrow Express from Paddington station to the airport was opened in June 1998 by Prime Minister Tony Blair. Construction had begun in 1993 with the design-build consortium Laing Bailey and architects Couves producing the infrastructure and Wolff Olins with Design Triangle controlling the overall design concept. Sleek, comfortable trains are equipped with TV news and information services and telephones. Since 1999 luggage can be checked in at Paddington before boarding the trains, which run every fifteen minutes. Even though the journey only takes fifteen minutes the rigid hierarchy of Second and First class seating persists, apparently at the request of Club Class passengers and airlines.[52] Premium fares mean that a single ticket from Paddington to Heathrow now costs £12.00 for the 17-mile journey.

With the apparently inexorable expansion of Heathrow it is inevitable that another rail link will have to be made should the proposed fifth terminal go ahead, increasing airport capacity to 80 million passengers a year. A number of options are possible including a further extension of the Piccadilly line, a second Heathrow Express station or a direct connection into the proposed CrossRail network. If the Piccadilly option is preferred it is expected that the new terminal would be connected by tunnels west of Terminals 1,2 and 3, with the westbound tunnel passing beneath the Terminal 4 loop. However a problem may arise in that there will be no direct link between all five terminals as the Terminal 5 station will not be on the Terminal 4 loop.[53] Yet another scheme called Airtrack posits a 1.9 mile rail link from the national network to the south at Staines to join with the Heathrow Express route at the airport. This would enable direct services to be run from Waterloo or Victoria and via Reading to the Midlands and North including Birmingham and Manchester airports.[54]

THE CHANNEL TUNNEL RAIL LINK

Work began in late September 1998 on the £5.5 billion high-speed Channel Tunnel Rail Link (CTRL), which is intended to cut the journey time from London to Paris to two hours twenty minutes. The first 43-mile section will run from the mouth of the tunnel near Folkestone to Ebbsfleet in north Kent. It is expected that this phase will take a further three years to complete. The second phase is due to commence in mid-2001. The terminus at St Pancras is expected to open in 2006 and the whole south-east section in 2007. This phase would require a tunnel to be dug beneath the Thames between Ebbsfleet and West Thurrock. On the north side of the river the line will disappear below ground once more near Barking to run the twelve miles under East London to St Pancras in twin single-track tunnels, apart from a short stretch of cutting at Stratford. The construction work is being undertaken by London & Continental Railways in association with Railtrack. In the early months of 2000 the sleek Medway Viaduct was efficiently taking shape on 22 concrete piers across the river valley. The Channel Tunnel Rail Link has not been received with great enthusiasm by those living close to the proposed route, but is likely to be the engineering project that will have the greatest impact on London in the next ten years.

Footnotes for Chapter Six

[1] The long gestation of the Jubilee Line Extension is comprehensively covered in John Willis' *Extending the Jubilee Line, The planning story* (London Transport, rev. ed. 1999).

[2] See Willis, 13-14. Although the tube link with Fenchurch Street has never been made, the former Surrey Docks area, with a station at Canada Water, was included in the Jubilee Line Extension. A connection with Lewisham has been effected by the most recent Docklands Light Railway Extension completed in 1999.

[3] It is interesting to speculate as to whether Thamesmead would have achieved the popularity expected of it in the late 1960s had the River Line been built. No doubt its use as the setting for Stanley Kubrick's film of *A Clockwork Orange* (re-released in the UK in 2000) did it no favours.

[4] 'DLR driving into City' *The Railway Magazine* June 1988, 360-361.

[5] Bank is not the deepest station on the Underground network. That honour is reserved for Hampstead on the Northern Line – 192 feet below the surface.

[6] *The Railway Magazine* June 1988 *op. cit.*

[7] Peter Semmens 'Docklands Light Railway heads fast to the future' *The Railway Magazine* August 1991, 556-563.

[8] Parliamentary powers for the construction of such works and the compulsory acquisition of land are secured through a Private Bill and Act for the benefit of a company or local or public authority, as opposed to the majority of legislation passed by the Government through Public Bills and Acts. For the Jubilee Line Extension legislation see Willis *op.cit.*, 86-87 & 95.

[9] *Jubilee Line Extension: Project Update* (London Underground Ltd, 1991) for full details.

[10] *ibid.*, 87.

[11] In use in Europe for forty years, but untried here until these projects, NATM allows large tunnels to be dug swiftly in firm ground with the exposed tunnel walls being sprayed with quick-drying 'shotcrete'. A permanent lining is installed later. The spaces carved out beneath Waterloo and London Bridge were cavernous.

[12] Keith Harpur 'Balfour Beatty fined £1.2 million for airport tunnel collapse' *The Guardian* 16 February 1999, 5.

[13] Alastair McLellan 'Jubilee Route March' *New Civil Engineer* 6 February 1997.

[14] Rajeev Syal 'Tunnel network threatens Big Ben' *The Sunday Times* 30 October 1994, 28.

[15] Charles Batchelor 'Mind the gaps in the Jubilee Line schedule' *Financial Times* 23 February 1999, 10.

16 The Jubilee Line Extension website is at http:// www.londontransport.co.uk/jubilee/

[17] The architects of the stations on the Jubilee Line Extension were: Westminster – Michael Hopkins & Partners; Waterloo – JLE Architects; Southwark – MacCormac Jamieson Prichard; London Bridge – JLE Project & Weston Williamson; Bermondsey – Ian Ritchie Architects; Canada Water – JLE Project and Herron Associates; Canary Wharf – Foster & Partners; North Greenwich – Alsop, Lyall & Stormer (formerly Alsop &

Stormer) Architects; Canning Town – John McAslan & Partners (formerly Troughton McAslan); West Ham-van Heyningen & Haward; Stratford – Wilkinson Eyre (formerly Chris Wilkinson) Architects; For full credits see Martin Pawley & Roland Paoletti 'Going Underground' *The Architects' Journal* 3 February 2000, 26-37.

[18] For Frank Pick see Christian Barman *The Man Who Built London Transport* (David & Charles, 1979).

[19] The best history of the architecture and design of London Underground stations is David Lawrence *Underground Architecture* (Capital Transport Publishing, 1994).

[20] Angela Patmore 'The dark at the end of the tunnel' *The Independent* 17 January 1995.

[21] Catherine Slessor 'Underground Jubilation' *Architectural Review* May 1999, 55.

[22] Coincidentally an exhibition of Ken Adam's work was held in London as the Jubilee Line stations were opening. See *Moonraker, Strangelove and other celluloid dreams: the visionary art of Ken Adam* (Serpentine Gallery, 1999).

[23] Lisa Russell 'Stratford's metamorphosis' *New Civil Engineer* 6 February 1997.

[24] Kester Rattenbury 'West Ham united' *Building Design* 11 June 1999, 12-13. See also 'West Ham sandwich' *Architectural Review* May 1999, 62-64.

[25] 'Canning Stack' *ibid.* 65-66.

[26] See Iain Sinclair's scabrous and often hilarious essays on the troubled history of this peninsula and the development of the Dome in the *London Review of Books* – 'Mandelson's Pleasure Dome' 2 October 1997, 7-10 and 'All change. This train is cancelled' 13 May 1999, 14-18. Recently collected together and supplemented in one volume *Sorry Meniscus, Excursions to the Millennium Dome* (Profile Books, 1999).

[27] Peter Excell 'Rail Roots on site of Dome' *The Railway Magazine* January 2000, 44-45.

[28] David Bennett 'Tunnelling out of Trouble' *Contract Journal* 12 January 2000, 12-13.

[29] Quoted in David Bennett 'Gateway to the Millennium takes shape in Greenwich' *Concrete Quarterly* Summer 1997, 2-5.

[30] Robert Bevan 'Let there be light' *Building Design* 3 September 1999, 15-16.

[31] Keith Miller 'Saving Isis from Crisis' *The Times Literary Supplement* 14 January 2000, 23.

[32] Andy Cook 'Stiff upper ellipse' *Building* 14 February 1997. Within weeks of the station's opening the view up

from the escalators to the glass canopy had already become a photographic cliché.

[33] 'Going Underground' *The Architects' Journal* 3 February 2000, 31.

[34] Museum of London Archaeology Service *The Big Dig* (MOLAS, 1998) 16-31.

[35] Mary Miers 'Light at the end of the line' *Country Life* 4 November 1999, 113.

[36] *The Big Dig op.cit.*, 4-15.

[37] Statistics taken from *Focus on London 1999* (The Stationery Office, 1999), 19 & 117.

[38] Charles E. Lee 'Useful but unloved – the story of Ludgate Hill Station' *The Railway Magazine* December 1964, 872-879. Ludgate Hill station closed in March 1929.

[39] Adrian Gray 'Snow Hill Awakes' *The Railway Magazine* November 1985, 524-525.

[40] C. Baker *The Metropolitan Railway* (Oakwood Press, 1951), 11-15

[41] It was at this time that a second rail bridge was constructed parallel to the previous LC&DR structure. This earlier bridge was dismantled in 1985 with one bridge abutment adorned with the company's crest remaining, together with the forlorn cast-iron piers in the river.

[42] Neil Sprinks 'Thameslink Services a Century Ago' *The Railway Magazine* June 1988, 363-365.

[43] Alan Jackson *London's Termini* (David & Charles, 1969), 204.

[44] Tim Sherwood 'Mr Punch's Railway' *The Railway Magazine* February 1988, 88-89.

[45] *CrossRail: East meets West* promotional brochure April 1993.

[46] BDP architect quoted in 'CrossRail: what could have been (and still may be)' *The Guardian* 'Space' supplement 19 February 1999, 10.

[47] Quoted in *Time Out* 17-24 March 1999, 11.

[48] 'The changing face of London's railways' *The Railway Magazine* March 2000, 50-54. Also John Glover *London Underground* (Ian Allan, 1997), 83.

[49] Tony Aldous 'Crossing the river from a different angle' *The Architects' Journal* 12 March 1998, 10-11.

[50] CGL Rail's sponsor companies are John Mowlem & Company, Hyder, London Electricity and Mitsui & Co. Ltd.

[51] *The Railway Magazine* March 2000 *op. cit.*

[52] Jonathan Glancey 'Is this the future for British rail?' *The Guardian* 15 June 1998, 10.

[53] John Glover *op.cit.*, 85.

[54] *The Railway Magazine* March 2000 *op.cit.*

Select Bibliography

Ashton, John *The Fleet: its river, prison and marriages* (Fisher Unwin 1888)

Barker, Felix & Hyde, Ralph *London as it Might Have Been* (John Murray, 1995)

Barker, T C & Robbins, Michael *A History of London Transport* (Allen & Unwin, 1976)

Barman, Christian *The Man Who Built London Transport* (David & Charles, 1979)

Barton, Nicholas *The Lost Rivers of London* (Historical Publications, 1992)

Bayliss, Derek A *The Post Office Railway* (Turntable Publications, 1978)

Berkeley, Roy *A Spy's London* (Leo Cooper, 1994)

British Geological Survey *British Regional Geology: London and the Thames Valley* 4th ed. compiled by M G Sumbler (HMSO, 1996)

Bruce, J. Graeme & Croome, Desmond F *The Twopenny Tube, the story of the Central Line* (Capital Transport, 1996)

Buxbaum, Tim *Icehouses* (Shire Publications, 1992)

Campbell, Duncan *War Plan UK* (Paladin, rev. ed.1983)

Churchill, Winston *The Second World War Vol II: Their Finest Hour* (Cassell & Co, 1949)

Connor, J E *London's Disused Underground Stations* (Connor & Butler Specialist Publications, Colchester, 1999)

Day, John Robert *The Story of London's Underground* (London Transport, 1979)

Day, John Robert *The Story of the Victoria Line* (London Transport, 1969)

Dickinson, H W *Water Supply of Greater London* (Newcomen Society, 1954)

Douglas, Hugh *The Underground Story* (Hale, London, 1963)

Duncan, Andrew *Secret London* rev. ed (New Holland, 1998)

Eitan, Karol & Allibone, Finch *Charles Holden Architect 1875-1960* exhibition catalogue (RIBA, 1988)

Errand, Jeremy *Secret Passages and Hiding Places* (David & Charles, 1974)

Fitter, R S R *London's Natural History* (Collins, Glasgow, 1945)

Follenfant, H G *Reconstructing London's Underground* (London Transport, 1974)

Foord, A S *Springs, Streams and Spas of London* (Fisher Unwin, 1910)

Glover, John *London Underground* (Ian Allan, 1997)

Graves, Charles *London Transport Carried On* (LPTB, 1947)

Greater London Council *London Rail Study* (1974)

Hadfield, Charles *Atmospheric Railways: a Victorian Venture in Silent Speed* (Sutton Publishing, 1967, repr. 1985)

Halliday, Stephen *The Great Stink of London, Sir Joseph Bazalgette and the cleansing of the Victorian Metropolis* (Sutton Publishing, 1999)

Harrison, Michael *London Beneath the Pavement* (Peter Davies, 1961)

Heaps, Chris *London Transport Railways Album* (Ian Allan, 1978)

Hollingshead, John *Underground London* (Groombridge & Sons, 1862)

Horne, M A C *The Bakerloo Line, a Short History* (Douglas Rose, 1990)

Horne, M A C *The Victoria Line, a Short History* (Douglas Rose, 1988)

Horne, Mike & Bayman, Bob *The Northern Line* 2nd edition (Capital Transport, 1999)

Howson, H F *London's Underground* (Ian Allan, 1986)

Humphreys, Sir George *The Main Drainage of London* (LCC, 1930)

Jackson, Alan A *London's Metropolitan Railway* (David & Charles, 1986)

Jackson, Alan A & Croome, Desmond *Rails Through the Clay* (Allen & Unwin, 1962)

Jephson, H *The Sanitary Evolution of London* (Fisher Unwin, 1907)

Kohan, C M *Works and Building (History of the Second World War, United Kingdom Civil Series vol 7)* (HMSO and Longman, Green & Co. 1952)

Lambton, Lucinda *Temples of Convenience and Chambers of Delight* (St Martin's Press, 1995)

Lampe, David *The Tunnel, the Story of the World's*

first tunnel under a Navigable River dug beneath the Thames 1824-42 (George G. Harrap, 1963)

Lascelles, T.S. *The City and South London Railway* (first pub. 1955, Oakwood Press, 1987)

Laurie, Peter *Beneath the City Streets* (Granada, 1983)

Lawrence David *Underground Architecture* (Capital Transport Publishing, 1994)

Lee, Charles E *Sixty Years of the Piccadilly* (London Transport, 1966)

Lee, Charles E *The Metropolitan Line* (London Transport, 1972)

McCamley, N J *Secret Underground Cities* (Pen & Sword Books/Leo Cooper, 1998)

Mack, Joanna & Humphries, Steve *The Making of Modern London 1939-1945, London at War* (Sidgwick & Jackson, 1985)

Mathewson, Andrew & Laval, Derek *Brunel's Tunnel ... and where it led* (Brunel Exhibition Rotherhithe, 1992)

Meller, Hugh *London Cemeteries: An Illustrated Guide and Gazetteer* 3rd edition (Scholar Press, 1994)

Middlemass, R C *London's Main Drainage: Historical Background* (Thames Water, 1975)

Moore, Henry *Shelter Sketchbook* with a commentary by Frances Carey (British Museum Publications, 1988)

Museum of London Archaeology Service *The Big Dig* (MOLAS, London, 1998)

Nock, O S *Underground Railways of the World* (Adam & Charles Black, 1973)

North East London Polytechnic *Dockland - an illustrated historical survey of life and work in East London* (North East London Polytechnic & Greater London Council, 1986)

O'Brien, Terence H *Civil Defence (History of the Second World War, United Kingdom Civil Series)* (HMSO and Longman, Green & Co. 1955)

Passingham, W *The Romance of London's Underground* (Sampson Low & Co. 1932)

Pennick, Nigel *Bunkers Under London* 2nd ed. (Electric Traction Publications, 1985)

Pennick, Nigel *Tunnels Under London* 3rd ed. (Electric Traction Publications, 1981)

Rolt L T C *Victorian Engineering* (Allen Lane Penguin, 1970)

Rose, Douglas *The London Underground: a Diagrammatic History* (Douglas Rose, 1980)

Ross, Stewart *History in Hiding: the Story of Britain's Secret Passages and Hiding Places* (Robert Hale, 1991)

Standage, Tom *The Victorian internet: the remarkable story of the telegraph and the nineteenth century's online pioneers* (Weidenfeld & Nicolson, 1998)

Stevens, F L *Under London, a chronicle of London's underground lifelines and relics* (J M Dent, 1939)

Sunderland, S *Old London Spas, Baths and Wells* (J Bale Sons & Danielson, 1915)

Trench, R & Hillman, E *London Under London* rev. ed. (John Murray, 1993)

Weinreb, Ben and Hibbert, Christopher *The London Encyclopedia* (Papermac, 1983 rev. ed. 1995)

Welbourn, Nigel *Lost Lines, London* (Ian Allan, 1998)

Williamson, Elizabeth and Nikolaus Pevsner with Malcolm Tucker *London Docklands, an Architectural Guide* (Penguin, London, 1998)

Willis, Jon *Extending the Jubilee Line: the Planning Story* (London Transport, 1999)

Wright, L *Clean and Decent* (Routledge, 1980)

Ziegler, Philip *London at War 1939-1945* (Sinclair-Stevenson, 1995)

Newspapers and Periodicals consulted:
Archaeological Journal, Architect's Journal, Architectural Review, The Builder/Building, Building Design, Contract Journal, Concrete Quarterly, Country Life, The Daily Telegraph, Electrical Review, The Engineer, Financial Times, The Guardian, History Today, The Independent, London Archaeologist, New Civil Engineer, Railway Magazine, Sunday Times, The Times.